Text and Supertext in Ibsen's Drama

Text and Supertext
in
Ibsen's Drama

Brian Johnston

THE PENNSYLVANIA STATE UNIVERSITY PRESS
University Park and London

Library of Congress Cataloging-in-Publication Data

Johnston, Brian, 1932–
Text and supertext in Ibsen's drama / Brian Johnston.

p.   cm.
Bibliography: p.
Includes index.
ISBN 0-271-00644-7
1. Ibsen, Henrik, 1828–1906—Criticism and interpretation.
2. Criticism—Methodology.   I. Title.
PT8895.J588 1988
839.8'226—dc1988–12488

Contents

Acknowledgments

Most of this book was written in Beirut, Lebanon, and I wish to thank the American University of Beirut and Beirut University College for providing me with a wonderfully hospitable environment within which to work. With a courtesy and munificence of spirit typical of the Arab peoples, my colleagues tolerated my obsession with Ibsen at a time when they were undergoing actual tragedy on a massive scale and when our Western "culture" was not displaying itself in the Middle East with any degree of credibility, justice, or even human decency. My American and European colleagues, some, sadly, now hostages, some dead, always were of tremendous support in the dangers we shared with the Lebanese and Palestinian people.

When, with great reluctance, I was forced to flee Beirut, I was greatly fortunate to find refuge at Carnegie Mellon University, where this book was completed. To Akram Midani, Dean of the College of Fine Arts, to Mel Shapiro, then-Chairman of the Drama Department, to Don Marinelli, Assistant Dean, and to all my colleagues in the Drama Department, my special gratitude.

I also have been sustained in the writing of this study by the fine encouragement of Eric Bentley, Gerald Dugan, Rolf Fjelde, and Leon Katz, Rick Davis, and Michael X. Zelenak of the

American Ibsen Theater in Pittsburgh, which offered me drama-turgical shelter from the shelling in Beirut for two memorable summers in 1984 and 1985. All these are co-authors of the book's merits and unheeded counsellors against its defects. To John Stroupe, editor of *Comparative Drama,* and to the editors of *Ibsen News and Comment,* where some of the ideas of this book were first tried out, my special thanks.

Preface

In 1925 Hermann J. Weigand pronounced Ibsen "modern" and
his very influential study established a tradition that still holds
the center of Ibsen interpretation. Ibsen's modernity, it seemed,
lay in the nature of his *realism:* its psychological acuity, which
anticipated Freud, its unusual penetration into the ambiguity of
characters and motives, its unsparing and confessional self-
analysis in the last four plays. This was an Ibsen highly congenial to the times, whose famous remark, "I have been less the
social philosopher and more the poet" than his contemporaries
guessed, was assumed to imply "I have been more the psychoanalyst." This, it was felt, was a great gain. It removed Ibsen from
the often uncongenial arena of social and ideological controversy. It gave him a "timeless" quality; for though social problems might get solved and thus become dated, we would always
have psyches and these always would have problems. By an odd
maneuver, therefore, Ibsen became "universal" by becoming
smaller. By keeping to the core of the onion—the mystery of the
psyche—and not exploring beyond to the furthest dimensions of
metaphoric reality, Ibsen spoke to and for every timidly circumscribed self.

The cost of this maneuver has been to make Ibsen universal

but trivial. He shares with all of us our smallest range of human identity: something that is not true of Freud, who saw the history of the *species* within the drama of the individual. Furthermore, such interpretation has had to ignore Ibsen's *texts:* to discount their imagery, their range of reference, their cultural and historical reverberations, and their aesthetic nature as scripts written for theatrical performance before the European public of the nineteenth century. What is most ignored in such interpretation is the manner in which Ibsen, as an *artist,* is adapting and extending the terms of his artform—drama—in order to create authentic and ambitious artistic structures.

The rigors, limitations, boundaries, and difficulties that Ibsen imposes upon himself are the terms of his aesthetic performance; the tightrope he sets up defines and makes more consequential the nature of his artistic gestures. To hurry past all this difficult and elaborate artistry in order to get at a collection of psychopathological casebooks actually is to be operating—and not very arduously—in the wrong field of interest altogether.

Modern Ibsenists, in contrast to their nineteenth-century counterparts, tend to be academics: men and women who have learned to tame their imaginations and expectations to the requirements of institutions whose tolerance has its limits. To demonstrate that Ibsen shares their reasonable, responsible, conformist though "ambiguous"—a key value term—attitude (the sensibility of the fallen spirit) is the effort of interpreters anxious to make Ibsen one of their company. Wanting to see themselves on his stage, they have refashioned him in their own image.

But it was the nonacademic men and women of the nineteenth and early twentieth centuries—Bernard Shaw, Henry James, James Joyce, Oscar Wilde, Lou Salomé, Emma Goldman, Rainer Maria Rilke, Hugo von Hofmannsthal, Thomas Mann, and others—who better got the measure of Ibsen and who possessed the intellectual language to describe his art. And this was in the period in which performing an Ibsen play could be a revolutionary action, a daring defiance of the cultural norms of the time. To his contemporaries Ibsen was more like Jean Genet in our day.

People at home with their culture do not make extravagant demands upon it—of the order of "the third empire of spirit," whose coming alone would redeem our humanity. Such sensible people have elected to become interpreters of Ibsen, so their only recourse is to avert their eyes from Ibsen's larger strategies, to deplore, urbanely, Ibsen's odd tendency to make large ideological utterances, to deny the wide-ranging metaphoricity of his art, to refuse to see that in him which links him to the Greek tragedians, to Milton, Blake, Wordsworth, Goethe, Melville, Kafka, and Beckett, rather than to traditional realism.

It might be objected that playing a dramatist's larger intentions does not "work" in the theater. But until this is seriously attempted with Ibsen's plays, how can we know? And this should not prevent *interpreters* from establishing the full measure of Ibsen's art. The American Ibsen Theater established that it was worthwhile seeing what an Ibsen who sets out to rival Sophocles might provide us. Partisan feminist advocacy will keep *A Doll House* on the stage, and the rewards of the eponymous role will do the same for *Hedda Gabler*. But only a grasp of the great, poetic *supertext* in Ibsen's art will bring, for example, *Ghosts, The Wild Duck, Rosmersholm, The Lady from the Sea*, and the marvelous last four plays back into the modern repertory and so end the impression, gained from any perusal of lists of forthcoming theater productions, that Ibsen was the author of only two (feminist) plays.

In the pages that follow I will relate Ibsen's artistry to this "supertext" and demonstrate how it establishes both the scale and the intricacy of Ibsen's dramas. Ibsen is the heir to the great Romantic movement as much as the creator of the new realist drama. And it was Romanticism's genius to have created for itself a new mythology, uniting particulars to universals (supremely, in Hegelian philosophy), which is the precondition of a major dramatic art. This had been the great achievement of Greek culture, and of the medieval and renascence worlds: And it was with a consciousness of having inherited these two earlier, conflicting concepts of universal human identity, and of needing to effect a synthesis between them (Ibsen's "third empire of spirit") that Romanticism, especially in the Germanic world, constructed its new mythology. In this mythography new archetypes came to birth: the Zeitgeist, the Weltgeist, the Geistes des

Volkes, the national consciousness, and the continuing life of the spirit from earliest mythic, prehistoric times to the alienated spirit of the present. Human consciousness was seen as a conflict-filled continuum from origins to ultimate destiny.

The major philosophical work of Romanticism, the *Phenomenology of Spirit,* is saturated with such archetypal content. This content can be of incalculable advantage to a tragic poet, and Ibsen, at the end of the Romantic movement (which came later in Scandinavia than in the rest of Europe), had the imagination and intelligence to perceive the "great argument" opened up by his culture. Such a system of archetypes will come into being, be used to its utmost, and then be exhausted, as happened in classical Athens, in medieval-renascence Europe, and in the Romantic movement in Europe.

Whether Ibsen developed his version of this great argument because it creatively extended his tragic art, or whether his tragic art was the direct expression of his spiritual "investment" in the argument, is something we will never be able to establish. We can, at least, see that the two—the art and the ideology— were absolutely interdependent. For the important thing about the Romantic argument, we saw, was that it was saturated with myth. Charles Segal has observed the myth-saturated nature of Greek drama:

> The study of myth is both important and difficult for semi-otics because myth stands at an intersection of different sign systems. Myth comprises a system of symbols, verbal, visual and religious. Each myth is built up of already existing symbols and forms and, like all narrative, reforms and reorganizes those symbols into its own structures. Myth, as Roland Barthes suggests, is a "second-order semiotic system," which creates its own language, its own system of relations between signifier and signified, from the primary significations of cultural values and narrative forms.[1]

The creation, exploration, and exhaustion of such a system would be completed within a limited span of time—from Aeschy-

lus to Euripides, Marlowe to John Ford, Schiller to Strindberg—
so that the terms of a new functioning system would have to be
evolved that could extend, like a Peer Gynt's onion, the range of
the human and dramatic gesture through individual, familial,
societal, historical, national, natural, and supernatural dimensions of reference. In such a system, whose circumferences of
implication hold the whole structure together, like a spider's
web, the slightest trembling at any point causes the whole structure to be shaken. That is, any significant action involves all the
layers of reality simultaneously.

In the *Antigone* the unburied body of Polyneices will be an
agonizing wound in the *psyche* of Antigone, an event that brings
together and tears apart a *family*, that involves a *society* and a
nation and its *past*, includes actions within the world of *nature*
and is seen as watched over by the offended *gods*. The characters
in the drama "operate on" all these levels at the same time. This
also is true of *Macbeth* and of *Ghosts*, or *Rosmersholm* or *Little
Eyolf*.

Such cultural enterprises are, of course, always fraught with
"contradictions," gaps, ambiguities. They are not watertight and
"scientific" systems: They would not encourage creativity if they
were. The need to assert the existence of such a supertextual
dimension to human consciousness makes the enterprise a living, imaginative one. The fact that we can tell, from an unnamed
text, when it must have been written, and when it could not
possibly have been written, or whether it is an anomaly within its
culture, reveals that this cultural supertext is not an arbitrary
thing. While such a system is still in operation, artists, thinkers,
writers, continually sustain, invoke, and extend it. Even in his
insanity Nietzsche invoked both Dionysos and the Crucified
One—a version of Ibsen's Emperor and Galilean. In such a system, the identity of one element is fortified by its affiliation with,
or opposition to, another. As Segal writes:

> The totality of a corpus of myths may be read as a single
> text that possesses the internal coherence, autonomy, and
> coding processes of Barthes' second-order semiotic sys-
> tem. In reading the whole body of a society's myths in this

way, we are constructing the "megatext" of its mythic material. . . . This megatext is an artificial construct, necessarily invisible and unconscious to the society whose exemplary narratives and symbolic projections of what reality is are located within that system.[2]

What Segal here terms a "megatext" I have dubbed a "supertext": The meaning is the same. Within both the Romantic supertext and the megatext of the Greek mythopoeic systems,

myth is a narrative structure whose sign-and-symbol-systems are closely correlated with the central values of the culture, especially those values that express a supernatural validation, extension, or explanation of the cultural norms. Myth is also a more or less coherent system of symbols that express relationships between the human world and the forces of nature and the various forms of the unknown: the gods, the dead, the afterlife.[3]

The immense value of such a "system" for the poet is that it allows an alternative, more evocative and more wide-ranging *language,* a counter-discourse to the limited discourse of the everyday world. It can extend the terms of the artwork beyond those of the immediate, given present. Though coherent, in that it allows the artist to identify the "forces" he sees as operating upon human life, such a system is not wholly conscious and not in any way fixed. The universals of this system permit and encourage an extensiveness of exploration that every ambitious art requires.

What is interesting about the Romantic creation and deployment of such a mythopoeic system is that, unlike the systems of earlier periods, it does not extend and reinforce, but counteracts, the given cultural norms. This is an obvious aspect of the "Romantic rebellion" from William Blake to Richard Wagner. Its mythopoeic system is raised to oppose an "alien" and even "alienated" traditional order. The forces summoned by the poet, natural or supernatural, are often those denied or repressed by the given culture. It is for this reason that the typical Romantic hero

is *apolis,* set apart from society, like Byron's Manfred or Ibsen's
Brand. (In this, they recover the isolated grandeur of the heroes
of Sophocles' old age, Philoctetes and Oedipus at Colonus.) John
Gabriel Borkman, in Ibsen's Realist Cycle, is such a figure existing, I shall argue, outside the cultural norms that would seek to
judge him and explicable only on his own strange but impressive
terms.

One cannot possibly understand the nature of Ibsen's rebellion
and of his concept of a "third empire of spirit" unless one is aware
that he is conscious of having large metaphysical forces to "draw
upon." Without this awareness, that rebellion will seem to be no
more than congenital irritableness—with his society and with
himself. This would be as absurdly reductive as to interpret the
early Wordsworth's rebellion as based upon no more than a preference for hills over streets. Ibsen's Realist Cycle is a universal
battlefield in which one form after another of inadequate conceptions of reality—inadequate *worlds*—are defeated in combat with
the absolute spirit. Universals are not lifeless abstractions when
they are believed in: They become alarming forces animating
psyches and disrupting the world. Two of the most powerful
forces ever unleashed upon humanity—Christianity and Islam—
though abstract systems, intimately affect the life of much of the
planet's population. In Ibsen's cycle, as in his earlier, poetic
plays, his world of intimate particulars resonates with the terms
of his universal argument.

Ignoring the universal terms of his art makes unintelligible
much of his procedure, which then can seem somewhat clumsy,
as if it were apprentice work in the development of the trivially
sensitive, "ambiguous" realism that has no other ambition than
to simulate our ordinary experience of life. His art, like Jean
Genet's, is a subversive one, designed to unnerve us rather than
invite us to settle down, cosily, for a form of dramatized moralistic gossip. We still need to find the right performing terms for
that extraordinary sequence of masterpieces, the Realist Cycle,
that Eric Bentley termed "the crowning glory of tragedy in modern dress."[4]

If Ibsen is to survive in the modern theater other than as the
author of two "feminist" plays, it must be in terms that reveal the

immensity of his intention. He needs imaginative interpretation and presentation because his art is imaginative and intellectually daring. Biographies and studies of Ibsen that meticulously reproduce the social life of Skien, Grimstad, Bergen, and Christiania in the later nineteenth century forget that he inhabited, also, a far larger and more important world: the world of the imagination and of inherited culture and its universal conflicts. The idea of Ibsen as the careful photographer of his society simply does not make good sense. When he lived in that society, he mostly wrote "remote" historical dramas. During the writing of his Realistic Cycle he chose to live among the antiquities of Rome or in the historically consequential Germany of Bismarck. His eye, therefore, always seemed to be focused on a larger drama than the personal and social conduct of his compatriots. Ibsen had the misfortune to be born into a provincial, limiting, and repressive society from which he spent his lifetime liberating his imagination. It does not serve his cause doggedly to return his art reductively to such a milieu simply because biographical conjecture—gossip—is the least demanding of interpretive procedures.

1

Introduction

Behind the phenomena's multiplicity the artist catches glimpses of a unity; behind the confusion, a coherence; behind the forms, an idea; behind the casual, the essential. The artist's task lies in separating the essential and making it real for us.
— Sigurd Ibsen, *Human Quintessence*

Sigurd Ibsen's words quoted above express a currently unfashionable idea of art: that the artist, beginning with the confusions and contradictions of nonaesthetic discourse, achieves, through his or her artwork, a unity-within-plenitude, a coherence and totality, denied to ordinary discourse—the discourse, for example, of critical interpretation. By taking on a *genre* and developing a *style* the artist imposes upon himself limits and requirements independent of his individual personality and independent of the terms of discourse of everyday life. Significant aesthetic experience is the meeting ground of the self-forgetting artist and the self-forgetting audience. It is always possible to submit the artwork to the nonaesthetic language of critical interpretation and even to *reduce* it to the terms of a methodology, but, as anyone knows who has visited an art gallery, attended a concert or a play, or read a poem or novel, the experience of unity-within-plenitude always is recoverable. The attempt by interpretation to discover the unity-within-plenitude intended by the artist, if not *naively* pursued, still is worthwhile. This is what I attempt on behalf of Ibsen, asking myself at every point if my interpretation is plausible as a coherent intention by Ibsen.

This study is complementary to my earlier *The Ibsen Cycle* (Boston: Twayne Publications, 1975), and the reader's understanding of my argument will be greatly helped if he or she consults that work. In *The Ibsen Cycle* I claimed that the twelve plays, from *Pillars of Society* to *When We Dead Awaken*, made up a single cyclical work, an odyssey of the human spirit directly paralleling that charted by Hegel in *The Phenomenology of Mind*. That is, the scenes, characters, and actions of those plays, taken together, performed the gigantic task of recollecting the past of the race within the theatrical presentation of actions of Ibsen's own time. I claimed that, in Ibsen's own words, his plays formed a "cycle" with "mutual connections between the plays," one play being the dialectical development from its predecessor. The action of the recollection of the total past, which Ibsen's admirer, James Joyce, was to repeat in the novel, was the condition of our coming into our birthright as humanity. Truth and freedom required the repossession of that birthright, much of it forgotten, or forbidden, by the present. The memorable productions of the American Ibsen Theater were based upon this idea. In this book, I first survey those critical attitudes that still inhibit recognition of the magnitude of Ibsen's achievement, then present five "case studies," extending the methods I developed in *The Ibsen Cycle*. This study, therefore, represents a methodological advance over the earlier one, but it extends, rather than qualifies, the claims of the first book.

My primary interest is the Ibsen text; the *structures* the individual plays, and the whole Realist Cycle, reveal, and the *textures* the plays contain, in terms of imagery, cultural reference, impact of performance, and so on. That this structure and texture can best be revealed through the Hegelian worldview that Ibsen inherited is the sole reason why I employ Hegel in my

interpretation. I am not a Hegelian wishing to subdue imaginative literature to Hegelian terms: I am trying to explore the intellectual cosmos Ibsen inhabited.

Hegelian aesthetics represented a culmination of humanist
discourse (for Hegel sees art—and above all dramatic art—as one
of the supreme labors by which spirit comes to know, to objectify
itself, as in religion and philosophy). For Hegel artistic expression was an exploration of the collective discourse of humanity.
It was not the individual subjectivity of the author that Hegel
saw as significant in artistic expression but the way in which the
artist's work revealed our universal humanity. Ibsen, also, explored in the fullest and richest manner the ongoing discourse of
the human species. This discourse must include the significant
past, historical and cultural. His "text" is an "intertextuality"
which is fully aware of resonances within the text. These resonances derive from other texts, from our history, culture, my-
thologies, philosophies—from our total range of human expression, in fact.

I have preferred to use the term "supertext" (with its inevitable
contrast, for the drama student, of "subtext") than the term "intertextuality." But my account of the supertext is not so very different from that of "context" or the network of "connotation" invoked
by such writers as Roland Barthes: the "cultural code" from which
the signs are drawn and by means of which they take on expanded
meaning. If our language is shaped by both prelinguistic and
postlinguistic "inlays,"[1] then art, such as drama, employing both
linguistic and nonlinguistic "signifiers of connotation . . . subject
to the physical constraints of vision (different from phonotary
constraints, for instance),"[2] will set up a rich interplay between
such "inlays" and the spoken (and written) dialogue. As Keir
Elam, in *The Semiotics of Theatre and Drama*, observes,

> Even in the most determinedly realistic of dramatic repre-
> sentations, the role of the sign-vehicle in standing for a
> class of objects by no means exhausts its semiotic range.
> Beyond this basic denotation, the theatrical sign inevita-
> bly acquires secondary meanings for the audience, relat-

ing it to the social, moral and ideological values operative
in the community of which performers and spectators are
a part.[3]

Ibsen, far from being a determinedly realistic writer, extended
these "secondary meanings" as far as his imagination, operating
within the discipline of his art, could extend. The cosmic scope
of that imagination can be gauged from his notes to *The Lady
from the Sea,* as well, perhaps (for the relationship between the
father and the son was close), from Sigurd Ibsen's *Human Quintessence,* whose account of the human condition, taking in post-
Darwinian biology and the place of our human species in the vast
cosmos opened up by modern astronomy, reads like a gloss on
such an Ibsen play as *Little Eyolf.*

One contention of mine has encountered some resistance: that
only the context of the whole of the Realist Cycle allows us fully
to understand any individual play within the cycle. This means,
of course, that Ibsen was writing primarily not for his own contemporaries, who could not know the way in which each individual play contributed to the design of the whole, as for posterity:
But this does not contradict what we know of Ibsen as a man.
His contemporaries enjoyed one privilege we cannot share: the
shock of surprise and puzzlement at the arrival of each new play.
But we have the privilege, at least as great, of seeing each play,
even the earliest in the cycle, as one part of the total design.

The very elaborate, richly resonant "text" that Ibsen created
with his cycle confronts us not as an elaborate puzzle to be
teased out by generations of academics but as a potentially liberating discourse which would help to expand, to free, our own
consciousnesses, which themselves are inadequate, inauthentic,
or unexamined "texts." In Roland Barthes's words:

> The 'I' which approaches the text is itself already a plural-
> ity of other texts, of infinite, or more precisely, lost codes
> (whose origins are lost). . . . Subjectivity is generally
> thought of as a plenitude with which I encumber the
> text, but in fact this faked plenitude is only the wash of

> all the codes which make up the 'I', so that finally, my
> subjectivity has the generality of stereotypes.[4]

Ibsen's ambition was to bring back authenticity to this faked
plenitude by converting the terms of our everyday consciousness
from the stereotypical to that of forms filled with significance.

An interpretation of a play can proceed only on the assumption
that it can be demonstrated to embody an artistic intention (theatrical performance) which the director and the actors can attempt
to realize. It no longer is considered a "fallacy" to attribute intention to an author and "meaning" to a "text." Here, E. D. Hirsch's
distinction between "meaning" and "significance" will be useful.
"Meaning" represents the author's intention and is the proper
object of interpretation, which always seeks to establish the plenitude, totality, and unity of a work. An artist's meaning never can
be fully established, and deconstructive criticism has revealed
the radical instability of texts, but, as I will argue later, it is
possible to pronounce one interpretation superior to another as
better representing the author's intention. "Significance," on the
other hand, represents the new values and relevances a work
may acquire within our culture and will form much of the
noninterpretive, critical commentary upon an author and his or
her work. This particularly is true of drama, in which the ideal
performance seeks not merely to be faithful to the author's intention but also immediately to address the interests of a contemporary audience. Ideally, the new significance that is discovered in
a drama can be presented without violating the author's intention. When we hear the wounded soldier, Scarus, in *Antony and
Cleopatra* declare his readiness to sustain more injuries with, "I
have room / For six scotches more," we should not attach to his
words the significance they would acquire in, say, *The Iceman
Cometh*. Most of us would agree that to present *Oedipus the King*
or *King Lear* as rollicking farce is to attach inappropriate significances to these works. Once we are aware of how radically Sophocles changed the plots of the myths on which he based his own
stories of Oedipus and Antigone, or how drastically Aeschylus
altered Homer's account of Orestes' story for his tragic purposes,
we cannot discount the intervention of the author in his work.

These plays were not written by the culture in which the authors lived. On the contrary, the authors intervened consequentially in their cultures by means of their tragic art, altering the consciousness of the culture as effectively as the philosophers were to do.

Nevertheless, the best way to fathom the meaning and intention behind a work such as the Realist Cycle of twelve plays is to forget the author altogether when analyzing his plays, just as we should leave behind, as far as we can, our own subjectivities. The communal participation of an audience at a performance of an artwork involves the renunciation of the individual ego of our everyday lives, and the most satisfactory performance is that in which we feel that the renunciation is amply compensated for by a consciousness of "universal" meaning. The kind of "interpretation" which reduces the *dramatis personae* to the objects of the attention we give to characters from our everyday life defeats the whole purpose of the objective artwork, which is to confront everyday reality with an alternative, more alarming but more liberating, reality.

When faced with an artistic structure as ambitious and intricate as Ibsen's Realist Cycle (on which the artist worked for twenty-two years), one's first duty as an interpreter is to try to establish the unity and rich coherence of the work. As with all ambitious works, such as the *Iliad,* the *Commedia* of Dante, or Joyce's *Ulysses,* this will be an endless activity, for the intricacy of organization of these works, though it can always be guessed at, can never fully be known or expressed. For one thing, the interpretive activity is fundamentally different from the creative activity so that the latter cannot adequately be described in the language of the former. Indeed, interpretation renders the single discourse of the artwork in a plurality of languages. Any aesthetic work, say, a large canvas, a sculptural group, a cycle of plays, an organization of *cantos* into a poem, has a *telos* and achieves its intention through the structure it elaborates and organizes. The meaning of the work is not some correspondence to a "truth" outside the work but lies within the work as a pattern of contrasts, juxtapositions, similarities, formal disposition of the parts, formal conflicts and reconciliations, and so on: in fact, all the activities which make the man or woman an artist. The "ardor" or energy of the artist's desire for adequate expression only can be satisfied, as art, through the formal constraints the artist finds it valuable to set himself. The analogy often drawn between the linguistic pattern of signifier-signified, where the word or expression is a sign that seeks correspondence with a "signified," does not fit the aesthetic situation where the artwork does not point beyond itself but only to itself. The meaning of an Ibsen play is its own adequate performance and the audience's comprehension of the artist's total performance. Interpretation of art, therefore, does not claim to be the revelation of a "truth" which the artwork is "conveying"—a relation to a signified, lying outside the work which might once and for all be identified—but, instead, the interpreter's recording of the significance he discovers within the pattern created by the collision of "ardor" and "structure." Any external aid to interpretation, such as the discovery of the artist's employment of an intellectual system or worldview, only sends us back to the closed world of the artwork to see how its elements can be reconciled to this discovery. Long ago, Matthew Arnold insisted that, unlike the philosopher, the poet does not try to *discover* new ideas but only to "play" with ideas already formulated. As "play"—even ambitious play—the artwork has more in common with games such as chess or football than with scientific inquiry. When an artist brings the terms of a philosophy into his work, they are at once converted into artistic elements.

The artwork is a closed totality. The "primary text" of the artwork "needs" the "secondary text" of interpretation not because the artwork has failed to convey its "truth" but because the terms of the artist's performance—a poem, string quartet, or drama—are intricate and elusive and may baffle a contemporary audience or be forgotten by a later one: And also because it is in the nature of symbolic structures to be endlessly significant. The "need" is not in the artwork, which may have achieved the perfection the artist sought, but in the audience of the artwork. Consider the few lines that make up William Blake's "The Sick Rose":

O Rose, thou art sick
The invisible worm
That flies in the night
In the howling storm
Has found out thy bed
Of crimson joy
And his dark, secret love
Does thy life destroy.

Why is it that one cannot imagine that these few lines ever will cease to elicit new and significant commentary and that one never will feel that any one commentary is the final and definitive one? The poem is not so much looking at an object, which it is trying to get us also to "see," as creating its own object, a pattern of dramatic juxtapositions and actions into which it is drawing us. A good commentary will convey to us the richness and depth of the terms Blake is employing, but we know that no interpretation will ever hand us a definitive account of the poem's meaning, for the "meaning" of the poem is enacted only in its own language, which is not the language of interpretive commentary. All such commentary can do is to send us back to the poem more capable of responding to its terms and, perhaps, sharing the poet's own sense of the immense drama behind the terms he has raised. An awareness of Blake's own attitudes toward the sexual, social, and economic conditions of his own day, of his "program" for the regeneration of our "fallen" and alienated human identity, will increase our sense of the scale and urgency of the drama the poem is enacting while our knowledge of modern psychoanalytic theory may give the poem added significance, but these external sources do not orient the poem toward an identifiable "truth" outside the terms of the poetic performance. Such external "sources" are only the materials out of which the poet has constructed a new reality—the poem—or are the materials out of which the reader constructs his new experience—the reading of the poem.

Seeing a contradiction between the interpreter's claim that the artwork achieves perfect expression of its meaning and yet requires the work of the secondary text better to reveal its meaning, Wlad Godzich writes:

Although apparently granting the primary text the status of perfect presence that we saw in lightning, or, to speak the discourse of poetics, that of a symbol where the relation of sign to referent or signifier to signified, is fully motivated, the very practice of a secondary discourse is at least implicitly or unconsciously grounded in the belief that such a congruence has not been achieved, may not be achievable, or that it can be ruptured at will, since this practice proposes to substitute its own product—its text—as the vehicle for transporting the truth. Blindly, it sees itself as a better representation of the truth, whereas it is in fact engaged in an allegorical relation of mapping one sign with another, of sublating one sign by another.[5]

Interpretation should not be trying better to "transport" the *external truth* of the artwork by means of the different discourse of criticism—as if meaning, anyhow, could be separated from the means of expression. There is no substitute for Blake's visionary performance in creating "The Sick Rose," and all that interpretation can do is to try to get the reader to fathom the full range and depth of that performance. A drama text does not require interpretation because its language is inadequately transporting a truth: A dance, a mime, an action to which dialogue is added (i.e., drama), all require the same kind of interpretative attention—an awareness of the range and force of the artist's expression within the constraints of the chosen form. If that range includes areas of consciousness that we associate with psychology, sociology, history, philosophy, etc., these do not have the meanings they possess within their own disciplines: Once they are drawn into the artistic performance, they are transformed into the elements of the aesthetic intention. Even in an avowedly *didactic* work, such as one of the Brechtian *Lehrstücke,* the actors confront the audience only as actors, as performers, and not as, for example, economists or sociologists. It is this fact that made so many of the idealist and reformist dramas of the sixties, in Britain and America, so objectionable: for one felt that the status of actor or director, within society, did not carry the authority that would justify the hortatory stance toward the audience, while, at the same time, the performances frequently lacked the aesthetic authority of more conventional works. We all know this, on a little reflection: that what makes the artistic expression of a cause, an idea, or a message convincing is the adequacy of the artistic performance rather than the adequacy of the idea, so that interpretation will be concerned always, finally, to subordinate the latter to the former. An adequate interpretation must be aware of the intellectual content of the artwork, of its playing with ideas and concepts, of the worldview it is expressing, but only as the terms of the aesthetic performance.

A sentence in a poem or drama is more like a "line" in a drawing or painting or in music: that is, it has an aesthetic-thematic function and performs within the aesthetic structure a different purpose from that of communication in everyday life outside such a structure. If a man in the street should say to me:

> It is the very error of the moon.
> She comes more nearer earth than she was wont
> And makes men mad

I would be concerned to test the truth of this statement and would decide the speaker is an unreliable communicator. But, in Shakespeare's play, these lines evoke the great disorder which Othello's action has brought within the compass of the drama's expressive reach, and, as an articulation of the tragic consciousness achieved by the movement of the play, they seem superbly appropriate. Such statements have to be *earned* by the artistic structure just as, in *Little Eyolf* and *John Gabriel Borkman*, the soaring last statements of the characters are earned through the intensity of the *agons* they are made to suffer. The "primary text" cannot be replaced by the "secondary text" because it is a different order of reality. It stands to the secondary text as the meal does to the menu, and Hedvig Ekdal, in *The Wild Duck,* to give one example, was not satisfied with her father's semiological substitution! We cannot place the critical interpretation on the same level as the dramatic text to be performed, for the critical text does not impose upon itself the aesthetic constraints of the artistic text. It is for this reason that "secondary texts" (interpretation) are ephemeral and replaceable, and for this reason also that they are parasitic upon "primary" artistic objects or texts, which endure. The secondary text tries to tell us something about the primary text: The primary text does not tell us something, it *does* something. T. S. Eliot observed in *The Function of Criticism:* "I have assumed as axiomatic that a creation, a work of art, is autotelic; and that criticism, by definition, is *about* something other than itself."[6]

In *The Order of Things* Michel Foucault, describing what he believes to be a radical shift in the nature of thinking between the sixteenth century and the "Classical period" that inaugurates the modern world, observes that it is "the Classical age that separates us from a culture in which the signification of signs did not exist because it was reabsorbed into the sovereignty of the Like. . . :

> And yet throughout the nineteenth century, and right up to our own day—from Hölderlin to Mallarmé and on to Antonin Artaud—literature achieved autonomous existence and separated itself from all other language with a deep scission, only by forming a sort of 'counter-discourse' and by finding its way back from the representative and signifying function of language to this raw being that had been forgotten since the sixteenth century. . . . In the modern age . . . literature is that which compensates for (and not that which confirms) the signifying function of language. . . . That is why literature is appearing more and more as that which must be thought; but especially, and for the same reason, as that which can never, in any circumstance, be thought in accordance with a theory of signification.[7]

Analyzing literature either for what it signifies or "from the point of view of that which signifies," whether from a psychoanalytic or a linguistic mode, is "to be searching for it outside the ground in which, as regards our culture, it has never ceased for the past century and a half to come into being and to imprint itself."[8] To interpret a literary text, therefore, is to be responsive

to the fact that aesthetic language expresses a different intention, and performs a different function, from that of the language
of discursive thought Paul de Man observed:

> For the statement about language, that sign and meaning
> can never coincide, is what is precisely taken for granted
> in the kind of language we call literary. Literature, unlike
> everyday language, begins on the far side of this knowl-
> edge; it is the only form of language free from the fallacy
> of unmediated expression. . . . The self-reflecting mirror-
> effect by means of which a work of fiction asserts, by its
> very existence, its separation from empirical reality, its
> divergence, as a sign, from a meaning that depends for its
> existence on the constitutive activity of this sign, charac-
> terizes the work of literature in its essence. It is always
> against the explicit assertion of the writer that readers
> degrade the fiction by confusing it with a reality from
> which it has forever taken leave.[9]

Paul de Man chides Northrop Frye for taking over American
New Criticism's idea of the "intentional fallacy" in his own system. Frye's distinction between discursive and poetic language
as that of the difference between intentional and nonintentional
language is rejected by de Man. *Discursive* language, he agrees,
has an intention beyond the language act itself, but the artistic
act, though not having an intention beyond itself, nevertheless
"reflects back upon itself and remains circumscribed within the
range of its own intent." De Man draws an analogy "between
different intentional objects such as the tool . . . and the toy,"
and remarks that the "aesthetic entity definitely belongs to the
same class as the toy, as Kant and Schiller well knew."[10] This is
not a denigration of the artistic activity: On the contrary, Schiller, in *The Aesthetic Education of Mankind,* viewed "the play
impulse" as the highest exercise of our humanity.

This might be what Foucault had in mind when he claimed
that the language of literature set itself up as "a sort of counter
discourse," for, by converting the terms of worldly experience

into a demanding and, within the closed circle of the aesthetic form, a liberating *play*, the artist and his audience can escape the perpetual dialectic of sign and signified of discursive language.

When an artist creates with his art "images of reality," these function in his artwork in aesthetic-thematic terms, just like the *themes* of musical form. The more ambitious the artist, the richer these images of reality will be, and I believe it was Ibsen's lifetime's object to make his chosen art—dramatic form—gradually absorb, conquer, and transfigure (in terms of a counter-discourse) the widest-ranging content drawn from his reflection upon his experience of reality. He is not so much *communicating* truth as *making* truth. His work is not inquiry and exhortation but aesthetic self-realization: a thoroughly serious *playing*.

The cycle of twelve realist plays was the project Ibsen set himself within which he felt he could achieve the fullest artistic self-realization. As *artistic* self-realization this meant the successful creation of an objective, freely standing artwork in which the artist's individual subjectivity was as thoroughly abnegated as, Hegel insisted, the philosopher's individual subjectivity must be lost in the development of the Concept. The project involved a continual making and exploration, from the first play to the last, following through the logic implied by the project and the artist's own development within the project: Thus the process was the reverse of mechanical. (Far more mechanical—and monotonous—would be the repetitive expression of subjectivity.)

The most persuasive and complete interpretation of a work is one that is able to reconcile the greatest plenitude of significant details within the coherent intention of the form, or as Paul Ricoeur expresses it:

> The more probable [interpretation] is that which, on the one hand, takes account of the greatest number of facts furnished by the text, including its potential connotations and on the other hand, offers a qualitatively better convergence between the features which it takes into account. A mediocre explanation can be called narrow or forced.[11]

Totality and coherence, congruence and plenitude, are the values we cherish in the work of art. This explains why we always are gratified both by our re-viewing of the work and by the reviewing offered by an interpreter, for on both occasions we experience hitherto unrecognized aspects of the work within its persisting unity. This is the reason why the conductor of classical music can return to the same score, year after year, without losing his sanity. Any previously undetected meaning, or any new significance, can be accepted only if it can be reconciled with the overall unity of the work. For many years I had looked upon the lengthy scene in *Ghosts* in which Helene Alving and Manders discuss the advisability of insuring the Orphanage as the only (inexplicably) redundant passage in the play—for it seemed far too obtrusive merely to explain the "curtain" line of Act II. Then, recently teaching the play, it suddenly struck me that this scene was exhibiting, in both Helene and Manders, that very cowardice before public power, convention, and the stifling and *lethal* web of social deceptions and oppression that will bring about the *nemesis* of the play. The play needed the scene so that we could see this cowardice in action, for it encapsules Helene's whole past, from which the rest of the play will wrench her free. The new perception did not violate but better confirmed the unity of the play. (I am aware that this could be an example of the "hermeneutic circle": One seeks a unity and "worries over" a detail until it can be integrated into a unity. But unity *is* more likely to be an artist's intention.)

The dialectic between "force" and "totality," between "ardor" and "structure," creates that "interminable" debate[12] that ensures that new artistic forms will continue to come into being, impelled by the force that has shattered previous forms. Derrida quotes Nietzsche's Zarathustra: "Here do I sit and wait, old broken tables around me and also new half tables. When cometh mine hour?—The hour of my descent, of my down-going."[13] This dialectic between force and form, whereby forms come into being, is fulfilled, and then dissolve is, as Derrida is aware, the very Hegelian condition of the history of consciousness itself. One of the most famous passages in *The Phenomenology of Mind/Spirit* is an account of the dissolution of one such cultural form and the momentous emergence of a new form:

> For the rest it is not difficult to see that our epoch is a birth-time, and a period of transition. The spirit of man has broken with the old order of things hitherto prevailing, and with the old ways of thinking, and is in the mind to let them all sink into the depths of the past and to set about its own transformation. It is indeed never at rest, but carried along the stream of progress ever onward. But it is here as in the case of the birth of a child; after a long period of nutrition in silence, the continuity of the gradual growth in size, of quantitative change, is suddenly cut short by the first breath drawn—there is a break in the process, a qualitative change—and the child is born. In like manner the spirit of the time, growing slowly and quietly ripe for the new form it is to assume, disintegrates one fragment after another of the structure of its previous world. That it is tottering to its fall is indicated only by symptoms here and there. Frivolity and again ennui, which are spreading in the established order of things, the undefined foreboding of something unknown—all these betoken that there is something else approaching. This gradual crumbling to pieces, which did not alter the general look and aspect of the whole, is interrupted by the sunrise, which, in a flash and at a single stroke, brings to view the form and structure of the new world.[14]

The Phenomenology of Mind is in fact a succession of such dramas of the human spirit, a total structure built up out of the destruction of its successive parts, and this, I have contended, is true also of Ibsen's Realist Cycle, in which, from the first play to the last, we see both the erosion and evolution of spiritual forms. Before we hurry to detect "contradictions" in Ibsen's text, we first should recognize that contradiction is the dialectic condition of his art. By this means, Ibsen recovers the pulse and rhythm of universal history (the history of the human spirit) within the form and language of only one of its forms, his contemporary world: a feat achieved by Hegel, too, of course, in which he recovers the spiritual history of the race within the language of post-Kantian discourse.

The dangers of interpretation are, on the one side, of discovering a plenitude of detail and significance that cannot be organized into a unified intention, or, on the other hand, of discovering a unity of intention only at the cost of sacrificing the work's plenitude, as in, for instance, a facilely "feminist" reading of *A Doll House* or a psychoanalytic account of *The Lady from the Sea*. Here the emphasis upon one possible level of significance entails evading the rest of the text's intention. The intention or meaning of a work of art often can be different from the new significances discovered within it. Furthermore, the formal nature of the artwork means that it always will be of another order than the contemporary significance we find in it.

Ibsen's relation to Hegel's *Phenomenology,* as to his other sources, is always that of the artist transforming "material" into the terms of his dramatic art. But the mode of the *Phenomenology* itself is, surprisingly, similar to aesthetic "doing." Hegel conducts the education of the human spirit in the *Phenomenology* not only on the levels of metaphysical and epistemological discourse but, as Donald Philip Verene observes, on the levels of commonsense speech and, more surprisingly, in the poetic and tropic mode of metaphors, ironies, and "poetic-mythical image." Verene quotes from an early work by Hegel:

> I am now convinced that the highest act of reason, that in which it embraces all ideas, is an aesthetic act and that truth and goodness are siblings only in beauty. The philosopher must possess just as much aesthetic power as the poet. Men without aesthetic sense are our literal minded philosophers. The philosophy of spirit is an aesthetic philosophy. One can in no way be ingenious [*geistreich*], one cannot even argue [*raisonnieren*] about history ingeniously [*geistreich*] without aesthetic sense. Here it ought to become clear what it really is that men lack, who understand no ideas and who frankly enough admit that

for them everything is obscure as soon as it goes beyond the table of contents and the index.

Poetry gains a higher dignity, it becomes at the end what it was at the beginning—the *teacher of humanity;* because [when?] there is no philosophy, no history left, the poetic art [*Dichtkunst*] alone will survive all other sciences and sciences and arts. . . . I shall speak here of an idea which, so far as I know has never occurred to anyone else—we must have a new mythology, but this mythology must be in the service of ideas, it must be a mythology of *Reason.*[15]

If poetry should become "at the end what it was at the beginning—the *teacher of humanity*"—then it would occupy the place in our culture that Homer and the Greek tragedians occupied in Athens: the supplier of a nondogmatic mythology capable of generating ever-new concepts. Verene also quotes Hegel's letter of 1805 to Voss in which Hegel declared: "Luther made the *Bible,* you have made Homer speak German—the greatest gift that can be made to a people,"[16] where, we see, Homer is exalted above the Bible. But Hegel (and in this he is in accord with current theory) insisted on the collaborative and intertextual nature of art. His description of the role of the artist within his total culture, what T. S. Eliot termed "tradition and the individual talent," can serve as a clue as to the nature of Ibsen's strikingly similar achievement:

Mnemosyne, or the absolute Muse, art, assumes the aspect of presenting the externally perceivable, seeable, and hearable forms of spirit. This Muse is the generally expressed consciousness of a people. The work of art of mythology propagates itself in living tradition. As peoples grow in the liberation of their consciousness, so the mythological work of art continually grows and clarifies and matures. This work of art is a general possession, the work of everyone. Each generation hands it down embellished to the one that follows; each works further toward the liberation of absolute consciousness. Those who are called geniuses have acquired some special skill or other whereby they make the general forms of a people their work. . . . What such geniuses produce is not their invention, but the invention of a whole people, or the *finding* that a people has found its essence. What belongs to the artist as such is his formal activity, his particular skill in this kind of presentation and he is brought up to this in the general skill. He is like someone who finds himself among workers who are building a stone arch, the scaffolding of which is invisibly present as an idea. Each puts on a stone. The artist does the same. It happens to him by chance to be the last; in that he places the last stone, the arch carries itself. By placing the last stone, the artist sees that the whole is one arch; he declares this to be so and thereupon is taken to be the inventor.[17]

"Ibsen the Norwegian" is the first world-dramatist: the first dramatist conscious of having a world audience. Yet, after his "world-historical" drama, *Emperor and Galilean,* his "world" would always be the Norwegian provincial or suburban consciousness: for he recognized that this was a world-consciousness, a world-mind or world-soul—a *Weltgeist.* The paradox of his dramatic art, therefore, is that though it seems "bottomlessly bourgeois" and "provincial," as Henry James deplored in an essay that nevertheless conceded Ibsen's power, its subject is our humanity and its history. Just as Hegel in Jena or Kant in Königsberg could simultaneously inhabit their little provincial cities and inherit the totality of history, so Ibsen, in the creation of his great Realist Cycle, could address our entire humanity through dramas within the drawing rooms of one of the remotest parts of European civilization.

To do this he devised an art form which, while presenting actions that have all the *intensive* power of great reckonings within little rooms, at the same time, by means of a "supertext," reaches out *extensively* to discover within the local and limited action patterns deriving from the widest-ranging human drama upon the battlefield of our total past. This merging of the particular within the universal, this immersing of the individual within the history and discourse of the species, was Ibsen's aesthetic response to the intellectual world he inherited, in which the Hegelian idea of our cultural evolution as a species was linked to the Darwinian account of our biological evolution. This response was not a facilely optimistic belief in human progress: Ibsen's vision was, I believe, a "fatalist" (his own description) and a tragic one. The human dramas he unfolded in the Realist Cycle were not his invention: They were the work of the "whole people," which he, with his "special skill" as a dramatist, would consummate by adding the final stone of the arch and proclaiming "Pax vobiscum!"

2

Ibsen's Realist Aesthetic

Only insofar as it is candid *(expressly renouncing all claim to reality), and only insofar as it is self-dependent (dispensing with all assistance from reality), is appearance aesthetic. As soon as it is deceitful and simulates reality, as soon as it is impure and requires reality for its operation, it is nothing but a base tool for material ends and can prove nothing for the freedom of the spirit.*
    —Friedrich Schiller, *On the Aesthetic Education of Mankind,*
Letter 26

. . . we may assume that we are merely images and artistic projections for the true author, and that we have our highest dignity in our significance as works of art—for it is only as aesthetic phenomena that we are eternally justified.
    —Friedrich Nietzsche, *Birth of Tragedy*

"Sois réaliste. Faites l'impossible."
    —Slogan of May 1968

"Be a realist. Ask for the impossible."
    —Cited by Jan Kott

Ibsen extended the Realist aesthetic far beyond the range of reference usually associated with realism. It is obvious that he shared much of the artistic attitude of many major realists; of Flaubert, Turgenev, Henry James. If we set the work of these realists against that of such *realistic* authors as Balzac, Dickens, George Eliot, we are aware of a difference of approach on the part of the realists: a new stringency of form, a new rigor which, sacrificing much of the expansiveness of reference and detail of the older writers, achieves that quality that James thought to be the essence of art—*intensity*. The fewer details of realist art seem richer in implication, the "terms" of the method more loaded with significance. The older, looser method of a Balzac or Dickens or George Eliot seemed to address itself to a possible "general public": The new Realism seems a product of, and for, the alienated consciousness of the modern spirit, whose origins can be traced in postrevolutionary European thought. This new literature of the alienated spirit stands in highly critical relationship to the social reality it portrays, as an attack upon that reality or, in Michel Foucault's phrase, as a "counter discourse" to it. A study such as M. H. Abrams's *Natural Supernaturalism* reveals the emergence of this alienated spirit in British and German Romanticism, Schiller's essay *On Naive and Sentimental Poetry* and Hegel's *The Phenomenology of Mind* being classic documents of the movement on the Continent. We see the continuation of this movement, in the theater, in the works of Schiller, Kleist, Buechner, Richard Wagner, and Ibsen, up to the avant-garde dramatists of modern times. Realism was an expression of this movement, one of its significant stages, and it is because of the peculiar richness of the realist aesthetic as an expression of this modern spirit that Ibsen remains as central to the modern tradition as, say, Manet and Cézanne remain central to the tradition of modern painting.

In a recent study of Realist painters, Charles Rosen and Henri Zerner observe that, in the authentic realists, the "subject" loses its importance, while the *artistic act itself* becomes the subject, assuming, in fact, the place of honor once held by the subject.

> If contemporary life was to be represented with its banality, ugliness and mediocrity undistorted, then the aesthetic interest had to be shifted from the objects repre-

sented to the means of representation. This is the justification of the indissoluble tie of mid-nineteenth-century Realism to art for art's sake; and though it is sometimes seen as an odd contradiction in Realism, it is, in fact, the condition of its existence.[1]

In literature, too, the realist aesthetic raises the *rendition* of reality to supreme importance while similarly relegating the *subject* to a lower status. When, in one of his early critical pieces, Ibsen insisted that "the ordinary person's character is by no means trivial from an artistic point of view; as represented by art, it is just as interesting as any other,"[2] he was expressing a belief that we can see as fundamental to Romantic ideology (which Realism inherited), as in Wordsworth's choice of the simplest figures for the subjects of his *Lyrical Ballads*. This realist aesthetic could be the basis of the most ambitious artworks, as with Ibsen's Realist Cycle, or James Joyce's *Ulysses*, where the largest "archetypal" presences are summoned up by means of the most everyday scenes, characters, and actions.

Whereas neoclassicism insisted on the dignity of the subject of the artwork, Romanticism and its offshoot, Realism, saw any subject as suitable for artistic rendition, and, indeed, the choice of simple, undignified, "unpleasant," or painful subjects (as in Géricault's studies of corpses, amputated limbs, or lunatics), by so transgressing the bounds of conventional artistic decorum, became itself a reinstatement of the "subject" in a new and radical sense. The objection that the portrayal of a beggar is in no way more realistic than the portrayal of a nobleman is valid: But realism at its best answered this objection by evolving an aesthetic that was truly indifferent to the *status* of the subject.

The new attitude, which was to have great influence on the development of realism and naturalism, elevated art above the subject, for it was the artist who made the subject significant, not the subject which gave dignity to the artwork. While this might always have been "secretly" true of art, it was never before clearly stated: And at no time before (at least since the age of classical Athens) was the artist accorded so high a social or cultural status as in the Europe of the nineteenth century. In the

Introduction we saw how this high evaluation of the artist's status was pronounced by Hegel; and the artist-seers who then emerged in Europe—and Ibsen was a central presence among them—were not at all diffident about acknowledging this status.

At first it seems a paradox that, just at the time when the artist and his work was given such high cultural value, there should arise a movement in the vanguard of this artistic community which would relegate the ostensible subject of art to the humblest objects and figures, and that this should be accompanied by a renunciation, on the artist's part, of the dignifying rhetoric of the older artistic styles. In the novels of Flaubert, for example, "the aesthetic liberation from rhetoric has its parallels in the work of the great Realist painters from Courbet, Manet and Degas to the Impressionists."[3] Previously, "rhetorical figures of speech, conceived pictorially, [were] the idealising formulas for pathos, for a whole repertory of poses and gestures that the renaissance artists derived from classical statuary and reliefs, and invented in new forms."[4] Ibsen, himself a painter and a collector of paintings, was surely aware—especially during his years in Rome and Italy—of the continuity of *subject* from the ancient, classical world, up to the aesthetic movements of his own day. Though Realism represented a break with this rhetoric with its reliance upon the "stock responses" such rhetoric could evoke, the *content* of the old rhetoric often was not abandoned. It is well known that many of Manet's paintings of modern life were in fact modeled on earlier or classical works, and we will discover that Ibsen, while abandoning the rhetoric of Romanticism, nevertheless retained the essential *content* of the spiritual past of the race within the metaphors of modern realism.

There are interesting parallels between Ibsen and Flaubert which might deserve a study someday. Flaubert's realism, too, "is derived from his Romantic inheritance and is, at the same time, a partial renunciation of it."[5] Though he insisted that writers should see things as they are (a requirement echoed by such realists as Ibsen and Joseph Conrad), he nevertheless held that "there is not an atom of matter that does not contain thought: and let us get accustomed to considering the world as a work of art, of which we must reproduce the processes in our own work."[6] Both Ibsen and Flaubert turned in disgust from their own bourgeois cultures to find salvation in "remoteness of subject," as we will see later in this chapter. There are affinities between the Flaubert who could write the realist novels *Madame Bovary* and *The Sentimental Education* and then create such Romantic works as the exotic *Salammbô* and the fantastic *The Temptation of St. Anthony,* and the Ibsen who could write the early Romantic and historical plays, and *Emperor and Galilean,* and then proceed to the realism of *Hedda Gabler.* Above all, the two authors share a supreme fastidiousness as to the aesthetic dimension of their work. They take the artistic act itself, its authenticity and subtlety, with the utmost seriousness.

In Flaubert, the aesthetic dimension is exhibited, as much as anywhere else, in the famous *style;* in the irony, for example, with which the author icily transfixes the banal world of the Bovarys. The irony is earned by artistic stringencies and self-denials that, again, recall Ibsen's method. Ibsen's way of making the artistic act itself the subject of each play is achieved by an artistic stringency even more severe than that of the novelist. As with Flaubert, such artistic stringency is a form of aesthetic heroism in defiance of a world indifferent to such values.

Rosen and Zerner usefully remind us of the difference between Realist and "realistic." The latter always has been present in art in some form; in the skillful rendition, for instance, of objects or people, in the plausibility of characters' motives and forms of expression. In *this* sense, Defoe's *Moll Flanders* is more realistic than Henry James's *The Ambassadors,* which is a highly accomplished work of Realism. Shakespeare's prose speeches, and much of his verse, often are more realistic than Ibsen's duologues, which, as in *Rosmersholm* and *Hedda Gabler,* two eminently Realist plays, are highly stylized. The Realist movement in literature and painting was a conscious aesthetic effort to attain artistic authenticity by renouncing the rhetorical devices of a tradition that had lost its validity. Such a concern for authenticity is evident in Ibsen's defense to Edmund Gosse of the new realist method he had employed for *Emperor and Galilean:*

> The illusion I wished to produce was that of reality. I
> wished to produce the impression on the reader that what
> he was reading was something that actually had hap-
> pened. If I had employed verse I would have counteracted
> my own intention and defeated my purpose. Speaking gen-
> erally, the dialogue must conform to the degree of ideality
> which pervades the work as a whole. My new tragedy is
> not tragedy in the ancient sense. What I wished to depict
> were human beings, and therefore I would not let them
> talk the language of the gods.[7]

To be faithful to the experience of reality, to render it with
truth, became the most demanding of *aesthetic* disciplines, not
an evasion of art. The old rhetorical devices, together with the
"heroic" subject and the "heroic" style, by becoming overfamiliar
as expansive gestures, had evoked stock responses that permitted the indication of areas of experience which the art actually
had not authenticated, had not searched out, and tested, from
the deepest and most problematic levels of the artist's and the
audience's experience. It is when this discrepancy is felt that
new forms are evolved, in that dialectic of "ardor" and "form"
mentioned by Jacques Derrida. The new forms frequently attempt to rescue, and maintain, the *old* values in the only terms in
which they can exist in the contemporary context. Such a passing of the spirit from older cultural forms was described by Hegel
in the passage from the *Phenomenology* I quoted in the Introduction; and it is this experience in fact that Ibsen records so deeply
in the story of Julian in *Emperor and Galilean*. In the twelve
plays of the Realist Cycle we watch one form evolving and dissolv-
ing, passing into a successive one, from the first play in the cycle
to the Epilogue, which brings the long dialectic to a close. Just as
Ibsen's Realist aesthetic, therefore, was his recognition that the
old form of drama had ceased to be valid, so his Realist Cycle is
the dramatization of this very process: the struggle of the human
spirit to achieve greater authenticity and adequacy as it journeys
forward, taking up and abandoning one spiritual drama after
another. This action, wrote Paul de Man, can be found in the
work of Mallarmé, with its "Hegelian overtones" of the theme of

"the universal historical consciousness."[8] The movement of Mallarmé's *Un Coup de Des* is "a dialectical movement of becoming. Each successive failure knows and remembers the failure that went before, and this knowledge establishes a progression. . . . Subsequent works can start on a higher level of consciousness than their predecessors. There is room in Mallarmé's world for some form of memory; from work to work, one is not allowed to forget what went before. A link is maintained, despite the discontinuities, and a movement of growth takes place. The impersonality is the result of a dialectical progression, leading from the particular to the universal, from personal to historical recollection."[9] This Hegelian "program" in fact could as well be a description of Ibsen's Realist Cycle.

The new nakedness of the realist aesthetic, as it renounced the older rhetorical gestures, greatly increased the artist's difficulties. The old rhetorical mode had disguised or condoned much actual implausibility. Critics willing to swallow the contradictions and improbabilities of *Hamlet* or *King Lear* can yet be heard indignantly protesting—or agonizing over—minor implausibilities in *Ghosts* or *The Wild Duck*. They do not reflect that they are actually demanding, and expecting, a greater degree of artistic finesse from Ibsen than they demand and expect from Shakespeare.

In *The Rhetoric of Fiction*, Wayne C. Booth claimed that "the typical demand for realistic effect is likely to clash with the typical demand for a pure rendering of the ideal aesthetic realm," for the "typical purist is likely to see moral problems and human emotions as the prime source of literary impurity."[10] Booth regrets that the modern Realist novelists, antagonistic toward the rhetorical devices of earlier fiction, have thereby sacrificed much of the moral and human content of the earlier fiction. This is a complaint very similar to that made in England against Ibsen's dramas when they first were performed in London in the last two decades of the nineteenth century. Much recent academic criticism, anxious to portray Ibsen (of all artists!) as a sturdy champion of bourgeois values, has tried to claim rich moral and psychological content for Ibsen's realist aesthetic, to reverse the counter-discourse of his art into something far more comfortable and congenial. Modern novelists, Booth contends, by concentrating on the artistic act itself, have suffered a damaging limitation of the amount of reality the novelist is permitted to present.

Because Booth sees the drive for aesthetic purity and the drive for realism as opposed, he is somewhat surprised by their actual convergence. The Realist quest for verisimilitude, for the authentic rendering of experience, quite perceptibly increased the difficulty of the artistic act. An artistic action and perception earned with such difficulty obviously was increased in *value*. The more genial and easygoing realisms, in the novel and the theater, of a Fielding and a Sheridan, a Dickens or a Bulwer-Lytton, belonged to an aesthetic consciousness confident of the adequacy and security, as well as the wisdom, of the idea of reality it shared with the great public. The new philosophy of revolutionary Europe, however, was to put all in doubt and completely to undercut the older confident and ample worldview.

The Realist aesthetic derived from a highly critical or skeptical attitude toward conventional ideas of reality, seeing as highly problematic what the great public was happy to take for granted. The open hostility between artist and public, taken to the length of public prosecution of the artist, as in the cases of Baudelaire and Flaubert and threatened against Ibsen's *Ghosts* (banned from public performance in Britain for many years), indicates only the extreme points of the estrangement between the new aesthetic and the culture in which it evolved. The great broad consensus of middle-class moral and aesthetic opinion on which the English novelists and the French *boulevard* playwrights depended broke down, confirming in the world of the theater the cultural division already apparent in the realms of literature and the visual arts. It is no accident that Ibsen should have found it convenient to exile himself from his culture for much of his creative life.

The Realist aesthetic, deriving from a number of causes— social, philosophical, historical, and moral—took up a posture of hostility, quickly reciprocated, toward conventional society. The public adherents of the new realism often were socialists, feminists, aesthetes, "advanced" thinkers of all kinds, so that when they assembled in such houses as Grein's Independent Theatre in London in 1891, it was not difficult for the critical spokesmen of the conventional press to identify and deride the "long-haired men and the short-haired women" who gathered to applaud Ibsen's plays. The gulf between the avant-garde and the conventional cultures is, today, taken for granted and treated with indifference, but on its emergence in the nineteenth century it was seen as a dangerous development that had to be suppressed, if possible.

The radical new realism and the new aestheticism were therefore reconcilable within the same cultural minority, as Booth is forced to concede:

> Curiously enough, both the quest for realism and the quest for purity, even in their most extreme forms, yielded the same attack on rhetorical impurities in fiction. . . . If fiction is to seem *real*, it must not be laden with signs of artifice. . . . If fiction is to be *pure,* if it is to "catch up with poetry," if it is to have anything like equal status with the more obviously pure arts, the author must somehow find a way to create a cleansed object which can speak for itself. Just as many poets in the modern period, whether symbolists, imagists or whatever, felt that the "natural object is always the adequate symbol," so the novelists and critics of widely different schools have echoed again and again the belief of Flaubert that the fully expressed "natural" event will convey its own meanings far better than any explicit evaluative commentary might do.[11]

Where Booth sees two quests converging, there was really only one, for realist art at its best was always a search for aesthetic purity. Flaubert's long agonizing over bringing off a quite ordinary meeting between Emma Bovary and her priest, getting the reader to "see" the entire scene "without one comment or analysis (all in direct dialogue),"[12] has its parallels in numerous actions in Ibsen's realism. To maintain the audience's sense that what it sees actually is happening, Ibsen must plausibly assemble, within his carefully delimited space, just those characters who will embody his dialectical "arguments," making carefully unobtrusive their archetypal traits, and impelling them to actions that will build up the perfectly shaped dramatic form of the play. He must get his characters to enter and exit "on cue" without seeming to (many of his characters make their first entrances just after their names and personal histories are mentioned, but this is so demurely done that audiences are not disturbed by this convention) and get them to act and react passionately and histrionically in ways appropriate to both the "human" and the "archetypal" levels of the story. To maintain the packed, symbolic fatefulness of scene, Ibsen frequently avoids quite natural changes of location— and, as the melodramas of his day reveal, frequent scene changes were well within the capacity of the nineteenth-century theaters. One such case is that of Krogstad's meeting with Kristine at the opening of Act III of *A Doll House.* The symbolic juxtaposition of the anguished couple, *below,* moving together to unite in joy, and the seemingly joyful couple, *above,* dancing happily and obliviously, soon to face anguish and disunion, is a metaphor Ibsen wishes to retain for his overall meaning; and for this purpose, he risks the incongruity of having Krogstad meet Kristine in the Helmer home, of all places. Grosserer Werle's meeting with his son, Gregers, in the Ekdal living room, forcing all the other characters to vacate the room where they are in the middle of a meal, is another such instance: here plausibly prepared for by the mess that Gregers makes of his own room. The confrontation of father and son must be enacted onstage for Ibsen's meaning, and so Ibsen turns his dramatic problem to good symbolic account, for Gregers's clumsiness in his room is a metaphor for his more fateful clumsiness within the household. These are stratagems and rigors that the lover of dramatic art appreciates, but they are easy for interpreters to overlook.

Hedda Gabler is a finely virtuosic display, to those who attend carefully, of the art of assembling the most improbably diverse group of characters who represent, thematically, the widest-ranging cultural "argument" (no less than that of *Emperor and Galilean*), making this group undergo the most violent of actions, plausibly, within the decorous environment of a middle-class drawing room, which must contain a multiple carnage that resembles a miniature *Götterdämmerung:* the deaths of Aunt

Rina, Løvborg, Løvborg's and Thea's "child," Hedda, and Hedda and Tesman's unborn child. With Ibsen's "classic" realism in which characters, actions, and dialogue are subjected to the shaping requirements of the classical dramatic structure, with its conflicts, crises, confrontations, peripeties, anagnoreses—the *structure* of classical drama without its rhetoric—the artist must all the time maintain our faith that all this elaborate artistry really is presenting us with "authentic reality" however "transformed." And what drives Ibsen to these extraordinary aesthetic rigors? His determination to bring into the image of his contemporary, fallen world of appearances the great universal human drama that he sees lying behind it, obscured by it. Ibsen's realism therefore is a denial that our *everyday* lives are "real" and he is determined to rescue reality from what we have made of it. In the long tradition of Idealist thought from the Greeks to the present day, Ibsen believes that essential reality lies behind the appearances, the phenomena, and that a genuine Realism, far from imitating our experience of everyday life, would have to reorder and reshape that experience until it became invaded by universal reality. This gives rise to the objection that Ibsen's plays are not "like life"—which is true if what is meant is the "unawakened" life from which Ibsen's art seeks to rescue us.

Some interpreters insist that Ibsen's dramatic method is that of the *pièce bien faite,* or well-made play,[13] but it is more rewarding, and more accurate, to see Ibsen as taking from the well-made play (*if* he took anything at all) only those elements it had in common with classical drama. The sequence of Exposition, Complication, Crisis, and Resolution of the well-made-play structure does not fit any play in the cycle after *Pillars of Society,* which one might see as representing the conventional theatrical structure Ibsen sets about subverting and transcending. In *Ghosts,* for example, exposition, complication, and crisis are continuous throughout the play (as in the *Oedipus Tyrannos*) and resolution is not attained. *A Doll House,* which Quigley reads as an ironic well-made play, does not fit the pattern either. Exposition does not cease until close to the *end* of Act III, *after* the final crisis, when Nora recounts her life with her father and her husband; and the play, notoriously, ends without a resolution. And where would one locate the *complication* in a play where complication is continuous? In a *dialectical action,* in which the discovery of multiple complexity (social, ethical, cultural, metaphysical) is ceaseless to the end, there is no point at which exposition, complication, or crisis can be shown to end. To read the play in terms of the *pièce bien faite,* that is, of a *conventional* aesthetic structuring of reality, is fundamentally to misunderstand its *radical* structure.

Richard Hornby observes that Ibsen really creates an "allegorical realism" which enforces continuity of space and time upon his actions. He notes that, from the stage space of, say, a drawing room, there are carefully maintained connections to a plausible surrounding space: other rooms, a kitchen, a stairway, doors opening onto a garden and from which visitors can be seen before they appear onstage; a topography, including a landscape and a town inhabited by watchful citizens, and so on. This is unlike the fluid stage space of Shakespearean drama, or the Chamber, Antechamber, and Exterior that Roland Barthes has seen as the unvarying scene of Racinian tragedy (though Jan Kott, for one, notes a resemblance between the "closed rooms" of Racine and Ibsen, the spaces in which the characters are trapped, fatally).[14] The Ibsen scene has its own unique history. The house of Bernick, the Torvald apartment, the house of Alving, and the rented house of Thomas Stockmann, to take the scenes of only the first four plays in the cycle, each defines the lives of its inhabitants and undergoes its own often-violent change. The scene frequently constrains and stands between the characters and their potential development; or is a refuge (*The Wild Duck*) from threatening reality, or a hostile environment invaded and subdued (*Rosmersholm*); or an environment only reluctantly inhabited by the alienated spirit (*The Lady from the Sea; Hedda Gabler*). The stage scene not only is a believable habitation for the realistic *mimesis* dictating its own rules as to what can be permitted to be shown; it also must be a *symbolic* space which, by the interplay of its interior and exterior locations, and by its often emphatic use of verticals, can establish, as Asbjorn Aarseth has argued, symbolic and metaphoric meanings.

The *temporal* continuity Ibsen maintains is equally as stringent as the spatial. Hornby notes that Ibsen's method cannot permit temporal discontinuities, from the rising to the falling of the curtain, for each act. In *Ghosts,* for example, the playwright implies the unfolding of a definite period of time—about five or six hours—which, though totally convincing to the audience, actually is impossible for an action that begins before lunch and ends with the sunrise. Ibsen's *symbolic* action requires the contrast of the mist and rain for Acts I and II and of the rising sun of Act III. A continuous action in which Mrs. Alving must receive Manders at a reasonable hour to discuss business before lunch, converse with the carpenter, her maid, and her son, witness the slow burning of the orphanage and her son's collapse at dawn, can be continuous within three hours of only briefly suspended theatrical action only by much sleight-of-hand. It is obvious that in *Ghosts,* just as in Greek drama, from which much of its argument and structure derive, the rules of the dramatic action are governed not by the terms of the everyday world and its chronology outside the theater but by terms of the symbolic drama.

Three major temptations that faced the new Realistic aesthetic, according to Rosen and Zerner, were those of "the sentimental, the picturesque and the anecdotal."[15] Each of these represented a relaxation of the stringent discipline of Realism, an attempt to compensate for the loss of the old sustaining rhetoric by a technique of ingratiation: a technique which the grand style of the older rhetoric had discouraged. British and American realistic drama in particular, lacking the ideological dimensions of the best continental drama, frequently resorted to these ingratiating devices.

When Henry James applauded Ibsen's depiction of Hedvig, in *The Wild Duck,* for the total avoidance of sentimentality in the portrait, this was a commendation by one major Realist artist (the author of *The Awkward Age* and *What Maisie Knew*) to another for maintaining the high standards of the Realist aesthetic at a point where its debasement would have been so easy—and so popular. Sentimentalism, one imagines, is just about the last charge anyone would make against Ibsen's method. The Romantic tradition of the use of the child as a symbol of (inadequate) Innocence (Blake) or of modes of perception lost to the corrupted adult consciousness (Wordsworth) lifted the themes of the child and of child-death far above the sentimental, and it is Ibsen's transmutation of this tradition into the terms of his new Realism that makes his thematic child-deaths, as in the superbly "Romantic" *Little Eyolf,* so far removed from any taint of sentimentality. One can imagine no British playwright of the period capable of taking up this theme in such depth and with such fine austerity of purpose.

With the second temptation, anecdotal art, the viewer's focus of attention is dispersed and scattered onto innumerable peripheral and incidental details, a notable weakness of Victorian art in which such a lifeless plenitude compensated for a "committed" decisiveness of plot or design. Instead of exploring, establishing, and responding to the logical fatefulness of events within the aesthetic structure, anecdotalism happily provides a profusion of inert details, or ornamentation, which merely embroiders the wholly conventional design. When this is wedded to a conventional moralism (which usually is the case in anecdotal literature), the result is to reinforce the public's most commonplace ideas of reality while giving those ideas the appearance of richness and complexity. The Realist aesthetic, on the other hand, did not seek to reinforce, but to unsettle and awaken, the public's perceptions, and this could be done not by offering a profusion of conventional detail but by selection, "point of view," startling and unsettling juxtaposition, reduction of detail to basic principles and elements, by loading a few terms with immense implication.

Anxious to detach Ibsen from the taint of what he believes to be "Hegel's abstractness, his obsessive systematizing," Hornby claims for Ibsen's art "a delight in the particular."[16] This is an eminently pragmatist idea of what is good in art, but it praises Ibsen for a quality in his realism which, I believe, he does not possess to any great degree, except in the essentially *novelistic* drama, *Emperor and Galilean.*

A delight in the particular seems to be a very good thing to have, but it does carry the danger of developing into the delight in the irrelevant clutter of, for example, Victorian genre painting and melodrama and into the dreary "realisms" of the modern stage and television screen, where, it seems, no tic, however trivial, is omitted from characters and their actions. The verisimilitude and detail which are rightly admired in reportage are out of place in an aesthetic work which succeeds by consequential selection, omission, juxtaposition, shaping—a tendency toward significant abstraction in fact. For Ibsen's *symbolic* realism is forced to be selective in its use of details which cannot remain inert but must be "charged" with illuminating significance at appropriate moments in the play. It is precisely this selectivity and spareness in the use of "props" that gives the dramas' details such metaphoric power. This also points the way to producing the plays by eliminating much of the "clutter" of realistic verisimilitude. Each detail, each "prop," should *earn* its place on the stage.

The anecdotalism that doted on "rich character study" was positively the major disease of Victorian drama, where figures sentimental or comic, pathetic or heroic, impossibly virtuous or luridly villainous, often with no connection with the design— such as it was—of the plot, were furnished with "racy" or "lifelike" idiosyncratic styles and mannerisms—exacerbated, in British drama, by class considerations—and with "interesting" or "endearing" little traits, in order to satisfy the audience's "delight in the particular" at the expense of any *universalizing* function of the artform. The best illustration of this in fact is the actual conversion of Ibsen's dialectical *A Doll House* into the anecdotal *Breaking a Butterfly*. Harley Granville-Barker records the instructive event:

> The scene is laid in some English country town. Nora becomes Flora, and to her husband, rather terribly, Flossie. He is Humphrey Goddard and we find him gifted with a mother (quite unnecessarily) and a sister (wanted for the piano playing *vice* Mrs Linden who disappears). The morbid Dr. Rank is replaced by a Charles-his-friend, called, as if to wipe out every trace of his original, Ben Birdseye! He is not in love with Nora-Flora, of course; that would never do. But Dunkley, alias Krogstad, had loved

her as a girl, when Humphrey Goddard stole her young
heart from him; so love has turned to hate and revenge is
sweet.[17]

We see the purpose of the changes wrought upon Ibsen's text.
The unconventional rendering of reality is returned to a conventional interpretation whose commonplace though simplistically
abstract quality is disguised by "enriching" superfluous detail.
Humphrey Goddard, in the adaptation, behaves as heroically as
Nora, in her most Romantic mode, had dreamed and so Flora
stays at home, chastened and awed by her husband's example.
(It is obvious that an analysis that reduced both texts to a seg-
mentation into "dramatological units," semantic or otherwise,
and did not see the two as representing radically different *intentions* would be overlooking the most essential characteristics of
the texts.)

As for the *third* temptation confronting the Realist, the *picturesque,* Ibsen's procedure can be seen as more than usually free
from the fault. Setting plays in such versions of the picturesque as
the fashionable drawing room, the bohemian quarter, or in the
exoticisms of the glamorous and the squalid were temptations to
which many Realists succumbed. Henry James, who joined many
in deprecating the "dreariness" of Ibsen's Norwegian bourgeois
settings, often himself preferred to haunt Belgravia or Bohemia;
while that offshoot of Realism, Naturalism, showed a preference
for the extravagant miseries of the lower depths of metropolitan
life—scenes which are far more attractive or sensational than
Ibsen's demure bourgeois domestic settings. Yet, until his last
play, *When We Dead Awaken,* Ibsen kept to these settings
throughout the Realist Cycle. This feature is so constant in Ibsen,
in contrast to other modern realist dramatists (and to his own
earlier work), as clearly to constitute an intention behind the cycle
that calls for interpretation. When we remember how Ibsen, for
much of the time preceding and during his writing of the cycle,
actually lived in such bohemian and exotic locales as Rome, Capri, and Gossensass, the absence of the "picturesque" from his
work is all the more striking. The extensive landscapes of *The
Lady from the Sea, Little Eyolf,* or *When We Dead Awaken,* for all

their beauty, are not exploited to add glamour to the plays but, instead, chart the full spiritual "areas"—from sea depths to mountain peaks and beyond—that the plays are exploring. The *scale* of Ellida's spiritual renunciation, or of Allmers's and Rita's exploration of their loss, or of the "earthlife" that Rubek and Irene invoke in their death-union require, for visual identification, just such landscapes as Ibsen, in these plays, specifies.

In Ibsen's realism the stage space is symbolically "charged," undergoing its own epiphanies, even in so prosaic-seeming a setting as that of *Pillars of Society,* which depicts a symbolic space invaded by spiritual forces just as much as the overtly more symbolic *John Gabriel Borkman.* Without any heavy "signaling" Ibsen can use his realistic scene to infiltrate upon it his larger universal "argument." Much of the symbolic power of Ibsen's scene comes from the fact that it is being dialectically subverted, undermined, destroyed, from the beginning. Given reality is seen as false appearance to be supplanted by universal truth: a movement that reminds one of the actions of Sophoclean tragedy. Furthermore, the Ibsen action does not record a dis-Order after which the violated original Order is restored, as in Shakespearean drama; rather, it follows the pattern, inaugurated by Aeschylus, where false and inadequate reality and inadequate concepts and convictions are, through suffering, painfully discarded and more adequate principles, or truths, evolved. This is the dialectic pattern of each play and of the entire cycle. Indeed, one can say that the dialectic exists both in the minutest action or insight within a moment of the individual play and within the giant single action of the cycle in its totality: that the dialectic action is the pulse-beat of Ibsen's cosmos, informing the microcosm of the individual moment and the macrocosm of the Whole. Being dialectical, Ibsen's text is made up of contradictions, of negations, which are the conditions of evolution. We now see the reason for Ibsen's nonpicturesque settings: The Ibsen scene is a habitation of the spirit, created by the spirit we will see unfold before us on the stage, containing its memories, its guilt, and its aspirations. To be convincing it must be solid and substantial, for the alienated and erroneous spirit has created a false *world* which it now uneasily inhabits. Because this world is an expression of the alienated spirits of the protagonists, who represent aspects of ourselves, such a world can be exotic neither to the protagonists nor to us; for we are to recognize ourselves in the reality presented and annihilated. Paradoxically, therefore, the "father of modern realism" is unremittingly engaged in exposing the falseness of, and demolishing, all given configurations of reality.

The recognition of forgotten or repressed powers, entailing also the recognition of realities and values often in opposition to those the protagonists had put their whole faith in, is what Ibsen means by we dead awakening. It is this subversion of all claims to represent reality that makes Ibsen's realism radically different from that of all other realists in the modern tradition.

Rather than striving to give back to us our experience of everyday life, Ibsen's method, on the contrary, seeks to shatter it. It is a realism that sets itself against "given" reality, and all attempts to perform the plays as if they offered us a faithful record of our unawakened life experience can only produce a false effect. If, however, we learn to see that realism as far more devastating to our conventional perceptions than the method of Brecht; closer, in fact, to such a method as that of Jean Genet, we may, by discovering the power of the Ibsen action, discover its effectiveness with audiences.

A deep dissatisfaction with the bourgeois reality within which they found themselves confined was shared by a number of realists, and Ibsen's expressed regret that he had not been around to torpedo the Ark is just one of the more violent expressions of this dissatisfaction. Flaubert observed that he could find refuge from the contemporary society that disgusted him only in the remote and exotic world he brought to life in *Salammbô*. Ibsen, similarly, lamenting that he found himself, in Dresden, "in a society well-ordered to the point of boredom," took no comfort in his imminent return to Norway. "What on earth will happen when I settle at home? I shall have to find salvation in remoteness of subject. That is when I intend to begin *Emperor and Galilean*."[18] Flaubert, turning in disgust from the world he dissected in *Madame Bovary* to the Phoenician world of ancient Carthage, and Ibsen, turning from the stifling parochialism he had dissected in *The*

League of Youth to the Byzantine world of Emperor Julian, were seeking a liberation for their spirits, constructing larger worlds for their imaginations than given reality could provide.

This idea that an artist, rather than imitating the world given to his immediate perception, instead constructs an alternative world, a "counter-discourse" to the world's (and one interpreter has suggested that this is Hegel's procedure in the *Phenomenology*), is close to the idea of the artist expressed in *Human Quintessence* by Ibsen's son, Sigurd. It would be improper, of course, to claim that in this book Sigurd Ibsen is proclaiming his father's philosophy (though we know that father and son were close in thought): But it is at least remarkable how Sigurd's ideas (a form of Nietzschean Socialism not unlike Shaw's) resemble the idea of Ibsen's art that I have been promulgating since *The Ibsen Cycle* (1975).

One first of all is impressed by the cosmic *scale* of Sigurd Ibsen's thought. His book begins with an account of our human species as inhabitants and products of a post-Copernican universe, aware of the immensity of the surrounding cosmos where other planets in other solar systems presumably are undergoing similar or different development. In our imaginations, Sigurd Ibsen observes, we try to populate this immensity with creatures that might resemble humanity. Though, mentally, we can accept this cosmos, it has not "penetrated into our emotions."[19] These new scientific concepts have not "succeeded in changing our motives, our ideals, our egos."[20] Thus our humanity frequently can be seen as lagging behind our intellects (a condition explored in such Ibsen plays as *Ghosts* or *Little Eyolf*). Darwinism has brought home to us "the common origin of all organisms: all plants and animal forms are twigs of one and the same genealogical tree, the race of man a shoot of the vertebrate animal branch."[21] Due to the contradictions between our scientific knowledge and our older inheritance, we create an ironic disparity between our actual situation in the cosmos and the social and personal realities by which we still live. (This discrepancy is the basis of Ibsenian tragedy and Shavian comedy.) We have other contradictions, also. For all the pull of our otherworldly religions, we are creatures of the earth: Humans "have wanted, above all, to live; their kingdom has been of the earth, only."[22] These words seem to echo, even to rephrase, the words of Allmers and Rita, Rubek and Irene.

Darwinism, Sigurd Ibsen (with his father's grimness) points out, has been misconstrued as equating natural selection with progress. But it is very likely that better "germ forms" (what today we might call gene pools) "bearing in them richer possibilities than those our species can realize have gone to waste."[23] Nature has no purpose, and we can understand Nature only through our own categories which, as Kant insisted, are denied access to the "thing-in-itself." "The attributes ascribed to Nature are given by us."[24]

Culturally, mankind, alone among species, "remakes himself within nature, departing from nature"[25]—a major (Hegelian) theme, I claim, of *The Lady from the Sea*. Our social systems, however, lag considerably behind our intellectual understanding. Only within the world of art are we able to escape the limitations of the alienated reality we have constructed around ourselves. The end of human endeavor, however, is not art but heroic individualism, and the heroes of the past serve to remind us of heroic possibilities within a new form of humanity: an idea closely resembling Henrik Ibsen's "third empire of spirit." Any such new heroic identity (where all conflict would be spiritual, a sublimation of the present forms of physical conflict) would need to remember its past, from which it would gain ideas of its spiritual possibilities.

Human Quintessence seems a quintessence of Ibsenism, its thought ranging in the bold manner of the late nineteenth and early twentieth centuries. In his account of the function of art, Sigurd Ibsen propounds a thesis very close to that I am proclaiming in this book, for he sees a direct antagonism between art and everyday reality:

> The artificial makes amends for nature's exterior insufficiency, the artistic supplies its lack of inner coherence. It is just on account of its lack of coherence that life, as we see it about us, the life of both individuals and society, offends us at every step.[26]

Far from rendering, or recording, the reality they see before them, artists can "move into another world to which they give a meaning and where their ideals can be realized. . . . Life is disproportion, chaos, arbitrariness; art is balance, symmetry, conformity to law."[27] Even more strikingly close to my thesis is Sigurd Ibsen's insistence that art depicts archetypal forces and powers that are not expressed in the rhythms of everyday reality. Art "gives liberty of action to forces and possibilities to which life does not grant the chance of coming into their rights," revealing "life to us as it should be." "Nature shows us only fragments, art collects these fragments into an entity."[28] Far from imitating life, art actually corrects the errors of our experience of reality:

> Behind the phenomena's multiplicity the artist catches glimpses of a unity; behind the confusion, a coherence; behind the forms, an idea; behind the casual, the essential. The artist's task lies in separating the essential and making it real for us.[29]

Or, as Arnold Rubek tries to explain to Maia (who, in these matters, as in others, is a thoroughgoing pragmatist) when explaining his interest in the playing of a group of children:

> Der er noe harmonisk—nesten som musikk,—i de bevegelser, en gang imellem. Midt i alt det klossete. Og de enkelte gange er det morsomt å sitte og passe på—nå de kommer.

> There's a harmony—almost like music—in their movements, every so often. Right in the middle of all the gawkiness. And it's amusing to sit and watch for those special moments—when they come.[30]

The philosopher and the poet, Sigurd Ibsen concludes, have similar purposes; "the one, just as well as the other, will give us a glimpse of the coherence of things."[31] These are large claims for the artist, but they belong to that European (and especially Germanic) Idealist tradition which, I claim, lies behind Ibsen's Realist aesthetic. Sigurd Ibsen does not once mention his famous father in *Human Quintessence*. He does not have to. Both the author's own identity and the title of the book, with its seeming reference to Bernard Shaw's famous study of Ibsen's plays, makes Ibsen's presence felt on every page. The book, indeed, reads like a tribute from the son to the spirit of the father. As to the subject of this chapter, Ibsen's Realist aesthetic, we find Sigurd Ibsen writing: "One can talk as much as one will of naturalism in art, yet it will always be only a question of manner of presentation; for according to its very nature all art that deserves the name will be idealistic."[32]

Realism, as an aesthetic, did not set out to offer a photographic image of everyday reality either in painting or in literature. In Ibsen's hands Realism was the means whereby the artist could create, in terms of consummate and demanding art, an account of the human condition that, in scale of exploration, can rival any in European culture. Ibsen's realistic art was his counter-discourse to that of the world in which he found himself: his means of creating an alternative and more significant world possessing the coherence and the display of archetypal and exemplary spiritual qualities that the actual world frustrated or obscured. The idea that given reality may fail to realize its truth, the Absolute Idea it should express, is the very radical message of Hegelian philosophy: that that which has been completed as Idea, as thought, has yet to be fulfilled as actuality, and that the facts and institutions of our everyday world are only the imperfect means whereby we may attempt to attain our true self-determination. Though the heroically lived life was, for Henrik Ibsen as much as for his son, the primary requirement, in art, if the artist is daring, disciplined, and visionary enough, the obstacles to our self-fulfillment may be fought and overcome and the powers and forces necessary to our liberation summoned. But before we can "see" this great function of Ibsen's art, we first need to search out, and confront, those approaches that obscure and frustrate its recognition.

3

Text and Subtext

The rat, the mouse, the fox, the rabbet watch the roots; the lion,
the tyger, the horse, the elephant watch the fruits.
            —William Blake, *Proverbs of Hell*

Anyone connected with the theater at some time is going to have
to confront the concept of the "subtext." This takes the given,
surface text as being an inadequate expression of the full situation. This seems to be the same as what I claim for the supertext:
the network of larger referents behind the words that subvert
everyday reality's claim to express sufficient truth. However, I will
claim that the supertext exists objectively as a pattern of references, a conscious "intertextuality," linked to a clearly existing,
inherited cultural and ideological "argument" continually invoked
and exploited by art—indeed being the very *condition* of much
European art. In supertextual interpretation, one would link the
phrase "joy-of-life" in *Ghosts* to a pattern including Osvald Alving's art, the champagne, sexuality, Hellenism, the sunrise, and
so on and see it as one side of a "binary" system which includes, on
the other, the phrase "duty" linked to a pattern including social
repressiveness, denial of sexuality, Pauline Christianity, the rain,

and other related metaphors. One finally would hope to get another rational individual to agree that these patterns are present, are linked to such patterns in other Ibsen plays, and must influence our way of seeing the play's intentions. Subtextual criticism, on the other hand, does not ask us to clarify the referential nature of these words and metaphors to see how they are linked significantly in a pattern of meaning, but, on the contrary, to see these words as standing for "unconscious" or unstated and unacknowledged drives of supposedly real individual psyches. Supertextual interpretation aims for a precision which can be assented to by anyone willing to concede, after considering the evidence, that the terms of Ibsen's art do have this referential quality. It accepts that this never can be a wholly exact or definitive procedure, but it sets out to overcome the imprecision all interpretive writing must encounter. Subtextual criticism, rather than seeing imprecision as an obstacle, flourishes in it.

To the performer, needing to "believe in" and make others believe in his or her role, subtextual criticism is of value, as it is for the director anxious to make the performance humanly credible to an audience. Anyone who has been involved in a production knows the importance of this and would not scorn the typical comment of the actor: "What I think this character *really* feels in his or her heart is . . ." One cannot act an idea or a symbol, one is told, even if, as in a play like *Everyman* or a German Expressionist play, the *dramatis personae* are labeled with purely symbolic names. (Though one cannot imagine Good Deeds asking "What's my motive?")

Works of art are careful, consciously wrought metaphors that extend into a surrounding world of previous art forms and into the text of the world's recorded history, remembering what the everyday world contrives to forget. The almost inexhaustible significance of a poem, a play, a painting, by a major artist is the way in which its intricate iconographic structure refers to an entire world of art, culture, learning, philosophy, and ideological expression and conflict. To turn away from this intricate pattern of reference and to speculate on the subjective motives of individual characters within the composition is to turn away from the artwork altogether. If all human discourse is an intertextuality, art is special because, by its principles of selection and arrangement, by subjecting itself to very special rules of manifestation and expression, and by its insistence upon aesthetic unity, it stands aside from, comments on, and provides an alternative to the world's discourse.

Texts are made out of other texts, but a major artist is not merely "spoken by" his culture (or written by its language); his intervention in his culture's discourse is decisive and, if he is innovative within his art form, he is asking his audience to reconsider and reexamine the conventions by which that art form hitherto has been understood. That is, a supertext does not only reflect an intertextuality; it reorganizes and revaluates and transforms it whether or not the continuing discourse of the culture takes note of this. Much of this was set out in T. S. Eliot's *Tradition and the Individual Talent*.

Subtextuality, by subordinating the *objective* referential purpose of artistic language, denies the artist the very powers which prompted him or her to become an artist in the first place: the ability consciously to absorb, master, and modify the ongoing development of a tradition of art. There already is a general tendency in people, unwilling to respond to the more demanding aesthetic intentions of an artwork, to confuse its terms with those of their more familiar "real life" equivalents, and "psychologism" in interpretation only encourages this confusion. If the artwork is to succeed with us, we have to meet the artist on his own terms.

The individual artist, in his life's work, has established the manner in which his art orients itself toward the culture and the aesthetic conventions from which it emerged, and interpretation seeks to make this orientation more clear. When we confront such an artist's work, we should first agree to accept this orientation as a condition of judging the work's success. We might reject the whole artistic endeavor, but we should at least attempt to understand the objective nature of what it is we are rejecting. We should try neither to convert the artwork into something more congenial nor to dismiss it for not doing what it does not set out to do.

In subtextual interpretation dramatic characters become like icebergs, of which only a fraction is seen above the surface and whose greater masses are moved by strong, invisible currents at finally unfathomable depths. There are fascinations in this procedure, but they are anti-aesthetic ones. It is not the purpose of art to offer us half-completed puzzles hinting at the inexplicability and mysteriousness of reality but, as Sigurd Ibsen insisted, to correct reality's confusions and inadequacies. Even in a minimalist dramatic method, such as Harold Pinter's, in which the unstated implication exists within a "pause," the device is a controlled effect on the part of the dramatist, not a throb of independent psychic life within the dramatic character. The disparity between what we sense the situation to be and the inadequate or inappropriate response of the characters to this implied situation is an "objective" tactic of dramatic art, as we more clearly see in the plays of Samuel Beckett. That it frequently encourages subtextual speculation in certain critics is due to the human weakness of readers to amplify the writer's fiction. Ibsen once remarked that his readers were often more "poetic" than the poet himself. Dramatic *performance* is likely to be more successful in counteracting this tendency to daydream over a text.

Subtextual and psychologistic interpretation of Ibsen was given an extraordinary fillip by Freud himself, who wrote a very imaginative, beautifully written but ultimately misguided analysis of the character of Rebekka West of *Rosmersholm*. As someone who admires many of the writings of Freud, I do not take issue with his analysis from any belief that this discipline has nothing to contribute to literary studies. Freud's piece on Rebekka West is the best psychoanalytic account of an Ibsen character we possess, so that its wrongness of approach is very instructive for interpreters. And Freud himself cannot be held accountable for the way in which his method has been taken up by less sensitive interpreters of literature, who use the methodology as a substitute for the more demanding requirements of an aesthetic discipline. Evident from the start of Freud's analysis are two features that will emerge less discreetly in later neo-Freudian subtextual interpretation of Ibsen:

    1. He pays no attention to the dramatic-theatric structure of the play. The sequence of stage events, in which

actions, speeches, and memories of actions are presented to the theater audience as an artistic *unfolding,* creating the experience of the artwork, is simply set aside and another, biographical sequence is substituted—inferred events as they presumably occurred, chronologically, in Rebekka West's "life."

2. Freud treats Rebekka West as a real person whose theatrically presented identity hides a hidden and unconscious identity.

In the first approach Freud resembles many critics and interpreters who, not really interested in dramatic art, rearrange Ibsen's structures with their careful sequences and replace them with another, *novelistic* one. This leads to the frequent observation, first made by Georg Lukács, that Ibsen really was a novelist, whose genius overburdened the stage's capacity for *showing* in order to present something of the modern novel's richness of psychological/social exploration. Against this, we must protest that if Ibsen had wanted to present the modern novel's subject matter he would have chosen the novelistic form. This form was sufficiently well developed in his own culture for him to adopt; whereas the much inferior development of the theater presented him with immense obstacles against his self-realization as an artist. Ibsen was not trying to create the equivalent of the novel's richness and complexity for the stage: He set out to create a different art form—above all a *performing* art form—altogether. The sequence of events as they unfold in time on the stage is the only sequence the interpreter should consider. Rebekka West is made to remember, or confess, an event when she does because that is the appropriate moment in the drama's movement/ structure for that illuminating detail, which contributes to the total artistic design, in time and space, that is taking shape before our eyes. There is no "reality" to the characters outside the frame of the stage space and the two or three hours of their ritual performance. When it is not realized that Realism is an aesthetic, this misconception (which is less likely to trap interpreters of, for example, Greek classical tragedy, where Aristotle's

distinction between "story" and "plot" is well established) becomes a common one.

It is the second approach that creates the more fundamental
confusion in interpretation of both the drama and the novel.
Freud is partly aware of this confusion, conceding at one point,
"So far we have treated Rebekka West as if she were a living
person and not a creation of Ibsen's imagination."[1] Even after
this self-admonition, however, Freud continues to psychoana-
lyze Rebekka West as if she *were* a living person. He constantly
wavers between the fascinating possibilities opened up by seeing
the character in real-life terms and the glimpses that now and
then break through, that this is the artistic creation of a playwright. It reveals in the greatest of the Freudian interpreters an
inability to decide with what kind of reality, aesthetic or actual,
he is confronted. It is the fallacy of the actual that finally takes
over his discussion:

> If we resurrect Rebekka's past, expanding and filling in
> the author's hints, we may feel sure that she cannot have
> been without some inkling of the intimate relation be-
> tween her mother and Dr. West. It must have made a
> great impression on her when she became her mother's
> successor with this man. She stood under the domination
> of the Oedipus complex, even though she did not know
> that this universal fantasy had in her case become a real-
> ity. When she came to Rosmersholm the inner force of
> this first experience drove her into bringing about, by vig-
> orous action, the same situation which had been realized
> in the original instance through no doing of hers—into
> getting rid of the wife and mother, so that she might take
> her place with the husband and father.[2]

The story Freud so brilliantly tells is a fascinating one and, furthermore, it has the neatness and symmetry of the Oedipus plot:
of Rebekka journeying, like Oedipus, to a place where she will
discover she stands in danger of *again* performing the Oedipal
drama of displacing one parent and sleeping with another. But it
is not the story that Ibsen shows us, and no amount of "filling in

the author's hints" can justify replacing Ibsen's action with another. The aesthetically impure business of deconstructing the
story in nonaesthetic terms, then reconstructing it, filling in
hints, is something we anyhow are unable to do as theater audiences: And out of the theater, where no Rebekka West exists, we
are merely daydreaming over the text if we do so.

The characters and events in a dramatic structure, just like
the moments in a string quartet, exist only for their contribution
to the unfolding design of the performance. As iconographic or
symbolic figures they can gesture outward, to the larger "text" of
our cultural heritage and situation, and they will derive much of
their meaning from this larger text, as we shortly will see when
comparing a psychoanalytic interpretation of a passage from
Rosmersholm with an interpretation linking this passage to other
Ibsen texts. To gesture inward, teasingly, to a realm of implied
psychological reality would destroy the unity of aesthetic attention which the work is seeking from the audience. Freud's procedure requires so much conjecture that the dramatic structure
Ibsen is presenting to us dissolves. It further dissolves because
this account ignores all the other members of the dramatic ensemble (of which Rebekka is only one element). Rosmer is only
incidentally mentioned; there is no account of the dramatic function of the important figures Kroll, Mortensgaard, Brendel, Mrs.
Helseth.

Freud, of course, did not set up to be an interpreter of Ibsen; he
"used" the example of Rebekka West to illustrate a psychic disorder encountered in everyday life. He read Ibsen's play as if it were
a precocious Freudian novel. Derek Russell Davis discards even
this concession to aesthetics and treats the Ibsen dramas as case
histories written with the lack of clarity forgivable to a pioneer in
psychoanalysis. Looking at *Ghosts*, for example, he sees not a
structure of ideas, a cultural intertextuality behind the particular
details, but only a collection of *facts*—mainly medical ones—
which he proceeds to attend to, or to ignore, according to their
serviceability to his psychoanalytic thesis. Thus he brusquely dismisses the evidence for inherited syphilis "as an aetiological fac-
tor" behind Osvald's collapse, and, filling in the background of the
Alving family's early history and of Osvald's probable reaction to

the probable miseries of those years, Russell Davis discovers evidence for a classic case of schizophrenia.[3]

Such "attention" to Ibsen's text reveals no tragic insight, no larger vision of our human condition, but only a pitiable and squalid history of unhappy and undistinguished individuals at a loss to understand themselves or others. This is the exact opposite of what an experience of a *performance* of *Ghosts* should offer, though any director following Russell Davis, if he should think a performance worth attempting (which is unlikely), would no doubt fight Ibsen's structure at every point. The Ibsenists who like this sort of thing because it seems to make their man significant to all sorts of areas of human interest—and Russell Davis goes on to discover similar clinical symptoms in other Ibsen plays—are sacrificing Ibsen the dramatic artist to Ibsen the topical subject. Ibsen's great lifework was to liberate himself, and those of us dead capable of awakening, from the confusions of our everyday world into a perception, through and above these confusions, of universal, rational powers of the human spirit that give meaning and coherence to the human condition. As an artistic project it is no more typical of *our* modern world than the projects of the Greek tragedians, Dante, or Goethe; but it is also no less valuable in confronting us with dimensions of artistic endeavor that our world may have lost sight of. Psychoanalytic criticism that has fastened itself like an incubus on the Ibsen text reduces the artistic enterprise of the Realist Cycle to a collection of pitiable case histories.

More recently, Russell Davis, in colloquy with a fellow Freudian, has turned his attention to *Rosmersholm*, though *Ghosts* is not forgotten, for he confides, "My own suspicion is that Osvald's collapse into a catatonic state explains very clearly why Ibsen never went back to his mother's house." The colloquists then proceed to analyze the psychopathological condition of the characters of *Rosmersholm*, finding particularly lurid significance in the passage in which Rosmer's former tutor, Ulrik Brendel, tells the apostate, Rosmer, that Rosmer's "victory is assured,"

> But—please observe—on one immutable condition . . .
> (*taking Rebekka gently by the wrist*) That the woman

who loves him will gladly go out into the kitchen and lop
off her delicate pink-and-white little finger—here—right
at the middle joint. Moreover, that the aforesaid loving
lady, just as gladly, cut off her incomparably formed left
ear. (*Releases her and turns to Rosmer.*) Farewell, John,
my conquering hero.[4]

One can see why the psychologizing interpreter would be
roused by this passage so that, as with other such passages in
Ibsen, it is all the more important, before speculating on its
subtextual significance, to see if we can "place" it in the context
of Ibsen's objective supertext. Both the circumstance onstage
and Brendel's phrasing would tell the reader familiar with Ibsen's works that this is a rephrasing of a crucial speech by Julian
in *Emperor and Galilean,* in which Julian, also an apostate, turns
upon his halfhearted pagan followers, spelling out the only terms
in which he can believe they genuinely are his supporters:

> These Galileans, I tell you, have in their hearts something
> I dearly wish you would strive for. You call yourselves
> followers of Socrates, of Plato, of Diogenes. Is there one of
> you who would gladly go to his death for Plato's sake? Do
> you think Priscus would sacrifice his left hand for Socra-
> tes? Would Chytron let them cut off his ear for Diogenes
> sake? Of course you wouldn't.[5]

The apostate Rosmer doubts that his "pagan" follower, Rebekka, though she has professed conversion to the Rosmer way of
life, has the self-sacrificial resolution of the "Christian" Beate,
who killed herself for Rosmer's sake. Brendel, though he does
not know it (the alert in the audience do), is speaking out
Rosmer's unconfessed doubts, and in more lurid and "theatrical"
terms than the finer-toned Rosmer could; and Brendel's utterance will, at last, give Rosmer the courage to speak out. The
theater audience can detect this, if it attends carefully, for it is
"there" in the objective structure of the play's argument, which,
for over two hours, it has been following closely. It also is likely
that many in the audience will know Ibsen's other works and will

pick up the link with *Emperor and Galilean* and its concept of the "third empire of spirit." This is the kind of attention an imaginative writer desires and it is how a supertext operates: If we do not attend to this, we are denying Ibsen the terms of his artistry. To Russell Davis, Ibsen's text does not invite him to explore the patterns of meanings and associations discoverable in Ibsen's whole artistic program but, instead, to explore quite different possibilities:

> Finger and ear are well-known Freudian symbols for male and female sexual organs. Rebecca, who has taken on the thrusting role of the male in her relationship with Rosmer while still longing to be penetrated as a woman, must kill both desires in herself.[6]

Here, Ibsen's text and all its careful connotations within his total work have disappeared, to be replaced by a subtext that is a Freudian code to be decoded. This procedure is by no means an aberration in Ibsen interpretation. It therefore will pay to examine the presuppositions of an approach whose popularity with Ibsen interpreters is the greatest single obstacle to establishing, by means of the supertext, the *scale* of Ibsen's achievement.

In the present instance, is Russell Davis claiming that, in Ulrik Brendel, Ibsen has created an uncannily perceptive (and precocious) psychoanalyst who detects Rebekka's libidinal condition and then proceeds to utter Freudian runes about it? Or that Brendel knows not what truth he speaks, but that Ibsen does and is out-Freuding Freud, who did not mention *these* compulsions in his study of Rebekka West? Or that Ibsen quite "unconsciously" gives Rebekka these symbolic associations which had to wait, for explanation, until the establishment of psychoanalytic procedures in literary interpretation? And then, what of Julian's followers? Do they, too, all long to be penetrated as women? Or does one apply the Freudian interpretive kit quite arbitrarily? Certainly Russell Davis hardly can claim to be interpreting Ibsen's intentions. As Charles Altieri observes of the Freudian interpretation of Shakespeare:

. . . for Shakespeare to accept a particular Freudian concept would entail his knowing the entire system (unless, of course, one manages to state the insight in terms we believe a Renaissance man could understand). Freudian readings of Shakespeare, then, are usually readings of the text's significance, not its meaning. This does not mean that such readings are wrong. It does, however, suggest they are subsidiary to, and responsible for, a prior description of meaning, and it entails their being subject to different criteria, criteria created by the discipline of psychology rather than constructed to account for authorial purposes.[7]

In a similar vein, E. D. Hirsch, objecting to Freudian interpretations of *Hamlet,* observes that it is irrelevant for recognitive interpretation—which seeks to establish the author's meaning— that the play permits a Freudian reading. This might be part of the text's "life" within our culture, but it cannot be seen as any part of the poet's intention.[8] The main objection to such readings is that they proceed serenely without ever feeling accountable with regard to the *aesthetic plausibility* of their claims; that the author actually could have intended such meanings to be extracted from his artwork. Of course, there is always recourse to the "unconscious" intention, that very convenient convention of psychologizing interpretation. The Unconscious is a capacious magician's hat into which inconvenient surface meaning—the text—can be stuffed out of sight and from which lurid alternative meaning triumphantly can be pulled. As the Freudian code can be seen to proliferate over the entire field of discourse, no text whatsoever is exempt from such transmogrifications into something rich and strange. Not just fingers and ears, but toes and mouths, noses (notoriously) and eyes, arms and legs—everything, indeed, but the *pudenda* themselves, which, being forthrightly what they are, now become the most innocent of organs. Any fictive writing that is not a direct and unadorned presentation of copulation is likely to be decoded as deviously sexually symbolic and the artist denied any other enterprise.

In the everyday world the honorable purpose of psychoanalysis is to bring its unhappy—or self-indulgent—subjects to well-being and social adjustment. But this is far from the purpose of most significant dramatic—and especially tragic—art. An Antigone, well adjusted to her family history and to the new polity of Creon, happily marrying Haemon (and this, it seems, *was* the mythic story that lay to Sophocles' hand), was of no use to Sophocles' tragic purpose. An Antigone such as Sophocles reinvented her, obsessed with a corpse and the world of the dead, rating brothers higher than husbands, though abnormal and even pathological from the moralizing psychoanalytic point of view, was perfect for Sophocles' purpose of demonstrating a heroic norm from which we, in our daily pusillanimity, have fallen. The "awkward," rather than ingratiating, aspects of Ibsen's major characters, is a Sophoclean feature of his drama.

There is, then, a grave absurdity in the conclusion of the colloquists on *Rosmersholm* that Ibsen's tragic protagonists have succumbed to a destructive psychic fantasy "in which they are acting neither maturely nor responsibly to each other."[9] Now, it is in the nature of major tragic heroes and heroines to be immature and irresponsible in this way. The passionate Achilles, the hot-tempered Ajax, the stubborn Philoctetes, the extravagant Lear, the malcontent Hamlet, and so on, all do much and say much that mature and responsible middle-class citizens would not and could not say and do—and are all the more impressive for it. The *Antigone* itself actually incorporates this view of its immature and irresponsible heroine in the figure of the eminently responsible Ismene, who is as well adjusted and as insignificant as any psychologizing interpreter could wish. Yet, strangely, Sophocles has permitted his irresponsible heroine to rebuff her well-adjusted sister:

> Go away, Ismene: I shall be hating you soon, and the dead
>   will too.
> For your words are hateful. Leave me my foolish plan:
> I am not afraid of the danger; if it means death,
> It will not be the worst of deaths—death without honor.[10]

It is doubtful that an *Ismene,* written on psychologizing and moralizing principles to proclaim the blessings of maturity and well-adjusted responsibility, would challenge the tragic status of the *Antigone*—but one would like to see the experiment carried out!

And, in a sense, this is what Errol Durbach, using the psychologistic and moralistic approach, claims Ibsen has done with this very play, *Rosmersholm!* There is much in Durbach's book that is perceptive and interesting: If I select what I think are his less successful contributions to Ibsen interpretation, this is to advance the argument of this chapter rather than to characterize his book as a whole. Employing the same criteria as Russell Davis (which demonstrates my point that the subtext never can be established), he claims that Rosmer and Rebekka, in fact, exhibit a truly admirable responsibility and maturity, splendidly deserving the moral awards Durbach lavishes on them. However, the smile of approval changes to a scowl of disapproval when Durbach turns to such feckless pairs as Solness and Hilde, Rubek and Irene, or the completely reprobate John Gabriel Borkman, all of whom receive stern reprimands for their moral shortcomings. We, from our positions of safety in the theater of the moral majority, can smugly note the psychological and moral shortcomings of the *dramatis personae* in the cycle as they are paraded for our inspection. Like the spectators of a psychopathological gladiatorial show, we can doom or reprieve the contestants according to our moral prejudices. The fallacious concept of the "tragic flaw," with its pharisaic assumption that tragic characters must somehow be seen to deserve their suffering, is here most drearily manifested. Walter Kaufmann long ago derided the attempts of critics to demonstrate that Sophocles' tragic victims, all noble, admirable, and innocent, were in some way justly punished. The concern that the cosmos should conform to our moral predilections is an attitude antithetical to tragedy, and moralizing Ibsenists are, in effect, attempting to remove the tragic dimension from his art. When this bourgeois attitude is applied to Sophocles or Shakespeare, its ludicrous conclusions— that Oedipus's "hot temper" or Cordelia's initial "pertness" merit the appalling suffering they, and those surrounding them, must endure—are apparent. It should be just as apparent in criticism of Ibsen's plays.

For why should Ibsen spend a lifetime's arduous artistry constructing such a dismal and spiritually deadly theater in which there would be precious little beauty or joy—except the unholy joy of a modern Tertullian relishing the spectacle of the psychically damned? Such a theater, instead of being one in which we dead are awakened, would be a public menace; each staging of the cycle would constitute a pharisaic festival. And, in fact, the very first play in the cycle, *Pillars of Society,* is, precisely, a massive attack on this form of pharisaism.

How can one account for the extraordinary metamorphosis of Ibsen, in academic interpretation, from the anarchist who scandalized all Europe and who was fiercely denounced in the publications of the respectable bourgeoisie, into the sturdy champion of bourgeois values who saw his main function as a dramatic artist as that of sniffing out deviations and abnormalities that might disturb the even tenor of middle-class life? For this is the extraordinary thesis underlying the interpretive procedures of many Ibsen commentators. How can a dramatic enterprise, self-avowedly conceived, in the bold nineteenth-century way, as an instrument of spiritual liberation on the largest scale, be reinterpreted as nothing but a succession of rather mean-spirited retrenchments? The Ibsen who regretted he was not around to torpedo the Ark, and of whom Bernard Shaw could remark that he was one of the grimmest artists since Beethoven, has been transformed into a benignant moralist anxious to protect the values of the bourgeois nuclear family:

> Like Solness, Brand and Allmers, Borkman cannot make his substitute faith viable because his own humanity is so crucially defective, because his conception of himself as redeemer is merely an aspect of that personal insufficiency. The greatest failure of all self-appointed prophets in Ibsen is always, on the most private and individual level, the inability to enact their projects as living realities in friendship, marriage, or in familial relationships with children, parents and siblings.[11]

In Chapter 9 I offer an interpretation of *John Gabriel Borkman* that totally opposes Durbach's judgment. This is not just a disagreement as to the nature of a character: It represents a total disagreement as to how one should read a dramatic text. The moral-psychological concerns that many interpreters believe so natural to bring to a text come from assuming a vague subtext behind the text. It is vague because, as we saw with *Rosmersholm*, two interpreters employing this approach can come to exactly opposite conclusions. If, however, the text is seen as creating a pattern of objective references, an intertextuality of cultural connotations found in that artist's work and in the work of others, then, I believe, agreement and collaboration in interpretation become possible. My moral or personal approval or disapproval of a dramatic character finally is a valuation inaccessible to disproof, for the "character" about whom I feel thus is someone I have constructed, in a wholly subjective way, out of the elements of the text. The character does not exist except in this wholly arbitrary and inaccessible way.

If the true supertext is not to be an arbitrary and subjective thing, a series of undemonstrable associations on each interpreter's part (a mere game to be played with the text), but, instead, is to be revealed as a firmly established structure of intended historical, cultural, and ideological references and connotations, then our business as interpreters must be to serve this structure by clarifying it for the reader. Of course there will be much room for disagreement; but the disagreement will be about the validity of interpretations that point to the text and its relation to other texts and pronouncements by the author, to the nature of the *genre* and its requirements, to detectable patterns, and to the way in which the interpretation of any detail clearly contributes to establishing a coherent intention by the whole work as an artistic unity. This, though it can never be an exact procedure, is not subjective and arbitrary either—any more than philosophy or historiography. One interpretation can be challenged—and displaced—by another, but only if it manages to bring a greater number of details of the work into a coherently unified intention.

The parallels and connections I shall make between Ibsen's "text" and the "world" it is drawing into its total act or performance are, I shall hope to convince, conscious, rational artistic decisions on Ibsen's part. This "world" is our human identity and its history within the cosmos as it has been revealed in discourse and as it is available to the artist's reflection and molding. Nor does the artistic performance try to "transport" a truth to us that lies behind language or the terms of the performance. The truth it presents is the truth of the performance itself: its attainment of significant plenitude and coherence through the imaginative and authentic extension and deepening of the dramatic ritual.

We first should reverse the traditional notion of the relation of the dramatic performance to the story. The performance does not exist in order more or less successfully to embody a story which then spills over, as in Freud's analysis of Rebekka West, beyond the theatric presentation into a wider world where art and reality become blurred. On the contrary, the story exists only to realize the dramatic performance which is the culmination of the clarifying creative process. We do not unpick the text to get at a richer human reality; we "assemble" it as a conductor assembles a symphony, to arrive at the greatest richness-within-unity of a performance. Aristotle's clear distinction between "plot" and "story" should be called to mind. The plot is the performed action within the limited time and space of the theater, the story the wealth of incidents preceding (and sometimes succeeding) the performed action: Oedipus's fatal conception and birth, his life up to the moment, on which the play opens, when the citizens approach him urging him to discover the reason for the plague at Thebes, and, after the performance ends, the life of Oedipus in exile. The performance is the glare of the spotlight into which these elements are drawn for intensely ironic and, above all, aesthetic configuration. Beyond both story and plot is the "argument" of the play: the dialectic of universals we perceive behind the particulars. The Realist Cycle as a whole is but one massive performance. The great richness and variety of the stories that emerge from this performance should not tempt us to overlook the theatric terms which give to Ibsen's great argument an intensity and urgency unattainable by other literary forms.

4

Text and Supertext

Hegel remains the first thinker to have set forth the aim of representing in logical form the rise of consciousness as it gradually unfolds from bare sense-perception to Reason as absolute knowledge of the world and all there is in it. This unfolding is not simply that of the individual's self-education to philosophy. It is at the same time the record of Mind's long travail, for Man's self-education reflects and recapitulates the story of Mind's manifestation in nature and history. The various levels of consciousness traversed by Mind and Spirit are stages in the self-realization of Man, and the individual repeats the process by raising himself from ordinary perception to philosophy.
— George Lichtheim, Introduction to Hegel's
The Phenomenology of Mind

Hebraism and Hellenism,—between these two points of influence moves our world. At one time it feels more powerfully the attraction of one of them, at another time of the other; and it ought to be, though it never is, evenly and happily balanced between them.
— Matthew Arnold, *Culture and Anarchy*

Are we Greeks? Are we Jews? But who, we? Are we (not a chronological, but a pre-logical question) first Jews or first Greeks? And does the strange dialogue between the Jew and the Greek, peace itself, have the form of the absolute, speculative logic of Hegel, the living logic which reconciles formal tautology and empirical heter-

> *ology after having* thought *prophetic discourse in the preface to the* Phenomenology of the Mind? *Or, on the contrary, does this peace have the form of infinite separation and of the unthinkable, unsayable transcendence of the other? To what horizon of peace does the language which asks this question belong? From whence does it draw the energy of its question? Can it account for the historical* coupling *of Judaism and Hellenism? And what is the legitimacy, what is the meaning of the* copula *in this proposition from perhaps the most Hegelian of modern novelists [James Joyce]: "Jewgreek is Greekjew. Extremes meet"?*
>
> —Jacques Derrida, *Writing and Difference*

We are confronted with the text. In the case of a dramatist, this means not just the words on the page but also actions on a stage shaped into a unified performance: a controlled rhythm in time, as in music, and in space, as in dance. The aim of interpretation of a dramatic text must be that which envisages the most complete and most coherent—unified—performance. Thus, when we read a playtext, we should imagine not a "real-life" situation but an ideal *theatrical performance*. Furthermore, the text of one of the realist plays of Ibsen, like a canto from Dante's *Commedia,* however complete and unified, is only a part of a larger and more intricate structure—the twelve-play cycle. Not only does the individual play contribute to this larger structure: It derives much of its own meaning from its position within the whole cycle. In chapter 8, for example, I will claim that there is a very profound reason why the central play of the cycle, *The Lady from the Sea,* takes place in what is described as a "turning point" (*knutepunkt*) of the world.

I believe that Ibsen sought his own individual salvation through his art. The history of the world, he once observed, resembled a sinking ship, and the only thing to do was to save oneself. "Let those who can save themselves," Hegel wrote, disclaiming any ambition to "instruct the world against its will."[1] By saving himself as indvidual artist Ibsen was saving human art itself, "redeeming," as it were, the identity of dramatist in the world, as Dante redeemed the identity of poet by writing the *Commedia* and as James Joyce was to redeem the identity of modern novelist. Redemption through engaging one's "talent" on the highest possible task, even at the cost of the public's bewilderment and discomfort—this Brand-like posture (for Ibsen wrote that Brand could have been an artist as much as a priest)—does fit the man who wrote the following words to his friend Georg Brandes:

> What I recommend for you is a thoroughgoing, full-blooded egoism, which will force you for a time to regard yourself and your work as the only things of consequence in this world, and everything else as simply nonexistent. . . . There is no way you can benefit society more than coining the metal you have in yourself. I have never really had a very great feeling for solidarity. In fact, I have allowed it in my mental cargo only because it is a traditional article of belief. If one had the courage to throw it overboard altogether, one would be getting rid of the ballast that weighs most heavily on the personality. There are actually moments when the whole history of the world reminds one of a sinking ship; the only thing to do is to save yourself.[2]

Such an artist is unlikely to be scolding or trying to reform the world, nor is he likely to be engrossed in the psychological aberrations and peculiarities of his neighbors. The world Ibsen imaginatively created is a world of sublime *showing,* in which he is the master magician calling up, summoning, the spiritual powers or shapes—*Gestalten*—as did Goethe in the Dedication (*Zueignung*) to *Faust:*

> Ihr nahr euch wieder, schwankende Gestalten!
> die früh sich einst dem trüben Blick gezeigt.
>
> (You come again, you hovering forms, as earlier,
> Appearing to my clouded sight you shone.)

The idea of Ibsen as a theater magician (like Faust before the Emperor) conducting a grand séance with his Realist Cycle is not as extravagant as it might seem. In one of the best books on Ibsen, Jennette Lee's *The Ibsen Secret* (1907), the author reminds us that Ibsen's first, childish theater was a magician's one. She quotes from Jaeger's *Life of Ibsen:*

> He got leave to appear, on certain Sunday afternoons, as a magician in one of the rooms of the house, and all the neighbours around were invited to witness the performance. I see him distinctly in his short jacket, standing behind a large chest that was decorated and draped for the occasion, and there he presided over performances that appeared like witchcraft to the amazed spectator. Of course I knew that his younger brother, well paid for his assistance, was inside the chest.[3]

There is a sense in which Ibsen's theater was always a magician's one, and, though it might look like "real life" to the naive spectator, the dramatist well knew the devices, tricks, and deceptions that were necessary to create authentic artistic rituals. That the truest art is most feigning is always known by the best men of the theater, who know how little their procedure resembles real life. As I argued earlier, the Realist aesthetic entailed a greater degree of aesthetic—that is, of artistic—authenticity. It was not a flight from art.

Just as the shaman will artfully work upon the imagination of his spectators, devising the most cunning formulae to perfect his ritual—in which he seriously believes—so will the dramatist who is determined to make his art express the deepest and widest-ranging meaning. The connection between shamanistic rite and art was noted by the authors of *Dialectic of Enlightenment:*

> The work of art still has something in common with enchantment: it posits its own, self-enclosed area which is withdrawn from the context of profane existence, and in which special laws apply. Just as the ceremony of the magician first of all marked out the limits of the area where the sacred powers were to come into play, so every work of art describes its own circumference which closes

it off from actuality. This very renunciation of influence, which distinguishes art from magical sympathy, retains the magic heritage all the more surely. . . . It is in the nature of the work of art, or aesthetic semblance, to be what the new terrifying occurrence became in the primitive's magic: the appearance of the whole in the particular. In the work of art that duplication still occurs by which the thing appeared as spiritual, as the expression of *mana*. This constitutes its aura. As an expression of totality, art lays claim to the absolute.[4]

The shaman in his mask and costume and Ibsen in his top hat and frock coat are brothers under the skin; they have somewhat different means but similar ends. The shaman may call upon the powers to revive the land from drought while Ibsen may wish to revive a modern wasteland from spiritual drought. And both go about their work with equal seriousness and with equal concern with the authenticity, the rightness, of the ritual: of getting the right powers into the right place at the right time. That Ibsen used images taken from the people and events of his own time was an essential part of the ritual, of its two dimensions of operation; the "duplication . . . by which the thing appeared as spiritual, as the expression of *mana*."

It is this *shaped* and ritualistic aspect of Ibsen's modern realism that, when not understood, most disturbs those more at ease with, say, the more relaxed, "indirect" realism of Anton Chekov. To recover, and create faith in, this semiritualistic aspect of Ibsen's art will allow its power to be appreciated. If interpretation can get the director and the actor and actress to see how the Ibsen text calls upon them not to simulate the nuances of everyday reality but, instead, to attempt the more arduous but more exciting task of raising the performance to near-hallucinatory power, the "profession" will take up Ibsen's plays once again as ardently as it did in the years of their first appearance in the world. In those early Ibsen years it was felt that the performance of an Ibsen play would have the same impact upon the cultural life of Europe as any shaman could hope to have within *his* world.

Everyday reality and theater are polar opposites. Theater is the
art of apparitions. The curtain rises, and the startling presences
manifest themselves. Their appearance is their whole life:
Though they may talk of a past and a future, theatrical past and
future exist only in the present moment in which they are disclosed onstage. And they exist only to add to the "presence" of
the figures onstage. The dramatist endows his figures with just
so much theatrical identity and just so much history, and no
more, and of just such a kind, as will serve to create the "presences" necessary for the total dramatic ritual. There is no appeal
beyond this closed circle of appearance to a commonsensical or
"psychological" order of explanation. If we are to permit the dramatist the great advantages of his art—above all, the advantage
of the manifestation of presences—which compensate for what
that art, in contrast to the novelist's, does *not* permit, we should
always free ourselves, when confronted with a play, to respond to
its possible immensity of intention. This means we should be
prepared to extend to the utmost the imaginative dimensions of
the drama's terms. Not many dramatists will require this extension. Ibsen's theater belongs to the few that do, and it accounts
for what many have detected as the peculiar *intensity* of Ibsen's
dramatic actions; of their being engaged upon urgent and large-
scaled matters.

The actor, waiting in the wings, is a wholly different creature,
from a wholly different order of creation, than the "character"
who enters onstage with or without ritual mask and costume.
She or he immediately begins to exist, as real-life people do not,
in a highly controlled medium of aesthetic pacing, timing, regu-
lated self-disclosure, verbal patterning, and inevitable action.
Dramatis personae are totally without freedom: They exist only
to fulfill the aesthetic fate of the dramatic structure by which
they are held and sustained, minute by minute. Denied thereby
any "inwardness," any spontaneity, or any source of motivation,
they are not subject to our moral or psychological approval. The
only life they possess is what we are able, imaginatively, to give
them. They therefore are as great or as petty, as significant or as
trivial, as we are capable of perceiving. If, as William Blake reminded us, the Idiot and the Wise Man do not see the same tree,

they also do not see the same *Hedda Gabler, Little Eyolf,* or *John Gabriel Borkman.*

The creation, performance, and viewing of a dramatic work is a highly elaborate, greatly *conscious* aesthetic activity, a complicated act of collaboration on the part of author, director, actors, and audience. In playgoing, a form of spiritual transfusion has to take place between the audience and the play, in which the viewer, fully aware of the terms of dramatic performance, *enters into* the whole fictive world of the *dramatis personae,* endowing that world, and them, with substantial life while they, in turn, take possession of our imaginations. *They* live only as fully as, and as long as, we care to grant them life, and they have to *earn* their existence by proving themselves indispensable to our imaginative life.

A dramatic performance exists in a tense and heightened "now" where events fall into significant place in a way wholly unlike our experience of the everyday world. The proscenium arch and the stage space set up conditions for the aesthetic ritual that the performance will embody. In that space our imaginations enter an intensified present time that has abrogated the past and future. In the *performance* the recollected past becomes the present—*a present action of recollection.* Lieutenant Alving, and his tragedy, repossesses the stage *now* when Helene Alving resurrects his story. Just as the formula "Once upon a time . . ." permits the listener immediately to enter a timeless world, so dramatic art, too, exists in a timeless dimension. Roland Barthes observed how, at the very beginning, Greek drama set itself aside from ordinary time:

> Associated with the "loosening" of work time, the theater installed another time, a time of myth and of consciousness, which could be experienced not as leisure but as another life. For this suspended time, by its very duration, became a saturated time.[5]

As the curtain rises on a production of *Ghosts* or *Little Eyolf,* we immediately are ready to participate directly in the fateful action, recognizing that this separate and simultaneous *now* is responsive to forces and subject to laws wholly unlike our own world. The forgetting of this fact, and the attempt to make stage space and time resemble our own, is greatly responsible for the decline in the contemporary theater's power, which only is recovered in such "ritual" plays as Jean Genet's *The Blacks*. Worldly time, flowing continuously *outside* the theater, is not involved in the dramatic experience, an experience whose success indeed depends upon our suspending consciousness of the existence of the laws of the quotidian world. Everyone is familiar with the experience of having one's concentration, in the theater or concert hall, broken by the intrusion of the everyday order of time, and of trying to *get back into* the special, delimited, temporal conditions of the performance.

For his ritualist purpose, Ibsen invests his images of everyday reality with all the alarming potency and urgency that everyday reality tries to evade. It is for this reason, and not from any attachment to outmoded Scribean techniques, that his dramatic methods should so violate our experience of reality. Ibsen *intends* our experience so to be violated, so that we will respond to the forces he is summoning to his theatrical séance. The means by which these timeless forces manifest themselves within contemporary reality is far more important to the dramatist than any photographic fidelity to the appearances of nineteenth-century bourgeois Norway. That aspect of Norway already has passed away, revealing its inessentiality as a permanent human reality; but the potent archetypal and symbolic reality Ibsen forced this image of his society to reveal still powerfully works upon us.

In Ibsen's paradox, the "living" men and women, his contemporaries, were the "dead" who had to be awakened to recover their full human identity—their cultural and spiritual heritage; whereas the truly living powers, conventionally thought of as dead, as ghosts, stretched back to the furthest past and would still be with the race in the furthest future. They are the vast invisible audience of our daily lives. If his dead contemporaries refused to awaken, Ibsen would not live in *their* world but in the more adequate world he could bring to life by means of his art. He might use his contemporaries and their actions as "models," but, like Irene and the attendant figures of Rubek's sculp-

ture *Resurrection Day,* they would be totally transformed by
the medium in which he placed them.

Interpretation of the Realist Cycle has to be faithful to two
dimensions: to the grand and overall design, discoverable in the
books on the shelf—the collected plays; and to the immediate
intensity of the performance of the individual play. I am more
aware than before of how the dialectic of one play grows out of
that of the preceding and pushes forward to that of the succeeding play, repeating a feature of the dialectic of the *Phenomenology* in which:

> Any given stage of consciousness must have its preceding
> stage within itself. It must contain its own immediate ori-
> gin as well as the origin of consciousness itself. There is
> thus a recollective moment forever within absolute know-
> ing because of Hegel's sense of *das Aufgehobene.* When
> we look properly within the *Begriff* [Concept] we find
> there the *Bild* [Image], the product of *Erinnerung* [Recol-
> lection]. The *Begriff* is no monotone of itself, its own meta-
> physical categories in sequence. It is forever in friendly
> opposition to the image—its own origin, present in itself.[6]

This "friendly opposition" between image and concept, in
which the concept has its origin in the sensuous image, is
linked by Verene in his study of the *Phenomenology* to the
process of recollection. He describes Hegel's procedure in terms
similar to that of the "archetypal recollection" that I claim as
Ibsen's method. This is how he explains Hegel's constant use of
metaphor:

> *Archai* come from nowhere. They come when needed and
> they come from nowhere. They are drawn forth from con-
> sciousness suddenly and without method, that is, without
> some set procedure. Consciousness turns to itself and sud-
> denly has in its hands something of itself that it did not
> know was there in any explicit sense. The drawing forth
> of *archai* is like recollecting. It is in fact recollecting in its
> primordial sense.[7]

"The metaphor" Verene observes of Hegel's method "always shows us something from which consciousness can then withdraw and attempt to understand what it has seen" (24). There are innumerable places in the Realist Cycle also where we observe this process of the *recollection* of a potent *image* by the consciousness of a major character who then *reflects* upon and then attempts to understand "what it has seen." This anagnorisis is shown as a stage of the growth of consciousness within the play, a point from which there is no going back and which often is signaled by a reference to *seeing:* Helene Alving's "Now I see it all!" being only one of the more emphatic of many such instances. Looking back along the whole cycle, we can see how it resembles the long recollective vision also of the *Phenomenology:*

> For the consciousness that has in some sense reached absolute knowing, these metaphors are keys to the state of consciousness on any given stage of its course. Thus the metaphors or images in the *Phenomenology of Spirit* are not just any metaphors but the metaphors of consciousness itself, those by which it accomplishes the turning, the *Umkehrung,* of its being at any given moment. The *Phenomenology of Spirit* is a philosophical speech in which all the powers of language, its imagistic and its conceptual powers, are brought forth so that the reader may recollect. This recollection is the process of internal vision that all speculation requires. It is the constant companion, the friend, of speculation.[8]

In the second part of the *Phenomenology* Hegel recollects the spiritual biography of the human community; how it acquires Reason and ultimately arrives at perceptions of the divine. He insists that, to be fully human, we must reacquire this possession, relive this biography, for each of the stages and turning points has gone into the creation of our total identity. The impact of this idea of self-knowledge upon our contemporary world is evident. We find it in various forms in Marxian, Freudian, and Jungian theory, in the biological notion, reformulated by Freud, that "ontogeny recapitulates phylogeny." It informs much semiotic theory accounting for the rather wayward presence of Hegel in "deconstructive" texts. I believe it accounts for the power and unity of Ibsen's life's work and its absolute centrality to modern literature.

Any educated man or woman knows that his or her imagination is as much affected and molded by classical texts, art forms, scholarship, historical and cultural events, religion and philosophy, as by the busy immediate events of our everyday lives. A rediscovered papyrus of a lost masterpiece, a newly unearthed, richly furnished archaeological site, can create as much interest, at least, as a major battle or the private histories of our neighbors, for we feel that our total human identity is increased or modified thereby. This must have been even more true of Ibsen's time— the time of Schliemann's discoveries and of the Darwinian controversy—than of our own. Books that firmly set Ibsen in the physical surroundings of Skien, Grimstad, Christiania, or Bergen, giving us the photographed images of those places and describing their social settings, and so on, forget that the more important environment Ibsen inhabited was the invisible intellectual one, one that made him a somewhat restless inhabitant of our planet, an apartment-dweller notably uninterested in establishing himself civically within a local place and its community. It is in this larger intellectual environment that we will find the key to Ibsen's art.

What I call the "supertext"—the store of cultural reference a poet or thinker can draw upon and from which is derived his or her own identity—is a rational, sane, traditional sphere of reference for an art; an ongoing human discourse which all major artists and thinkers take up, contribute to, and extend. The writer of deadly closet drama fails to bring this supertext to life, to make it a vital part of his contemporary world. The major writer, like Ibsen, feels the importance of the supertext so keenly that he can see his contemporary world only in its terms. Instead of being relegated to a remote area of interest (scholarship), it is involved in the fabric of modern living; in personal relationships, in social realities, in political conflicts—all of which are more or less adequate as they reveal this universal content. I am convinced that, for Ibsen, the gigantic unresolved conflict of *Em-*

peror and Galilean continued to shape the life of his own time, as Matthew Arnold also believed, and as Jacques Derrida recently has reformulated it, drawing upon the work of James Joyce. It is also the theme of the work of Goethe and Schiller, of Richard Wagner, of Thomas Mann, of T. S. Eliot and others. The reconciliation of modern with Hellenic thought, of making the modern mind once again think in Greek terms, has been seen as Hegel's purpose, so that this might represent one of the major enterprises of the modern spirit.

Extended thus in *time,* Ibsen's cycle is filled with mythic, archetypal, cultural, and historical content and "quotation," deriving from this larger history of the race. These the poet sees as making up the psychic life of the present, erupting strangely and fatefully into the present. Extended in *space* on a similarly ambitious scale, this multilayered humanity would be seen as inhabiting a cosmos, from the depths of the sea to the distant stars. If all this is organized in an intricate, controlled, and imaginative way (and it would be all the better as art if it were so organized), then the cycle would reveal both a very elaborate objective artistic *structure* and a perceptible dialectic *movement* (the *life* of the structure) from the first play to the last.

Reading the plays, as Ibsen insisted we should, in the order in which they were written, detecting what he termed the "mutual connections" between the plays, does give support to the idea of the presence of a single, major, coherent intention—if we permit the supertext a function. The fact that similarly ambitious structures, many of them cyclical, exist in art and thought would show that I am making no outrageous claim. And I am claiming here quite *conscious* artistic intentions. It is possible that Ibsen's text could be shown to contain *unconscious* forms and archetypes and strategies: but we cannot know these until we are satisfied as to the extent of the *conscious* ones. Ibsen, in his letters and statements, refers to and quotes (and misquotes) Homer in *Emperor and Galilean,* had read Dante (offering advice on translating the *Commedia* into Norwegian), viewed the Sistine Chapel, knew of Wagner and Bayreuth (he lived close by, in Munich), and expressed his appreciation of Hegel. It is only too likely that the exiled author, like his disciple James Joyce, conceived his artistic activity (the only thing of consequence in the world) in similarly ambitious terms.

What might prove to be the really great thing about the cycle is the way it exists, like the *Commedia,* on the plane of universal, rational reality and, with equal urgency and intensity, on the plane of particular and passionate reality. It is precisely the capacity to feel keenly the rational and the universal and to see reason behind passionate phenomena that makes one an artist in the first place, as the earlier comments of Sigurd Ibsen and of Ibsen's artist, Arnold Rubek, stated. George Santayana insisted that the plane of universal reason—our supertext—is essential to the highest art, adding:

> The same powers of conception and expression are needed in fiction which, if turned to reflection, would produce a good philosophy. Reason is necessary for the perception of high beauty. Discipline is indispensable to art. Work from which these qualities are absent must be barbaric; it can have no ideal form and must appeal to us only through the sensuousness and profusion of its details.[9]

To establish that Ibsen's art builds up a great, visible, conscious, coherent artistic structure is to add momentously to the small stock of humanity's major artistic achievements. This means going continually to Ibsen's texts (each play and the whole cycle) and referring that text to the "world" (of cultural discourse) that Ibsen inhabited and inherited. By relating each detail of a play to the whole—the cycle—one contributes to the idea of the complex unity of the whole. Just as with any intricately organized, large-scaled structure, it would be wrong to give inflated prominence to any one part at the expense of the whole (the tragedy of Paolo and Francesca in the *Commedia,* for instance), so we should not forget that however deeply we respond to any single play within the cycle, that play occupies only one place within the structure of the whole. To "romanticize" the story of Paolo and Francesca by inflating its importance actually is to *diminish* it by removing it from the universalizing Whole; in the same way, to inflate the importance of any single play, or character within a play, in the cycle actually is to trivialize it.

The famous "retrospective" method of the cycle, for example, is not primarily a useful dramatic device for expressing events that cannot be fitted into the immediate realistic scene. It represents instead Ibsen's profound idea of the present: that it is a recollection and reliving, at every moment, of our total past, both as individual and as species. The return of the past within the present within an individual life becomes a metaphor (and a means) for the return of the *universal* past within the present. In a note to *Emperor and Galilean* Ibsen has Julian declare, "The individual must go through the evolutionary process of the race." Ontogeny recapitulates phylogeny, culturally as well as biologically. The age of Darwin is the heir to the age of Hegel and begetter of the age of Freud.

To a young man who wished to become a modern writer, Ibsen declared:

> You ought to make a thorough study of the history of civilization, of literature, and art . . . an extensive knowledge of history is indispensable to a modern author, for without it he is incapable of judging his age, his contemporaries and their motives and actions, except in the most incomplete and superficial manner.[10]

"Thorough," "extensive," "indispensable"—these words do not mean that Ibsen merely believes one should have an average idea of what has gone on in the world, nor are they the words we would expect the Ibsen of traditional interpretation to utter. They suggest instead a writer for whom the present cannot be understood at all unless it is seen as complexly textured with the entire past. The conviction that the present not only is textured with the past but is agitated by the unresolved conflicts inherited from that past is at least as old as the Renaissance. And in the European imagination this has been seen as a conflict between our Judeo-Christian and our Hellenic heritage. The ubiquity and persistence of this idea in the Western imagination, from the first pronouncements of Neoplatonists and Christian humanists

up to the passage from Jacques Derrida quoted in the epigraph to
this chapter is truly remarkable. (It is perhaps not as central to
the American imagination as it is to the European.) Certainly,
one cannot hope to understand any major expression of European art and thought (e.g., Milton's *Paradise Lost*) without taking this conflict into consideration, together with the attendant
idea that individual self-fulfillment requires the recovery of our
complete spiritual heritage. Consider the following passages:

> 1. The particular individual, so far as content is con-
> cerned, has also to go through the stages through which
> the general mind has passed, but as shapes once assumed
> by mind and now laid aside, as stages of a road which has
> been worked over and leveled out.

> 2. The historical sense compels a man to write not only
> with his own generation in his bones, but with a feeling
> that the whole literature of Europe from Homer, and
> within it the whole literature of his own country, has a
> simultaneous existence and composes a simultaneous or-
> der. The poet must be aware that the mind of Europe—
> the mind of his own country—a mind that he learns in
> time to be much more important than his own private
> mind—is a mind which changes, and that this change is a
> development that abandons nothing *en route*.

> 3. As he moves forward within his environment, Man
> takes with him all the positions that he has occupied in
> the past, and all those he will occupy in the future. He is
> everywhere, at the same time, a crowd which, in the act of
> moving forward, yet recapitulates at every instant every
> step that it has taken in the past.

> 4. We come across the remarkable circumstance that
> the mental processes concerned are actually more famil-
> iar to us and are more accessible to consciousness as
> they are seen in the group than they can be in the indi-
> vidual man. . . . At this point the two processes, that of
> the cultural development of the group and that of the

cultural development of the individual, are, as it were, always interlocked.

Each of these passages could have been written by Ibsen, who insisted that "the individual must pass through the evolutionary process of the race." They were in fact written by Hegel, T. S. Eliot, Claude Lévi-Strauss, and Sigmund Freud,[11] and what they have in common is the central humanist conviction that the individual, in his lifetime, both consciously and unconsciously recapitulates the history of the species: that we profoundly are the products of historical, cultural, and biological processes. This humanist conviction has been opposed by alternative convictions, but these, in their turn, have been absorbed by the humanist vision, which has a tougher digestive capacity than its opponents suspect. Romanticism, which was to witness one of the most ambitious extensions of the humanist endeavor to recover the total past, began at first with the Rousseauist, antihumanist quarrel between restorative Nature and corruptive Culture.

In Ibsen's own day this humanist tradition was fiercely attacked by that eccentric European Søren Kierkegaard, anxious, as always, to elevate the claims of subjective experience (his existential Christian drama) over all claims to objective value, whether in art, history, or philosophy. Rightly perceiving that, whatever Hegel cautiously proclaimed, Hegelian philosophy denied the absolutist claims of Christianity (for, to Hegel, Christianity was itself a Concept, *one* of the "moments" only, in the life of Spirit and thus capable of being comprehended by philosophy), Kierkegaard stubbornly set himself against the main tide of humanism:

The individual is without further ado supposed to be related to the development of human spirit as a particular specimen to its kind, just as if the development were something that one generation could bequeath to another; and as if spirit were a character belonging to the race and not to the individual, a supposition which is self-contradictory and ethically abominable. Spiritual development is self-activity; the spiritually developed individual takes his development with him when he dies. If an individual of a subsequent generation is to reach the same development he will have to attain it by means of his own activity, and he cannot be permitted to omit anything. But it is, of course, easier, cheaper and more comfortable to bluster about being born in the nineteenth century.[12]

Kierkegaard, of course, as is typical of his anti-Hegelian polemic, is not putting the issue fairly. Hegel would have agreed with Goethe that one must learn to *possess* one's heritage by *earning* it: That is the whole program of the *Phenomenology*, which has been seen by more than one writer as the first Existentialist work. But Kierkegaard would insist there is only one, overriding, indubitably certain reality that one can confront: each individual's need to be reconciled with the strict, authoritarian, punitive deity of St. Paul. All art, science, philosophy, and history are just a vain show, lacking all authority, compared with that imperative. However great the Genius, he insists in one of his later pamphlets, however persuasive or brilliant, his witness is nothing when compared with the least impressive utterances of an Apostle. The words of a Christ or of a Paul are to be believed not because they are persuasive but because they are by Christ or Paul; "a Christian priest would have to say, quite simply: We have Christ's word for it that there is an eternal life; and that settles the matter":

> There is no question here of racking one's brains or philosophizing, but simply that Christ said it, not as a profound thinker but with divine authority. . . . On the other hand, take the case of a man who racks his brains and ruminated profoundly on the question of immortality: would he not be justified in denying that this direct statement is a profound answer to the question? What Plato says on immortality really is profound, reached after deep study; but then poor Plato has no authority whatsoever.[13]

I wonder if those who find Kierkegaard a more congenial "thinker" than Hegel also accept this total abnegation of the intellect before dogmatic authority (whether Christian, Marxian, or any other). Kierkegaard denies one major tenet of art and philosophy: that the philosophic or poetic utterance *earns* its acceptability, its value, through its own *intrinsic* adequacy. In Kierkegaard's account genuine cultural evolution manifestly is impossible; humankind remains imprisoned forever in the same relationship with the same unyielding, unchanging Christian god, whose Authority alone validates utterance.

Is it not obvious that Ibsen, the poet of "the third empire of spirit," totally opposes Kierkegaard? His great historical drama in which, he declared, could be found his "positive world-philosophy" is titled not *Emperor OR Galilean* but *Emperor AND Galilean,* indicating not the Kierkegaardian choice, either/or, but the Hegelian synthesis, both/and. The Realist Cycle is, I believe, an exploration of the extent of the fragmentation and desolation of the human spirit resulting from the failure to re-solve the conflict of *Emperor and Galilean.* We remember Brand's account of modern humanity: the "stumps of broken souls / Torsos of amputated Mind / These separated heads and hands"—a metaphor taken from the remains of classic statuary, of former Hellenic wholeness, that Ibsen encountered in Rome. It is not surprising, therefore, that he would see his own age and its frock-coated, umbrella-carrying citizenry as by no means the most glorious phase of the long continuum of the human spirit and that he should set about trying to assemble a more adequate humanity out of these stumps of broken souls.

While it sometimes is conceded that Ibsen's scenes, with their vertical landscapes, his intense actions, and his even intenser characters, might embody to a greater or lesser degree (either admirably or deplorably) large objective purposes not associated with realism, his dialogue usually is considered to have narrowed down drastically the expressive range of drama. This was the charge brought against Ibsen by J. M. Synge and W. B. Yeats, and it has been repeated since, often with unfavorable compari-sons made between passages in Ibsen's prose plays and verse passages of Shakespeare.

To counter this, some Ibsenists have been eager to claim for Ibsen's dialogue an almost unequaled subtlety of *subjective* impli-cation within the form of *duologue.* Such duologues express "per-sonal encounter" and, usually ambiguously, represent the inner feelings of the characters. Such a view sees dialogue as the means by which characters communicate with each other, or the completed result of such communication; but this is an obvious fallacy. There just are no "characters" preexisting independently of the dialogue, to create and use it for any purposes whatsoever. *Dramatis personae* do not communicate with dialogue—they *are* dialogue. It is the dialogue which artistically creates them together with the whole "world" and its history surrounding them—as Samuel Beckett slyly intimated in *Endgame:*

> CLOV. I'll leave you.
> HAMM. No!
> CLOV. What is there to keep me here?
> HAMM. The dialogue. (*Pause*).

The scale of the characters and their situations will be as great or as small as the scale of *objective* (supertextual) reference the dialogue sustains. Dialogue is the medium through which the spoken drama exists, as much as the strokes of the paintbrush or the palette knife are the terms of the painting's existence. There is no Rebekka West eager to communicate to us or to other elements of the dramatic ensemble, independent of the words, spoken by herself or by others, which bring her into artistic being. She, and the other elements of the total dramatic design, exists only as long as the dialogue exists, between the rising and the falling of the proscenium curtain. (Ben Jonson merely carried to an exuberant excess this consciousness on the dramatist's part, of how his dramatic world and its characters are verbally sustained, minute by minute, by the poetry.)

Beyond the *ensemble* of *dramatis personae*, Ibsen's dialogue, through its careful choice of metaphors and cultural references, also creates and sustains a whole world-picture with its extensive history and scenography. We have seen that the Ibsen action frequently is the deconstruction of a false idea of reality, with all its contradictions, and the gradual perception of a more adequate idea, and that it is this artistic action of de-creation and re-creation that is the real "subject" of the Ibsen Realist drama.

If one refuses the full referential function and potency of dramatic metaphors, one might produce a coherent account of a dramatic action, but will not get hold of the world the play is bringing into being. Andrew K. Kennedy, in his book *Dramatic Duologues*, quotes Kierkegaard on the differences between ancient and modern tragedy. Ancient (Greek) tragedy, Kierkegaard observed, had a large degree of objective, "epic" content that could not be absorbed by the dramatic characters and therefore could not be rendered by dialogue alone. But the *subjective* nature of modern life means that, in dramatic art, dialogue can express "everything." Dialogue can express "everything" because Kierkegaard reduces everything to Christian *subjectivity*. Like many critics of realism, Kennedy seemingly assents to Kierkegaard's indifference to all attempts objectively to know (or change) the world, but at the same time seems to jettison Kierkegaard's Christianity—at least as an interpretive "control." Kierkegaard's subjectivism entailed a deep and agonizing relationship with his forbidding God, and this *depth* to some degree compensated for the *narrowness* of his idea of the essential human drama.

This emphasis upon subjectivity ignores Hegel's more authoritative and more interesting account of dialogue in modern drama. Also noting that, in modern drama, language had shifted to realistic dialogue, Hegel at the same time insisted that this dialogue not only expressed personal encounter but, just as much as the Greek choral ode and the Elizabethan monologue, *built up a substantive, objective world*. In modern dialogue, Hegel noted,

> *dramatis personae* are mutually able to express their character and aims, not merely relatively to their personal attitude to each other, but also to the substantive character of the pathos disclosed; they engage in conflict, and thereby actually advance the movement of the action. We may further distinguish in the dialogue between the expression of a pathos that is *subjective* and one that is *objective*.[14]

While poets rightly will be drawn to depict the subjective "unreconciled inward dissension of soul life" in dialogue, nevertheless the human soul is less affected by this "than it is through a pathos wherein at the same time a genuine objective content is evolved."[15] Hegel then praised the idealist dramas of Goethe and

Schiller, the dialogues of which depict whole cultures in conflict, as in *Don Carlos* and *Mary Stuart*.

It was because he accorded to the poet a supreme role in the creation of human culture that Hegel insisted that poetry establish an objective content. Poetry was "the teacher of mankind," and the modern age stood in need of "a new mythology" in order to give birth to a new art form:

> When in our time the living world does not form the work of art within it, the artist must place his imagination in a past world; he must dream a world, but the character of dreaming, of not being alive, of the past, is plainly stamped on his work.[16]

Ibsen, who spent so much of his creative life placing his imagination in a past world, gradually evolved his own mythology, a cosmos active with universal forces, that allowed him to endow his images of modern reality with universal power. For example, when we confront the text of a realist play such as *Ghosts,* we should be able to see how it builds up the widest-ranging historical/cultural argument by endowing its few individual characters with immense symbolic identity *when juxtaposed to each other*. Such juxtaposition reveals a striking thematic pattern (see diagram).

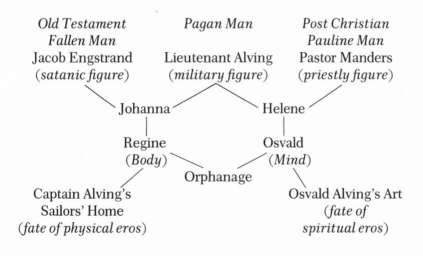

Old Testament *Fallen Man*	*Pagan Man*	*Post Christian* *Pauline Man*
Jacob Engstrand (*satanic figure*)	Lieutenant Alving (*military figure*)	Pastor Manders (*priestly figure*)

Johanna   Helene

Regine (*Body*)   Osvald (*Mind*)

Orphanage

Captain Alving's Sailors' Home (*fate of physical eros*)   Osvald Alving's Art (*fate of spiritual eros*)

This pattern emerged, gradually, from repeated analyses of the text; it "fits" the story while at the same time building up a clear "ideological" pattern, a pattern that only could emerge from a *dramatic* art of confrontation and conflict. That is, what I call the play's "argument" is not put forward by Ibsen as if it were a serious discursive treatise upon which we are meant to act; it is enacted, onstage, as a gathering together of spiritual-cultural powers and forces which Ibsen believes our theater should contain, as Greek drama could be saturated with its spiritual metaphors. That is, Ibsen inherited from cultural history the equivalent of the "megatext" of mythic/archetypal forces that, Erich Segal claims, the Greek dramatists inherited from their mythic traditions and, like the Greek dramatists, could draw upon certain archetypal figures to incarnate the universal dimensions of his dramatic argument.

The figure I designate "Old Testament" and "fallen" is named Jacob, has a deformed foot (associated with the "satanic" in Ibsen), speaks a *fallen language* of blasphemous oaths, of drunkenness and squalid sexuality. His action in the play will be, within the terms of this world, notably satanic, linked with the fiery entrapment of the priest. Pagan heroism, in Hegel and other writers and artists, is associated with the military identity; and the name *Alv*-ing also carries pagan associations, as does Alving's whole role in the play. A Pauline worldview would give to the *priestly* figure the identity and philosophy of which it most approves, and Pastor Manders's view of life requires, we discover, the renunciation of that *happiness,* of joy-of-life, associated with Alving and his children.

But Alving's offspring each has *two* fathers. Regine reputedly (mentally) is Engstrand's but biologically is Alving's daughter, while Osvald, biologically Alving's, has been given a (mental) father by Helene (through her lying letters), who is Alving remade in the image of Manders, to the extent that Helene actually claims Osvald has a priestly appearance about his mouth. Appropriately, from the nature of the dual fathers, Regine is physically fit but spiritually stunted while Osvald is spiritually creative but physically broken. Both children are linked to the Orphanage, and their destruction follows its own, a destruction attendant upon the revelation of the nature of the true father. Regine's future "ruin" is foreshadowed in her interest in Engstrand's brothel while the "joy-of-life" which Osvald has tried to objectify in art dies with his collapse.

This pattern reaches out to what Ibsen believed to be the major conflict of the modern world, one that he set out in *Emperor and Galilean* and which informs the entire Realist Cycle. Each play in the cycle contains the whole conflict, but in its own terms. Of course, the play is a good deal subtler and more moving than this paraphrase of its argument, and it is the continual interplay between the particular, personal drama and the universal drama that makes *Ghosts* a major work of art. To take away *either* dimension, particular or universal, would be drastically to reduce the stature of the play and to destroy the special poetry of the text.

There are criteria by which to tell whether one interpretation of a work of art is superior to another. As we have observed, that account is superior which is able to draw the greatest number of details into the most coherent artistic intention. It does this by looking at the *objective* implications of each detail of the play—the supertext—to see whether all the details taken together build up, in their own terms, an artistic statement which it plausibly can be demonstrated the artist could have intended. If a more fashionable, commonsensical, or realistic account of, say, *The Master Builder* feels obliged (with most accounts of the play) to leave unexplained why the hero is named after the sun; why there should be an imagery of sun and light throughout; why the hero should climb and fall at the autumnal equinox; why the play should consist of a rich pattern of triads (three acts, three scene changes, three repetitions of the basic action, three houses, three nurseries, three deaths from the tower, three women drawn to Solness, etc.); why the play should employ other striking images such as the fire-in-winter, nine dolls, dead twins, music in a churchyard, a little devil in white, harps in the air, vikings, trolls, a princess, a fabulous kingdom with a wonderful sky-castle, and so on; then we are not getting an interpretation of the play at all but, rather, on the "interpreter's" part, a failure to account for Ibsen's procedure. An interpretation—such as I offered in *The Ibsen*

Cycle—that brought all these, and other, details of the play into a unified artistic intention can be "refuted" only by a more *comprehensively unified* one.

I think it likely that Ibsen actually accepted the formidable challenge Hegel offered to the modern epic poet:

> The most exalted action of Spirit would be the history of the world itself. We can conceive it possible that our poet might in this sense undertake to elaborate in what we might call the absolute Epos this universal achievement on the battlefield of the universal spirit whose hero would be the spirit of man, the humanus, who is drawn and exalted out of the confusions of consciousness into the clearer region of universal history.[17]

Hegel did not believe a modern epic poet *would* write this absolute epic, but he knew he had completed something very similar with the *Phenomenology*. And the work of James Joyce and of Ezra Pound has shown a similar ambition, so that to claim that Ibsen took up this challenge is well within the bounds of rational interpretation. Admittedly it will prove immensely difficult to establish this supertext, but the difficulty of the task is no indication of its invalidity.

Each play in the cycle, and the cycle as a whole, takes on the form of quest and conflict. The subject of the cycle, the human spirit, assumes a succession of forms within each of which it struggles for ever-more adequate self-determinations in terms of truth and freedom. This quest, progressively, comes into conflict with alien worldviews, and their inadequacies, with which significant individuals are confronted. The archetypal or iconographic identities we detect behind the individual characters gives the action of the play its universal nature so that the *dramatis personae,* while enacting a plausible modern action, release onto the stage the forces of this larger, universal drama— a drama "built into" our modern identity. The dramatic *form* requires that conflicts are revealed, tensions created and heightened to crisis point, and *dénouements* achieved at the dialectically and the dramatically right moment, for it is a carefully structured work of art we are interpreting, not real life. The carefully maintained dramatic rhythm, obeying all the time the requirements of the form, moves to its *peripeties* (reversals) and attains its *anagnorises* (discoveries), involving all the elements of both the drama and of the argument in a controlled movement as disciplined as the sonata form.

Once we recognize that we are confronted, in the cycle, with a great work of *art,* intricately organized, we might proceed to detect the archetypal presences "behind" the individuals and their actions. These will be seen to be linked to temporal and spatial metaphors, placing the action within a cosmos. Season, climate, time of day and of year are all important indications of the larger meanings embodied by the play (as with the approaching cold and darkness of *The Lady from the Sea*) and not the accidents or inevitabilities of everyday life. The cycle as a whole, we now can see, is placing our human drama in extended time and space from the great overview of which we better can "place" the individual details. To see, for example, that *Ghosts* reenacts through the anguish of the personal drama an archetypal conflict within the race is to give to the play the rationality and universality essential for a *tragic* art.

Obviously there is a lot of work to be done before the extent of the cycle's achievement will be apparent. The cycle is not only a design, a pattern, like a richly elaborate Persian carpet; it also is a dynamic and dialectic *movement* within the pattern, a continuous process, as in the *Phenomenology*. It seems that the first four plays in the cycle, setting up their own design within the Whole, explore a condition of spirit belonging to a particular worldview—the Hellenic; that the more ambiguous second group reveals the presence of Christian and post-Christian conflicts; and that the third and final group, from *The Master Builder* to *When We Dead Awaken,* seems more "numinous," more responsive to multiple archetypal presences than the two preceding groups, just as the characters seem more *conscious* of the forces within themselves and surrounding them. In *The Ibsen Cycle,* I indicated how these last plays, in their last-act scenes, establish a *temporal* progression of Evening (*The Master Builder*), Late Evening (*Little Eyolf*), Night (*John Gabriel Borkman*), and Dawn (*When We Dead Awaken*), and showed how these four temporal stages are accompanied by four *spatial* increases in elevation, culminating in the mountaintop scene of the last act of the last play. I suggested that, by pondering these temporal and spatial metaphors, seeing them as the elements of an artistic intention, we would begin to be alerted to the great expansion of human space and time, of cosmic and cultural connotation, that informs Ibsen's dramatic art.

All this undoubtedly makes Ibsen a formidably *difficult* writer, a classic, in fact, who requires from interpretation a multidisciplined approach probably beyond the scope of any single interpreter. My own approach, to open up the plays by means of a Hegelian "code," is not meant to close off other approaches.

Each age tries to be self-sufficient and independent of the historical past, as if born yesterday, only to discover, at its deepest levels of reflection, how much it has been the product of the past. Toward the past we can attempt to forget it, or submit to it, or reinterpret it according to our perceived needs. Paul de Man, discussing Nietzsche's "Of the Use and Misuse of History," observes: "Modernity invests its trust in the power of the present moment as an origin, but discovers that, in severing itself from the past, it has at the same time severed itself from the present."[18] He quotes from Nietzsche's essay:

> Men and eras that serve life in this manner, by judging and destroying the past, are always dangerous and endangered. For we are inevitably the result of earlier generations and thus the result of their mistakes and aberrations, even of their crimes; it is not possible to loosen oneself entirely from this chain. . . . Afterwards, we try to give ourselves a new past from which we should have liked to descend instead of the past from which we actually descended. But this is also dangerous, because it is so difficult to trace the limit of one's denial of the past, and because the newly invented nature is likely to be weaker than the previous one.[19]

To maintain our history-derived identities against those forces that seek to remake us in more questionable or limited terms means to maintain the *conflicts* within, also derived from this history, and not facilely to proclaim ourselves free of them. This is a tragic acceptance, similar to Freud's, and it sets itself against the optimism of all utopianism. The liberation Ibsen's art offers us is not a liberation from tragic consciousness but a liberation into it: It is a promise not of Innocence but of Knowledge. We may be, in the present, severed from our full human identity and thereby "alienated" from the truth and freedom our lives should attain, but the "awakening" Ibsen's art offers us is to *tragic* self-knowledge.

Ibsen's Realist Cycle seems to combine the Hellenic art of dialectic drama with the Christian inwardly imaginative structure of the *Commedia:* that is, fusing the two supreme artworks of the two "empires." As a triadic *cycle* in which the human spirit, through selected representatives, struggles upward to truth and freedom, the parallel with the *Commedia* seems very close. Yet, though Christian mythology is prominent in the cycle, both the dramatic artistry and the concept of spiritual heroism are Greek; and the one play which reenacts the Christian myth in modern terms, *The Wild Duck,* seems to view the Christian *action* within the world with a great deal of skepticism. The concept of the "third empire of spirit" itself denies the Christian claim to have announced the final revelation, and a dramatist who, in the notes to *The Lady from the Sea,* can muse on our desire to communicate with other planets is exploring beyond a Christian cosmos.

If we are embarrassed by such claims for a dramatic art, that is only because we have learned drastically to limit those claims and to give theater a far more modest place within our culture. But Ibsen would not have agreed to this limitation of his art, and we must remember how he was able to occupy a commanding position within European culture ("it may be questioned," James Joyce wrote, "whether any man has held so firm an empire over the thinking world in modern times") more than comparable to that of the most wide-ranging and authoritative guru of the present.

The dualism which the "third empire of spirit" was to over-come was set out by that practical statesman of worldly politics, Lord Acton:

> Two great principles divide the world, and contend for the mastery; antiquity and the Middle Ages. These are the two of which ours is composed. All political as well as religious questions reduce themselves practically to this. This is the great dualism that runs through our society.[20]

This, indeed, is not the subject of our everyday thinking, but it is to *transcend* our everyday thinking, to become urgently aware of universal issues, that we engage with a major art or philosophy. Ibsen does not ask us to leave our homes only to return us to them when we enter his theater. He lived in a world in which, with whatever degree of sincerity, the great reactionary powers of Europe could form a "Holy Alliance" against the "pagan" forces unleashed by the French Revolution; in which revolutions were sanguinely suppressed, freethinkers were imprisoned, and institutions repressed dissent. Ibsen's friend Georg Brandes, himself a victim of discrimination at the hands of Danish academics, returns again and again, in his *Main Currents of Nineteenth Century Europe,* to this omnipresent collision between the reactionary, Christian powers and the pagan forces of enlightenment and liberty.

In the Realist Cycle, the Hellenic values are associated with the life-affirming, rebellious, often anarchic or violent energies within individuals: the erotic, aesthetic, intellectual, radical, "joyful" qualities. They are represented by such figures as Lona Hessel, the Helmers, Lieutenant Alving and his children, Thomas Stockmann, the fallen Ekdals, Rebekka West, Ellida and the Stranger, Hedda and Løvborg. These "Hellenic" qualities are more complexly synthesized with the Christian heritage in the characters of the last four plays in the cycle. The Christian values are represented by more ambiguous characters, due, probably, to the dominant yet defensive position of the powers of orthodox "Christendom" in Ibsen's time. These values are associated with duty, morality, authority, tradition, life-denial, earth-transcendence. Frequently they have infected the pagan "will," which can lead to a renunciation of life. A crucial text here is *The Lady from the Sea,* in which the major action is capable of two opposing interpretations (an appropriate situation for this Kantian play) according to one's ideological stance. While this might also be the case, to an extent, with other plays in the cycle, *The Lady from the Sea* makes this double-vision a condition of the experience of the play.

The dualism that informs the cycle and lies behind the dialectic action of each play, though transcending historical circumstances, found supreme expression, for the European mind, in Hellenic and Christian examples. The dualism is expressed, for example, in two famous speeches: Pericles' oration over the Athenian dead, reported by Thucydides, and Jesus' Sermon on the Mount, reported by Matthew. Not only the speeches but the occasions for their delivery form the strongest possible contrast as visions of life on earth. Pericles stands, according to Thucydides, in "the most beautiful" suburb of the most beautiful city perhaps the world has seen. The brilliant citizenry has assembled for a solemn funeral ceremony for those who have died for the state, seeing in the state, or *polis,* the supreme human value. From the Parthenon sculptures of the Panathenaea, one can imagine how beautiful such an assembly might have been, for the Greeks labored courageously to validate this image for us. It is an image of human possibility that still can strongly stir the modern spirit, for most of our cultural institutions, our arts, forms of knowledge, and physical values and recreations are derived from that source. Pericles' speech, too, is the model for all subsequent ones where a human community creates a collective image of itself that can elicit a loyalty unto death.

The speech is a hymn to civilization as quintessentially represented by the Athenian experiment: its democratic freedoms, its tolerance of human difference, its lack of dogma or fanaticism, its refusal to pass judgment on others, its love of beauty, its passionate commitment to the community's well-being, its nurturing, through education, of physical and intellectual excellence, its indifference to wealth in excess, its possession of courage without brutality. The city is physically beautiful and Pericles exhorts the assembly:

> Fix your eyes on the greatness of Athens as you have it before you day by day, fall in love with her, and when you feel her great, remember that this greatness was won by men with courage, with knowledge of their duty, and with a sense of honour in action who, if they failed in any ordeal, disdained to deprive the city of their services, but sacrificed their lives as the best offerings on her behalf.[21]

To be a citizen of Athens was to be taking part in the greatest happiness human life could offer, and (notable for a *funeral* speech) there is no mention of an afterlife. Undoubtedly Pericles was idealizing, but the speech, given the occasion, could not have been a travesty of the beliefs held by the community gathered there. Athens was praised as profusely by others (most movingly by Sophocles in *Oedipus at Colonus*), and even so severe a critic as Socrates preferred death to exile from her. The goddess of this civic ideal is Athene, "intellectual and active in the community," as Bruno Snell describes her.[22] The keynote of the speech is that civilization is a strenuous *activity*, a labor, with one generation inheriting what their predecessors achieved and handing on, themselves, an enriched legacy: the central humanist faith, in fact. Athens, says Pericles, is the touchstone by which other communities can be judged, and it has remained so. The supreme art form of this community was drama, an appropriately *tragic* drama of the heroic, active, life-affirming spirit.

No greater contrast, of occasion and of speech, could be imagined than the expression by Jesus of the opposite vision of life—the Sermon on the Mount. Not the community of the brilliant, beautiful, brave, and healthy within their lovely city, but crowds from unhappy, unfree communities, the insulted and injured, attend a sermon delivered outside the bounds of any city: "All sick people that were taken with divers diseases and torments, . . . and those who had the palsy; and he healed them."[23] It is to these that

Jesus performs his miraculous cures and gives his consoling message of the kingdom of heaven, to which the meek and the merciful, the mournful and the poor in spirit, the persecuted and the reviled—all the unfree—look for reward in an afterlife, for they can expect no joy or glory in this one. These words of comfort are mixed with words of stern moral prohibition, in contrast to the Athenian tolerance, and with threats of hellfire for the wicked. But with the threats goes the doctrine of the divine forgiveness of sins and of our forgiving the sins of enemies. Instead of eyes turned in love upon the beautiful city, these anguished eyes are fixed on a Father in heaven to whom Jesus teaches their possessors to pray. Life on earth, with all its miseries, is only a preparation for meeting this Father after death; thus, instead of strenuously laboring to create a civilization, we should be like the lilies of the field and the fowls of the air. Beauty in this world, Jesus tells his hearers, is what "the Gentiles seek," and, clearly, the Gentiles are wrong to do so! The supreme art form of this vision will be Dante's tripartite cycle, the *Commedia*, an ultimately "divine" comedy of the contemplative, earth-transcending spirit.

These opposing ideas of human aspiration seem to have been present to Ibsen's mind when he wrote *Emperor and Galilean*, whose opening scene, with its "beggars, cripples and blind men" at the doors of the Byzantine church, disputing doctrines, hunting out heretics, persecuting pagans, and hurling hellfire, is contrasted with the opening of the next scene (Act II), Athens, with its agora of colonnades, statues, and fountains and its attractive young students rationally seeking knowledge in *amiable* contest. But Athens is seen in the golden glow of a *setting* sun, and the attractive scene (reminiscent of Raphael's *School of Athens*) will soon reveal its contradictions and inward decay. Neither Christianity, nor Hellenism, it seems, can alone sustain a complete humanity, and *Emperor and Galilean* seems to envisage a creative synthesis. The Realist Cycle, Ibsen's next work, can be seen to explore the possibility of this synthesis or the extent of its failure. Only close interpretation of the plays, individually and together, will establish this. I think it is possible that Ibsen's *dramatic, tripartite cycle* deliberately synthesizes the artistic visions of the two "empires" of spirit into an art of the third empire. As we can see, we are only at the beginning of fathoming Ibsen's full intention.

To recapitulate the argument of this chapter: Ibsen's realist method presents us with a version of our contemporary reality which it then proceeds to subvert, revealing the falsity of its claim to truth by unmasking the deception and bringing into the dramatic action, through archetypal "echoes," the idea of a more adequate, possible human reality. The resurrection of these archetypal images is liberating, for it suggests that our human spirit actually is larger and capable of greater truth and freedom than the circumstances of the present allow, that we can inhabit unalienated reality. Such archetypal presences are not imaginative fancies: They are examples of the way in which the human spirit once was able to invest the phenomena of human experience with life-enhancing value or with transcendental significance even if in tragic form. As unimportant cogs of capitalist economy or of state power, we seem hardly capable of carrying such cargo, but Ibsen at least does us the honor of keeping the possibility open. This is an unfamiliar idea, both of Ibsen's art and of our reality, and its strangeness may be unwelcome to some. But one remembers what Roland Barthes wrote of the traditional reception of Racine, which sought

> to domesticate Racine, to strip him of his tragic elements, to identify him with ourselves, to locate ourselves with him in the noble salon of classic art, but *en famille;* it seeks to give the themes of the bourgeois theatre an eternal status, to transfer to the credit of the psychological theatre the greatness of the tragic theatre . . .

Barthes adds that we should

> renounce looking for ourselves in this theatre: what we find of ourselves there is not the best part, either of Racine or of ourselves. As with the ancient theatre, Racine's theatre concerns us much more, and much more valuably, by its strangeness than by its familiarity: its relation to us is

its remoteness. If we want to keep Racine, we must keep
him at a distance.[24]

This is not a popular—nor even a democratic—idea, but it
properly establishes the relationship between the major artist
and the public. Robert Scholes, criticizing the notion that teach-
ers should make a writer "relevant"—"to make Shakespeare our
contemporary"—observes, and I agree, that "it is much more
important . . . to try making ourselves Shakespeare's contemporaries, for a while, if only because it is a better exercise for the
critical imagination or, more importantly, because without such
attempts we lose history and become the pawns of tradition."[25]
I claim that Ibsen's supertext owes a great debt to Hegel.
There is nothing in this that need dismay Ibsen's admirers. To
have been aware of the Hegelian revolution in philosophy, a
philosophy that accorded to dramatic art one of the highest
places in human achievement, shows that Ibsen, like Mallarmé
and Joyce, was a highly intelligent and profoundly thoughtful
artist capable of perceiving the significance of a philosophic vision for his art. One might remember the words of T. S. Eliot
about F. H. Bradley: "True, he was influenced by Kant and Hegel and Lotze. But Kant and Hegel and Lotze are not so despica-
ble as some enthusiastic medievalists would have us believe and
they are, in comparison with the school of Bentham, catholic and
civilized and universal. In fighting the battles that he fought in
the 'seventies and 'eighties Bradley was fighting for a European
and ripened and wise philosophy, against an insular and immature and cranky one."[26] Ibsen more than once lamented the pro-
vinciality and insularity of Norwegian culture so that it is a particularly ironic injustice that tries to return him to the narrow
cultural context that he took such pains to transcend.
However convincing the interpretation, it cannot substitute for
an experience of the play itself, for that belongs to a different
order of attention altogether—to *aesthetic* attention. But it can
help to open our imaginations to the nature of the aesthetic
experience we are being invited, by the poet, to participate in.
The most wide-ranging argument, the most difficult of philosophical implications, the most convincing human characteriza-

tion, are, once they enter the magic circle which closes off the art work from reality, only elements in the total artistic design.

The small boy in Skien, amazing his spectators "with performances that seemed like witchcraft," and the world-famous dramatist, agitating and amazing Europe with enthralling yet mysterious artworks, were really doing the same thing. The cycle with its supertext does not attempt to convey a "truth" outside the terms of the artwork itself. It does not seek to have that kind of effect on the world at all. Instead it attempts something that first seems more modest but actually is far more ambitious: to open up our *aesthetic* perception of the human condition. This is all the artist, who is not a priest or a philosopher, can do. But it is much.

5

Providence in
Pillars of Society

Everything I have written is connected with what I have lived through if not actually experienced. Every poem (digtning) *has been a new process of spiritual emancipation and purification. For no man stands free of the guilts and responsibilities of his society* (samfund).
—Ibsen, letter to Ludvig Passarge, June 16, 1880

Pillars of Society (*Samfundets støtter*), opening Ibsen's cycle of twelve plays in 1877, inaugurated something wholly new in dramatic literature. And the play has the buoyant, energetic, large-spirited quality suitable to the launching of a great enterprise. Not coincidentally, this is the subject of the story: Bernick's launching of *his* greatest enterprise, which, like Ibsen's, will open up the ethical vistas upon which his society has turned its back. This is not Bernick's intention, but it is Ibsen's, and much of the fine irony of the drama derives from the great discrepancy between Bernick's intention and Ibsen's. Bernick is the unwitting agent whereby his community will be launched upon the long voyage to truth and freedom.

Far from morally distancing and judging his hero, Ibsen, together with the theater audience, *is* Bernick. That is, Ibsen's undertaking in the cycle is his own "process of spiritual emancipation"—a journey that will take him from the noisy confusions and frantic actions of *Pillars of Society* to the deeply reflective dialectic of *When We Dead Awaken*. Throughout the cycle, as the author visits one spiritual habitation after another, his objective will be the exploration of that human identity he shares with his fellows. This requires neither conventional nor unconventional moral judgment but the continuous opening up of consciousness into ever-more adequate, though still imprisoned, forms. Each household and its history that we visit is one of the forms, or structures, the human spirit has built around itself, the center from which a whole social order can be explored.

The title makes it clear that *Pillars of Society* is not about a single individual but a whole community (*samfund*): our communal humanity living a life that attempts to deny the active existence of universal powers and forces—of Reason—thereby evading both the possibilities and the responsibilities of our total humanity. The community therefore must be invaded, forcefully, by the powers it refuses to acknowledge; its complacent sense of its own sufficient virtue must be shocked into a perception of its radical lack of virtue. The drama's dialectic will overthrow a false consciousness, a false idea of reality, to prepare the ground for a more adequate form which, in turn, will reveal *its* contradictions in the succeeding play. This form of negative dialectics will be the living principle of the cycle, the spiritual heroism that refuses to compromise as it pushes forward to often desolate and tragic insight.

The play is composed on a lavish scale, with the largest cast of characters in the cycle, as if swiftly previewing the world that, in the succeeding plays, will come under more searching scrutiny. What is immediately apparent is the boldness of the play's symbolic artistry, its strange archetypal action with its near fabulous pattern of mortal danger and miraculous rescue. Such an action tells us at once that Ibsen's *realism* is of a special kind: It is shaped and molded by aesthetic imperatives that go well beyond attempting to simulate the patterns and rhythms of our everyday life.

On the eve of the hero's boldest venture and greatest possible triumph, two figures from the past (a decade's absence, which will be a recurring strategy throughout the cycle) suddenly return to create a crisis which will force the hero and his community to acknowledge guilt and error, together with the resolve to embark upon a new form of communal and ethical life. This is the large symbolic action which, enacted directly onstage, can be shared by the theater audience. The complicated story with its pattern of family relationships, past actions, and hidden secrets should not be allowed to obscure the archetypal clarity and directness of the theatrical action.

All the while that Bernick and his "virtuous" community were creating the labyrinth of untruth in the Old World, Lona Hessel, in the New World, had been creating what she describes, in direct contrast with Bernick's achievement, as *her* masterpiece, the truthbringer, Johan Tønneson, who returns with her to rescue both hero and community from the labyrinth. This is the large, positive action that the play is asserting: Any doubts as to the efficacy of this action belong outside our experience of the *performance* of the play. For the purpose of the performance, which must follow Ibsen's notation, such doubts would be as misplaced, *aesthetically,* as doubts (also otherwise humanly reasonable) as to the affirmative gestures of Beethoven's Ninth Symphony. Interpretation that requires performers to play the last scene of the play skeptically and cynically would be as misplaced as interpretation that asked the chorus to sing Schiller's *An die Freude* in this way. For the aim of both interpretation and performance is to release the full force and clarity of the artwork, not to render the work as confused and contradictory. The critic who desires to supply a text with a subtext that reflects the critic's own desire for "ambiguity" and skepticism in fiction is fighting against the artistic activity itself, which, rather than re-creating *our* world, in which such mistrust is called for, is bringing into being an alternative world, not subject to these doubts: for, in Sigurd Ibsen's words, "art gives liberty of action to forces and possibilities which life does not grant the chance of coming into their rights."

For part of the beauty of the Ninth Symphony—or of any major artwork—is that it creates for itself the right to speak out affirmatively, values and aspirations whose expression is baffled and thwarted in our actual, muddled, pragmatic world. The work of art will record the impediments to affirmation, and this will create the complexity of the work: But its impulse, or ardor, is to overcome these impediments, not cynically to exploit them. (Unless, of course, the work is an out-and-out satire, which *Pillars* manifestly is not.) Ibsen's art has its subtleties and its depths of human awareness which interpretation still needs to establish; but these are rendered by Ibsen with full artistic success: that is, with clarity. In our pragmatic world the Lona Hessels do not invade our drawing rooms on the eve of a major enterprise to impel us through guilt and anguish toward salvation. If Ibsen provides us with this blessing in his theater, our response should not be skeptically to squint at it as if the dramatist were offering us a morally dubious bill of goods.

To be cannily on guard against what we are being shown, or to believe that the author is having a secret joke, with the brightest of us, against his characters onstage and the dimmer members of the audience, is not to be in the proper frame of mind to enjoy a dramatic art. As my analysis will show, Ibsen *does* show his characters at times to be hypocritical or self-contradictory, or self-deceiving; but he is always clear about this, so that we can trust him and not fear that he is luring us into a quagmire of untrustworthy appearances and expressions. Major art aims at great clarity, even though it has a difficult thing to show; it is an "anecdotal" vision that wishes to load the artwork with myriad fussy complexities, nuances, and so on. The best art always strives toward clear symbolic symmetry, and Realism, as we saw in chapter 1, is no exception to this. Trust in what the dramatist shows us is a necessary condition of theater.

New World and Old World confront each other in the characters and in the wider ideological argument of the play, creating a symmetrical contrast of more than geographical significance. If America is depicted as not ethically superior to Norway, it is seen as at least wider, freer, and it functions as a force instigating a change of vision within the community. It is one of the play's clear ironies that it should be America, considered by the community to be wholly corrupt, that should bring about this change. In the symbolic contrast, the Old World represents the entire, un-critically accepted realm of reality which will be explored by the cycle as a whole: both its outward and its inward life, and its consciousness of its past—a consciousness that is shown to be crucially defective and selective. The human condition revealed is therefore that condition of multiple alienation first explored by Romanticism, where the self, within a variously repressive soci-ety, is severed from Nature, from its own natural self, from its true historical identity, and from any sustaining Absolute or God. The action of *Pillars of Society* explores beyond the immediate psychological and social situation to natural historical and meta-physical dimensions, recovering these for the modern realist drama for the first time.

Bernick is the most "advanced" level of consciousness in his society. The moral hypocrisy and capacity for "evil" he is brought to acknowledge are present in the other virtuous citizens—including the leader of the working men, Aune—and would emerge if they, like Bernick and Aune, were subjected to the same pressures. It is ourselves we see on stage. In the somewhat paradoxical Hegelian logic of the play, Bernick even is the hero of the action, a hero of consciousness whose journey into evil, like that of Margit in *The Feast at Solhoug*, signals, *for the entire community*, the death of one form of consciousness and the birth of a more adequate one. As always in the Ibsen drama, the spiri-tual condition of the central character marks the more developed sensibility, like the delicate antennae of an organism, of the total condition of consciousness made up by the other characters. That is, Ibsen's proscenium stage really can be seen as *one* mind and the individual characters as aspects of that one *gestalt* of consciousness.

As the most active member of his community, Bernick is forced beyond the impotencies of Rørlund's "virtue" or Hilmar Tønneson's aesthetic squeamishness to reveal his actual identity through his *actions*. This is the essential point insisted on in that section of the *Phenomenology* on which, I claim, Ibsen is draw-ing for the dialectic of *Pillars of Society*. In the dialectical drama necessary for the emergence of Reason, *The Animal Community and Its Deception*, Hegel insists that "an individual can never know what he is until he makes himself real by action." It is precisely the most energetic and gifted individual who will most reveal himself by his actions and, by doing so, will reveal the contradictions within his idea of reality, contradictions shared by his community; for his actions, and their results, will show themselves at variance with the principles publicly proclaimed *for* these actions. "Consciousness, then, in doing its work, is aware of the antithesis of doing and being."[1] In Bernick, awareness of this antithesis will be developed to an extreme, so that he becomes aware of having lost his "self" through the desperate actions he is driven to perform or contemplate.

Bernick's journey into evil is a process whereby, in T. S. Eliot's phrase, "Virtues / Are forced upon us by our impudent crimes."[2] The Hellenic goal of the play might be summed up in the Delphic injunction "Know yourself," and it will be a whole society, under the guidance of the Apollonian Lona Hessel, who will have to undertake this labor as the play closes. In Greek temple architecture the pillars or supports (*støtter*) hold up the entablature on which is displayed the community's idea of itself: its gods, heroes, and its ideal civic life, as on the Parthenon. If the pillars prove rotten, the whole structure will collapse. But though the pillars of Bernick's community *are* rotten, these self-serving hypocrites who profess the public good act wiser than they think or say; for, by forcing the exposure of their rottenness, they clear the way for the erection of sounder pillars upon which a better idea of society can be upheld.

For the virtuous community lives only a half-life, denying, on the one hand, its instinctual, animal life while also evading, on the other, its "divine" or ideal identity, paying only lip service to the realm of universal values. "Providence" is the key term in this pious fraud and is variously invoked by the hypocrites, who thereby assent to a usefully impotent concept of an Absolute that acts as no check or restraint upon their immediate self-interests. Ironically, therefore, the community's *self*ishness only stunts the self. The instinctual self is denigrated; in the Present, in the form of the Society for the Fallen Sisters, and, in the Past, in the prurient retelling of the details of past pleasures and sexual transgressions. The history of Dina Dorf's mother, who was starved and hounded to death, demonstrates the lethal savagery of the moral prejudices of the virtuous society. It is the same biting account of conventional society that we find in *Love's Comedy* and *Peer Gynt*.

Hypocrisy, however, is a promising moral symptom in a community, preferable, say, to an unashamed, bestial materialism, for it at least shows awareness of an "ideal" realm that actions may be transgressing. It thus has a potentially uneasy conscience that might be worked upon. When Bernick is forced to see the extreme disparity between the motives from which he acts and the virtuous intentions that he professes, he has *begun* the dialectical process which, in the plays that follow, will take the human spirit into ever more adequate, though no less divided, forms of consciousness.

It should be noted that while the levels of consciousness increase in terms of adequacy of vision as the cycle progresses, Ibsen's artistry at the early stages is as fine as at the final stages; for he surrounds the less adequate forms of consciousness with a wealth of ironic perspective. Each play is seen from the perspective of the Whole. In the same way, the reader of the *Phenomenology,* watching each drama of the spirit evolve into its "higher" successor, is aware at each stage of the structure of the Whole and reads the earlier stages with a considerable degree of ironic participation with the author. The actors, in Hegel's work, act "for themselves" and put on their own show for others, but are unaware that they also are putting on a show "for us." The greater the discrepancy between "their" consciousness and "ours," the greater the degree of irony of presentation on Hegel's part. In *Pillars of Society* this irony to a great extent depends, similarly, on the differences between the "show" the characters put on for each other and the show they unwittingly present to us—the spectators hidden in the darkened auditorium. The play, in fact, demands from its spectators a greater acuity and complexity of attention than one might at first suspect, and this has led hasty critics into a rash dismissal of the play for its "melodramatic" elements. It is excused for being the middle-aged Ibsen's "apprentice-work" in the new style of realism. But Henry James, long ago, indicated the rich density of the play:

Such a production as *The Pillars of Society* with its large, dense complexity of moral cross-references and its admirable definiteness as a picture of motive and temperament (the whole canvas charged, as it were, with moral colour), such a production asks the average moral man to see too many things at once. It will never help with the multitude that the multitude shall feel that the more they look the more intentions they shall see, for of such seeing of many intentions the multitude is but scantily desirous. It keeps, indeed, a positively alarmed and jealous watch in that direction; it smugly insists that intentions shall be rigidly limited.[3]

The play opens with a strong visual division: that between the interior garden room of a *private* house, whose glass wall looks out onto the *public* world of the street where strolling citizens are always within view. This scenic detail tells us that the Bernick family and their fellows are concerned to present a version of themselves to each other. The exterior space is bright and sunny, in contrast to the shaded interior, and is referred to as "out there" (*der ute*)—a phrase that will evolve to mean not only the immediately exterior scene but the entire world from which this community seeks to isolate itself. The favorite pastime of this community is the moral condemnation of others, a pharisaism for which these dwellers in glass houses will be terribly reproached.

Turning their backs on the sunlit street beyond the glass wall, the little group in the garden room also turns primly from a more liberal life in the past and from the example of larger and freer communities abroad. They thus deny themselves any spiritual extension, into past, present, or future, where larger and more generous and liberating ideas of human identity might be discovered. Instead, they vigilantly watch out for, and punish, any such manifestations. They gossip about such manifestations in the past with a blend of moral spite and prurient fascination: an activity that, while making for good, comedic *ensemble* playing, also drives home the judgment by the author against a way of life that is sickly and life-denying. Even before Lona Hessel makes her energetic and buoyant entrance, we feel that this society needs opening up to the qualities of health, courage, generosity of spirit—all of which she will bring.

We immediately notice something about Ibsen's realist art: how his scenes are simultaneously *functional* and *symbolic*. The characters in the garden room, turning their backs on light and life to listen to an idealist fiction read to them by Rørlund, live in a shadow world of the spirit, like the prisoners of Plato's Cave of illusions (as Rolf Fjelde has suggested) and will fiercely resent and attack those who return to the cave to liberate them to truth and freedom. The scene tries to shut out the spirit of truth and freedom, to exile it to a harmless distance, but this spirit will invade the stage space not just in the person of Lona Hessel but also by means of the dialectically evolving action which will have a momentum beyond Bernick's control. This movement will include a symbolic notation of sunlight, gathering darkness and storm, and a final clearing of the sky for the lovers' voyage to America, and for Bernick's own embarkation upon *his* voyage of self-discovery.

The family scene of the Bernick household exists between two transparent walls: the great glass wall behind which the fictive public is strolling in the sunlight, and the "invisible fourth wall" separating the stage from the auditorium. Bernick and his circle carefully play up to the fictive public, putting on a show of domestic harmony and virtue, and declaring their home a glass house open to anyone's scrutiny. Looking out, they approve of the world they see and are approved of by it—until the complications begin in Act II. *Then,* Bernick will be anxious to hide his domestic troubles and his public intentions from public inspection. But, while fraudulently "posing" to the fictive public, Bernick and his associates are "exposed" to us, the more critical public behind the invisible wall.

The poet's descent into the banal details of everyday reality— railway lines, new machines, ship repairs, sea routes, company shares—is possible because Ibsen can reveal universal conflicts by means of these factual metaphors: for the spirit must engage with its true opponent, the intractable-seeming materiality of modern bourgeois culture. In *Pillars of Society* we observe the first of the spirit's battles with the "fallen" material world, which will be continued throughout the cycle. In this play everyday reality is sundered drastically in two. Bernick and his society live by a despiritualized pragmatism, invoking "Providence" only as a moral cosmetic to cover their actions. At the other extreme are the "beautiful souls," Rørlund and Tønneson, the self-appointed spokesmen for, respectively, moral and aesthetic idealism: a fastidiously disengaged and therefore impotent idealism that comments upon but cannot affect practical reality. Both idealists therefore are relegated to the ladies' circle, which also is denied all practical power. Theirs is the high-sounding and usefully ineffective moralism and aesthetic idealism that endears itself to modern business and religion and which can declare its trust in God on the dollar bill. This separation of the real from the genuinely ideal, which is the condition of our modern world, is the reason for the crisis of the play. Because the major characters, the powerful males, have paid only lip service to universal principles while actually living as if such principles were of no consequence, their practical life itself, unpenetrated by spirit, is directionless and veers helplessly with every gust of adverse circumstance.

The larger scenography of the play emerges gradually through the dialogue, extending the total action beyond the little community to a landscape with valleys and mountains, across which a "branch line" will link the town to other communities; and a seascape at the end of which is the New World from which two figures from the past will emerge, also to open up the closed community. Another important extension of the here-and-now of the performed action is the recollected past with its oppressive and its liberating memories. Within this past is a "scandalous" history of sexual license and transgression, dance, theater, music, feasting, recalled with somewhat rueful disapproval by the moralist gossips of the present: a once freer, more creative past, ruthlessly repressed. Readers coming, as they should, from *Emperor and Galilean,* the immediately preceding play, might well associate this slandered past of joy-of-life-and-thought with the slandered past of Hellenism, which Julian tried to restore to his empire.

Evil, this community believes, is utterly alien to them; it is what *other* people do "out there" at the ends of railway lines and sea routes. But the dialectic of the play, by a cunning of Reason, will reveal that it is the pharisaic consciousness of virtue that is evil, whereas the acknowledgment of one's capacity for evil is the "good" that will be granted the community. This recognition of evil as not separate and alien but as existing within oneself is the major theme of the first three plays of the cycle and is explored with increasing intensity and depth until the final recognition scene of *Ghosts*.

Bernick boasts that the community can look right into his house and that his household can look back at the community, without shame; this, of course, is because neither will explore the real reasons for feeling shame, presenting only deceptive surfaces to each other. This smug and shameless mutual regard where each sustains the other's false identity in a proclamation of virtuous being (contradicted secretly, by the actual *doing*) is a false play-acting, a false form of theater.

The large cast of major characters, nine men and nine women and the child Olaf, is augmented by a still-larger one of "townspeople and other residents, sailors from abroad, steamship passengers, etc."—a crowd of citizenry and foreigners which, continuously moving and changing in the background, emphasizes the *civic* nature of the play's dialectic. The serious depiction of the civic and political (i.e., of the *polis*) spirit of the play is one of its "Hellenic" aspects, as it is of *An Enemy of the People,* the play that closes this first group. This is new in Ibsen. In none of the earlier plays is this political, or civic, dimension of reality treated with anything other than disdain: It is bypassed in *Love's Comedy* and *Peer Gynt,* dismissed as alien and unworthy in *Brand,* and satirized in *The League of Youth. Emperor and Galilean* does deal with political/historical realities but in terms of imperial Byzantium, and these dimensions are immediately lifted to ideological and metaphysical levels.

In the second part of the *Phenomenology* the dialectic engages the communal, civic, and political dimensions of human existence, exemplified, for Hegel, in the Greek *polis;* and the "animal community" brings about the crisis whose resolution will found the "rational" community of the *polis.* Hegel's analysis involves the resurrection of Greek myth, fable, and drama so that in his text, too, an account of the modern spirit is one in which the dead awaken and walk again. Ibsen's text gains immensely from the conjunction of modern political and ancient archetypal layers of reality, making the quest embodied by the cycle so much more substantial aesthetically than that of *Brand*.

When the curtain rises on the first act, we watch for a while the tableau of Rørlund with the ladies in the garden room, facing inward in a posture of rejection of the outside world; and it is only after we have contemplated this tableau for a few moments that the first dialogue takes place. This is between Aune, leader of the working men, and Krap, official agent of the bosses. Nowhere else does Ibsen take up this theme—the conflict between capital and labor—which was of such significance in the life and letters of his time. And his treatment of the subject, which is in striking contrast to that of other realists, such as Zola, Hauptmann, and Gorky, is a good indication of the nature of the Realist Cycle.

Though class division is present in the play, its significance is played down. Instead of presenting Aune as irreconcilably of a different social and ethical order than Bernick, the victim versus the oppressor, Ibsen in fact emphasizes the opposite: that Aune is inextricably part of the same spiritual community, with the same capacity for right or wrong action as the other prominent figures. Aune's career in "evil" parallels, in magnitude of guilt, and in timing, that of Bernick. Like Bernick, he is driven to contemplate the same crime, mass murder, in order to protect *his* interests. The Aune subplot therefore is fitted into the play's design to show us how the consequences of false consciousness are the same for everybody.

In terms of dialectical (and dramatic) development, Innocence is neither a very interesting nor a very desirable phenomenon. In Marxian thought, the proletariat, as the innocent victim of economic injustice, never can know guilt and so (in Ibsen's view) never would grow up. Marx and Engels proclaimed in *The Communist Manifesto* that the proletarian class was the only one in history that would come to power guiltlessly and would remain free of guilt, for its possession of the means of production would be at the expense of no other class. The proletarian passes from innocent suffering to guilt-free utopia. But Ibsen, who knew economic deprivation, insisted "no man stands free of the guilts and responsibilities of his society." The nobly indignant worker-victims of Hauptmann and Gorky, like the nobly indignant victims of much feminist or "minority" writing, are simplifications, and therefore falsifications, of our human psychology; one understands the reason for the simplification, but the artist concerned with truth cannot commit it. Is this not a reason for our unease with the innocent figures in the plays of Bertolt Brecht? In *The Caucasian Chalk Circle,* for example, both the characters of the (future) utopian Prologue and the victims of (past) Grusinia are *humanly* incomplete, whereas Azdak, whom Brecht depicts as *unfortunately* necessary for such hard times, is the only figure in which we can recognize ourselves.

Not being very interested in innocence, Ibsen cannot be very interested in evil, for neither innocence nor evil are stages of the growth of consciousness: They are the terms of a static ethical system. Both Aune and Bernick can learn from their contemplated crimes; if they could not, they would not be suitable for Ibsen's dramatic purpose, which is dialectical. Aune, therefore, is given the spiritual dignity of full accountability for his motives and actions, just as Bernick will be given the "grace" of greater self-knowledge.

The dialogue between Aune and Krap, revealing a conflict in society which the community refuses to acknowledge, now gives way to the comedic *ensemble* of Rørlund and the ladies, decorously removed from any close knowledge of such practical and problematic affairs. Instead, they are engaged upon charitable work for unmarried mothers. This, while ineffectually patching over the deeper rifts of the social fabric, agreeably sustains the ladies' sense of moral superiority, a conviction which Rørlund reinforces, likening their work to that of sisters of mercy who bandage the wounds of the morally fallen (*moralske fordervede*). The "fallen" condition of the morally lapsed women, however, and their desperate financial situation, is greatly due to the very *uncharitable* judgments and penalties created by the virtuous society. The history of Dina Dorf's mother, which we soon are told, reveals how lethally uncharitable the charitable circle really is. In all the numerous drafts of the play, which contain many substantial changes, this scene of the charitable circle with Rørlund is always firmly established. It must therefore be intrinsic to the meaning of the play.

In these earlier drafts, the book that Rørlund reads to the circle, *Woman as the Servant of Society,* is given more "escapist" titles: *Leisure Moments in Nature's Bosom* and, most tellingly, *The Community in the Forest,* a fiction that describes a community that actually retreated from the world into a forest to escape knowledge of evil. In similar retreat, Rørlund and the ladies can overhear the loud debate of the community's business leaders in the next room but have no knowledge of what important subject is being discussed. Outside, in the large world Rørlund deplores, the values of family life are undermined, everything is subject to doubt, and "a desire for revolution" (*omstyrtningslyster*) now confronts the most solemn truths. Rørlund's indictment could be describing the cycle of plays Ibsen now is launching!

The circle now is joined by Hilmar Tønneson, the aesthetic idealist, who shows himself to be as ignorant of practical affairs as the circle. Like Rørlund's, his idealism, risking no contamination from contact with unpleasant realities, is no threat to the business world. The businessmen have called a meeting to discuss the project of a railway line—a prospect from which, Rørlund gives thanks, Providence, through Bernick, had spared them, for the railway line means the possible contamination of the community from the outside world. (This is not an implausible situation: Emperor Francis of the Habsburg Empire, whose motto was "Law and Order" (*Ruhe und Ordnung*), had refused to allow the construction of a railway system in his empire for fear it would encourage revolution.)

The circle of ladies now settles down to gossiping about the past in order to instruct a relative newcomer, Mrs. Lynge, in the facts of the community. This is more than a conventional device for informing the audience, for the action itself allows us to get the measure of the group; for we note the gleeful prurience and the savagery of the ladies' denunciation of the pleasures of the past, of the sexual scandal surrounding the theater, and of the death of Dina Dorf's mother as a result of ostracism from the virtuous society. What is more, we already suspect what later will be confirmed, that the newcomer is being educated into untruth about the past: another instance of the multiple deceptions and self-deceptions practiced by the community. The scene is good comedy, but it also is a self-damning revelation of spiritual malice on the part of the charitable ladies.

At this point, Bernick and his associates enter to explain to the community why the morally undesirable railway project now is desirable despite earlier solemn assurances of their high-minded opposition. Therefore, they endorse their unscrupulous decision with high-sounding oaths: "In God's name," and "A Norseman's word stands as firm as the rocks of the Dovrefjord"—this for a decision that has broken their former word. Rørlund, who had declared that Bernick, in rejecting the railway, had been an agent of "Providence," shows uneasiness, so the "pious" Vigeland pronounces the formula that will assuage him:

> There's no denying that it's almost as if Providence (*for-synet*) had made the terrain for a branch line.
> RØRLUND. You really think so, Mr. Vigeland?
> BERNICK. Yes, I must say that I also find it providential [*jeg også betrakter deg som en styrelse*] that I traveled inland on business last spring and happened to go down a valley I'd never been before.
> (Fjelde, 32)

With such assurances, Rørlund's moral qualms are put at ease! Such an obliging Providence prevents or permits the railway scheme according to the business interests of the present moment. God is thus like a powerless constitutional monarch who can only set his seal on whatever his "subjects" require. Rørlund's acquiescence is so complete because he has no alternative concept of Providence: one that would insist that, far from obligingly going along with the demands of society, God, as in *Brand*, is likely to confront society with demands of His own.

Bernick's further claim that Providence (*styrelse*) led him to "a valley where I'd never been before" foreshadows perhaps the terrifying *moral* terrain he will find himself in, a valley of despair; for, near the end of the play, as he begins to climb out of this despair, he asks his family, "Where have I been? You'd be petrified if you knew" (Fjelde, 117). His journey into *this* valley will be part of the deeper design of Providence which requires that the leading member of the community be shocked into a perception of the calamitous inadequacy of the community's spiritual vision. Learning by shock will be one of the procedures of the cycle. Far from conveniently remaining ineffectually at a distance, Providence, in the course of the play, will prove to be painfully close, to be woven into the fabric of individuals and society. Furthermore, Providence will employ as its agents of enlightenment just the two figures, Lona and Johann, that the virtuous community would most vehemently dissociate from the divine (for Providence, like Hegel's Absolute, is highly ironic) and will employ them in a particularly shocking manner.

Bernick assures the startled circle that while the new railway line will create great material prosperity for the community, that community will remain immunized from contact with outside evil through the moral guidance of Rørlund, whose moral ineffectuality we have just witnessed. As great material change *must* create social and moral change, the businessmen's assurances obviously are hollow; but they are only dimly aware of this and, instead, congratulate themselves on the soundness of their own moral principles in contrast with those of the New World. "The individuals in this stage sense that they command no substantial reality in themselves, that they are just role-playing and they will play any role they can just to appear successful and real to themselves."[4]

When they receive the telegram from the American owners of the ship *The Indian Girl* urging that it be put to sea with the least possible repairs, their shock at this callousness is evidence of their self-ignorance. As the dialogue continues the theme of the moral turpitude of America, Bernick's son, Olaf, rushes into the room with the news that "a whole circus" has arrived with the steamer from America.

As with Mr. Sleary's circus in Dickens's *Hard Times*, the circus implies areas of the human spirit neglected by the pragmatist virtuous community: imagination, courage, physical grace, generosity, spontaneity, naturalness. These qualities will be conspicuous in Lona Hessel, who is, for a while, identified as "the circus-manager's wife." Reacting with shock and distaste to the "circus group" advancing in the street with their "horses and wild animals" and the jaunty strains of "Yankee Doodle," the group retreats from the window, drawing the curtains to shut out the offensive sight. "This is nothing for us," Rørlund primly declares, "Let us go back to our work." The circus theme will not appear after Act I, but, as a metaphor, it is important and is used forcefully by Ibsen. The *natural* response to the approach of a circus is Olaf's excited delight, whereas the virtuous circle's decision to shut out the sight and sit in semidarkness represents a clear repudiation of light and life. This rejection reminds us that this is the society that put an end to the festivities and the arts in the past, and it is not difficult to see in this a repudiation of the pagan and Hellenic aspects of the *Weltgeist*. In *The City in History*, Lewis Mumford describes how, after the collapse of the Roman Empire, the performers in the great pagan amphitheaters who once entertained the Roman public did not disappear:

> You would find them straggling over the highways of this old Roman world, stopping at a barbarian court, drawing a crowd at a fair: the weightlifter, the acrobat, the daring horseback rider, the men leading the bear. As an afterimage in the European mind, perhaps in the living linkage of the flesh, from generation to generation, handing on their arts from parents to children, sometimes greatly venturesome, but no longer committed to death, the old circus folk continued their play.[5]

These circus folk, along with the theater actors, were long denied the rights of Christian burial. Like the theater from which Dina Dorf originated, the circus could be seen as itself an act of defiant paganism, tenaciously holding onto existence, despite official disapproval and persecution, to reemerge in the modern European city. The community of *Pillars of Society* is to be ethically awakened by the reemerging spirit, but the humanity which that community must learn to repossess also is expressed in that metaphor of the circus and its ebullient joy-of-life. Lona's association with the circus, at this point, gives her this pagan aspect. Olaf, peering through the curtains, excitedly reports, "Mother, now the ringmaster's wife is standing by the fountain, washing her face" (Fjelde, 36). After this impropriety, which gives rise to outraged responses, and even the proposal by Rørlund that the police should intervene, the "strange woman" "comes in briskly through the door" of the room while the ladies, "in a frightened whisper," exclaim, "The circus woman! The ringmaster's wife!" (Fjelde, 36).

The scandal is only enhanced, however, when Lona reveals her identity, for she, together with Johan Tønneson, who has arrived in town with her, *is* the shocking past we have heard related to Mrs. Lynge; and this further reinforces the pagan associations of the circus-identity. So, too, does her name. I wrote to Dr. Einar Haugen asking him the origin of the name "Lona" without informing him that I hoped that, as with the names of the heroines of the next two plays, Nora and Helene, it would be significantly Hellenic. The reader will remember that I associate Lona with the Apollonian mission of self-knowledge—Know yourself! Dr. Haugen answered that, according to Bernt Stølen's *Norske Døbenavne (Norwegian Baptismal Names)*, published in 1887, "Lona (or Lone) 'is short for Abelone from Greek Apollonia, i.e. the divine, the one who belongs to the god Apollo.' " Those who have insisted that the many such correspondences I claim for the details of the cycle, contributing to its observable supertext, are "mere coincidences" will find that mere coincidence, right at the beginning of the cycle, seems capable of formidably significant creativity: so much so, in fact, that accepting conscious intention on Ibsen's part seems the more rational interpretive procedure.

If there also is a distinctly Dionysian aspect to Lona's entry, accompanied by wild animals and indecorous music, this also is likely to be intentional on Ibsen's part, for the union of Dionysos and Apollo would be the most appropriate way of inaugurating a great new theatrical enterprise. Nietzsche's *The Birth of Trag-*

edy, in which this divine pair is seen as essential for tragedy, was published five years before *Pillars of Society.* Ibsen, living in Dresden at the time, might well have heard of the book, which soon gave rise to academic scandal as outraged classicists, led by the young Wilamowitz, fiercely attacked the book and were attacked in turn.

One of the purposes of Nietzsche's book, a purpose he later was to repudiate, was to further the cause of Richard Wagner's music-dramas. While he was inaugurating *his* cycle with *Pillars of Society,* Ibsen was living in Munich only a few miles from Bayreuth, where Wagner was staging his great god-filled cycle, *The Ring of the Nibelungs.* Ibsen was aware of this (as he hardly could help but be, for Wagner was an unashamed publicist of his aims), for we find him mentioning it in 1876, a year before *Pillars of Society* was published. To think of Ibsen in the company of Wagner, as Thomas Mann did, and of Nietzsche is as fruitful for our interpretation of him as, like Jan Kott, to see him in the company of Freud.

And it is the example of Freud that allows Kott to see much of Ibsen's archetypal procedure. "Into the houses of Ibsen's imagination descend the ghosts of Oedipus, Electra, Orestes, and Iphigenia. . . . The summoning of Greek shadows reveals, once again, parallels between Ibsen and Freud."[6] In Ibsen's procedure, as in Hegel's and Freud's, more than one ghost can haunt an individual, just as, at a séance, a medium can speak with more than one voice. In the cycle, it is the significant action that raises the ghost and that allows the past to inhabit the present. A recollective art, such as Ibsen's or James Joyce's, therefore seeks quite consciously and masterfully to exhibit what one school of modern critical theory calls *intertextualité,* in which, according to Julia Kristeva, "every text takes shape as a mosaic of citations, every text is the absorption and transformation of other texts."[7] When this becomes the writer's *intention* and when the "citations" are controlled to realize the full meaning of the text, the interpreter must proceed warily. Knowledge of the intertexuality of the *Phenomenology* or of Ibsen's or Joyce's work is only the important first step toward understanding.

As important as the Apollonian identity of Lona is, I believe, the identity of Athena, "the virgin, intellectual and active in the community," who, with Apollo in Aeschylus's trilogy, guides the hero Orestes from tragic guilt to salvation and who, after Apollo's exit, also guides the community of Athens to new wisdom. As the cycle is not yet ready for Hellenic tragic consciousness, *Pillars of Society* is a pale ghost indeed of the *Oresteia*. Ibsen will have to train his public carefully to rise to the level of courage of the Greek audiences: and, indeed, when he did so confront his public, with *Ghosts*, it recoiled in dismay. We can see by this the extreme closeness between the social situation in *Pillars of Society* and the situation in Ibsen's actual world and how his vocation as an artist wishing to evolve an adequate dramatic art required the regeneration of his society.

The "divine" quality to Lona's action of guiding, while watching over, the developing crisis of the play, drawing it to its ethically "higher" ending, is augmented by the startling actions and words given her. She arrives to effect change, to bring truth, and to pronounce the terms of a new spiritual order for the community that will emerge from the old and false one; and at the same time to rescue the hero (*helt*) of her youth from the mortal spiritual danger he has fallen into. Her attitude toward the virtuous community throughout is "Olympian" and ironic.

Lona still is believed to be a member of the circus even after she identifies herself; but, disabusing the company, she commandingly takes over the room, chiding them for sitting in the darkness and "sewing these white things" which, she assumes, have to do with a death in the family. This idea of death will be elaborated, but, for the moment, her remarks are deflected onto the good (and telling) joke of mistaking the virtuous ladies for the fallen sisters. Then, recognizing their real identity, Lona returns to the death theme, this time implying a death of the spirit leading to a rebirth:

> Men fy, fy, fy,—dette moralske lintøy lukter så fordervet,— akkurat som livsvøp. . . . Vent, vent; vi skal nok komme opp av gravkjellern.

(S.V. II)

> . . . all this moral linen reeks of decay—like a bundle of
> shrouds. . . . Wait, wait, we'll make it out of the tomb yet.
> (Fjelde, 38)

The ladies, after all, *do* belong to the morally ruined (*moralske fordervede*), for, to Lona, straight from the air of the prairies, it is the *morality* that smells of corruption (*fordervet*) and death. Announcing that she has come to clear the air, she then proceeds audaciously to open the curtain to let the light into the room. Her startling entrance and these subsequent actions and speeches of swift and easy command have a larger-than-life quality. Like the implausible arrival of Hilde Wangel in direct response to Solness's utterance that youth will knock at his door, we are meant to feel this nonrealistic rhythm to full effect, to note its strangeness, and to follow, with some astonishment, Lona's quick assumption of authority within the world she enters. The Providence that the virtuous community exiled to an innocuous distance in the skies now has invaded the drawing room.

The "hero," through whose rescue Lona wishes to awaken this society, Karsten Bernick, is above all a man of practical abilities, of actions. With a vision of him standing strong and free once again, Lona even now forgives his guilt, at least that of which she is aware. He had thrown her over to marry the wealthier Betty and had allowed Johan to take the blame for the sexual transgression of which he had been guilty. But Bernick's energy-without-direction has further compounded this guilt (allowing Johan also to be suspected of theft) and, in the public realm, has enticed him to a daring and secret purchase of land along the route of the railway he is urging upon his community. At this moment of greatest public success, Johan and Lona unwittingly threaten him with total public destruction. The extreme coincidence of their arrival at just this time is another suggestion (we will meet many in the cycle) of a dimension of reality other than the everyday working upon events.

While it is true that it will be only under the threat of exposure by Johan that Bernick will be driven to his most appalling intention, this capacity for such action was always in him, as it is in us, waiting to be known and mastered. Only by a chastening self-knowledge of oneself can this mastery be gained, and Bernick, being a man of action, must learn of his self through his actions. From the very beginning of his career, in his matriculation essay of 1848, when he was twenty, Ibsen wrote:

> Of all the branches of thought the investigation of our own nature is among those in which the sharpest observation and impartiality are necessary if one is to arrive at that which is the goal of every inquiry, namely the truth. Self-knowledge demands the most careful study of ourselves, our inclinations and actions, and only by the results of such an analysis is it really possible for a human being to reach a clear and truthful understanding of what he really is. . . . Even if a man, by acquiring this self-knowledge, gets to know his worst characteristics, and thereby finds himself required to humble himself in his own eyes, such humiliation can in no way impair his self-respect, since it provides evidence of a strong will and an honest quest for what should be man's goal in life—the development of his spiritual gifts and a care for his temporal well-being.[8]

One is struck by the actual *lack* of humility of this statement and the implication, reminiscent of Freud, that the descent into one's depths entails the heroism-for-truth of a scientist rather than the abasement of a penitent. And self-knowledge is not only of our worst characteristics: It also would require our awareness of that in us which resembles the divine and which might require of us an even greater heroism. The cycle is not a long procession of spiritual crimes and evasions, sicknesses and errors; it also is a charting of freer and higher identities. The program of self-analysis is also one of liberation.

In Act II, the earlier intimations that the virtuous community could be uncharitable to its own members are borne out when we learn that the ladies assembled in the Bernick garden room now stay away from the family as it is involved in scandal. Even without the swift disclosure, in Act II, of Johan's innocence, the evident attractiveness of the disgraced pair would win the theater audience over to their side. Indeed, Dina Dorf and Martha Bernick will be won over to Johan *without knowing he is innocent of the serious charges against him.* Bernick, on the other hand, acts repellently before our eyes, both to his wife and to Aune. But he also reveals, in his dialogue with Lona, an interaction of private and public interests in which it is not easy to charge him with *conscious* hypocrisy. He is so much a public figure that it is inevitable his private and public interests should be so hard to disentangle. The self-interest from which he acts is perfectly natural: That is how actions in the world are undertaken. What is wrong is Bernick's concept of his self and its true interests.

So, also, is his concept of the community and *its* interests. In his quarrel with Aune, Bernick justifies displacing workmen with machines with the merely "Darwinian" reasoning, "the lesser has to give way to the greater. God knows (*i Guds navn*), the individual *has* to be sacrificed for the common good" (Fjelde, 46). Neither the idea of the "individual" nor the idea of the "common good" has yet received any searching definition: At the end of the play there will be an awareness that such definition is now imperative.

Bernick pressures Aune to repair *The Indian Girl* quickly so the community can be rid of the "Americans," whose scandalous behavior he thinks reflects badly on him. His accountability for their behavior is hard to understand, but Johan and Lona, also called the "Americans," *are* causing acute embarrassment to him by strolling round the town reminding everyone of their connection with the Bernick family. The crew of *The Indian Girl,* incidentally, was subject to drastic revision, as to their moral natures, between the early drafts and the final manuscript. In one draft they are given clearly Mediterranean (i.e., Hellenic) qualities: "playing and singing in the sunshine . . . real men, sunfilled like ripe fruit." This clearly connects the seamen to the joy-of-life theme of these first four plays, in *this* play now more appropriately represented by the circus. The drastic degeneration of the sailors, however, hardly makes less heinous Aune's and Bernick's willingness to send them to the bottom of the sea.

Bernick's public persona, represented by his public works visible about the town, impresses Lona and Johan, though they are unaware, as yet, of the price he has had to pay: We, however, can appreciate something of his lonely eminence from their commendations. To act the part of a moral pillar, in order to accomplish so much, he has had to distort radically his own nature; both its capacity for happiness and its possibility of living in truth. Without intending irony, Lona now compares *her* work with Bernick's: her "masterpiece," the free, honest, and courageous character of Johan, on which she has been working over the years while Bernick was shaping his *false* public identity. Johan's function as Bernick's opposite (*alter ego* or *doppelgänger*), the publicly guilty but actually innocent identity exactly reversing Bernick's, makes for some slight implausibility in the actor's role. Though about thirty years old, Johan has an adolescent naiveté very similar to that of his teenage soulmate, Dina Dorf. This is because Johan must be old enough, credibly, to be suspected of the affair with Dina Dorf's mother ten years back yet at the same time *now* be capable of experiencing first love for a young girl. The *coup de théâtre* of this act, when Bernick, in his expression of thanks to Johan, reveals that he was the guilty one and Johan, an object of horror to the community, is innocent, now brings the colossal hypocrisy of the hero, and by implication, of his community, out into the open so that now there are no more secrets to be revealed in the play; instead, we watch the corroding consequences of these deceptions as they work upon Bernick's character.

But Ibsen's argument is subtle. He is not proclaiming that Bernick's life should have been as virtuous as his public image; instead, he shows that this public image derives from a concept of virtue *that always must be a lie,* for the community's idea of virtue excludes as unvirtuous energies and values ineradicable from our full human identity, our birthright. The dialectic of the play is working on the public in the auditorium as well as upon its representatives onstage. What is wrong is not so much what Bernick *did* in the past, but that what he did cannot square with the identity he publicly acknowledges. His *virtuous* identity in the present can only perpetuate the lies that infect society, creating a defective, because inadequate, idea of the human identity society should sustain; whereas Bernick's desperately "evil" actions have the positive result of forcing consciousness to a more adequate self-understanding. And, I have noted, Dina Dorf and Martha Bernick can join forces with Johan while still believing him guilty of the transgressions that Bernick dare not admit to. The virtuous society's principles can be upheld only by the cloistered virtue of Rørlund.

Bernick believes he genuinely has served the public good, and Lona grants that he has been a force for good, socially, however much he may be destroying himself. He is at least honest enough to justify his work for its *practical* and not its *moral* value. And we have to remember that, at the time of the writing of the play, Europe was being transformed immensely by the practical energies of industrial capitalists even while the culture was deeply conservative, hypocritical, and fearful about its moral and spiritual destination, as is true of the United States today. The men who were transforming the world materially seemed quite content to abide by an outdated—and therefore conveniently unchallenging—idea of the moral/spiritual order, unaware that this contradiction within the culture, this dishonesty, left the moral/spiritual order helpless before the dynamism of the material and dehumanizing order. This was to be the burden of much of Bernard Shaw's political comedy, as in *Major Barbara*.

In *Brand* the hero sees how the "British smoke stacks" of the new industrial society pollute and poison fresh green life, how a new subhumanity, without spiritual direction, becomes deaf to all exhortation or prayer, forgetting Christ had died for them; giving up, in fact, its human identity. When the spirit of Agnes appears and calls on Brand to join her in flight from this smoke-filled vision of hell on earth to the sun and the south, Brand refuses and resolves to *live* and combat what he has so horribly imagined, "free and awake." As John Howard Lawson observes, citing this passage, "Ibsen remained true to this resolve. He never faltered in the bitter struggle to see reality 'free and awake.' "9

Without an active and authentic spiritual purpose, without *direction,* human energies can only end as the hollowness of identity of Peer Gynt or as the self-destructive network of lies in which Bernick becomes enmeshed. As the splendid edifices and public works rose up, creating his outward image, there also rose up, like the troll-brat's growth in *Peer Gynt*, their sinister counterpart, the edifice of lies which now threatens to destroy him. The moment of Bernick's greatest *public* triumph, therefore, to be signaled by the acclaim of the torchlight procession in his honor, will also be the moment of his most harrowing *private* collapse, the empty public illumination of his name in lights counterpointing his descent into a private darkness and desolation.

The complicated climaxes of Acts II, III, and IV, which are virtuoso displays of the simultaneous eruption of multiple crises, present us with the crowded confusions inevitable to the ethically unexamined way of life. Bernick can live life only as frantic *melodrama,* for melodrama is violence of action without reflective and universal (that is, philosophic) content. By removing Providence from the scene Bernick and his community have emptied the scene of meaning and value and have reduced actions to almost spasmodic reflexes: the condition also of farce.

Act III opens with an enraged Bernick entering onstage after having severely thrashed his son, Olaf, for attempting to run away. Olaf, with his attempts to flee the virtuous community, can be seen as an extension of Bernick himself, as his *natural* self that craves release from the world of lies. But it is this world of lies that Bernick insists Olaf should inherit. The rage with which he thrashed his son suggests a displacing of fury over his own predicament onto the boy. (The child, as a projection of the parent, will appear frequently as a metaphor in the cycle.)

The moral texture of the play now "darkens" considerably. Aune, to save his position as leader of his community, is willing to send the ill-repaired *Indian Girl* to sea and certain destruction, and Bernick, faced with the evidence of this, is genuinely shocked. But Aune's intention is only a foreshadowing of Bernick's, who soon is faced with Johan's resolve to clear his own name, which he can do only by ruining Bernick's. Though the plotting here is ingenious in the Scribean manner, the ironic artistry and symmetry go deeper; for the parallels and contrasts now being so skillfully juxtaposed are not to serve the mechanics of a fast-paced plot but to reveal the complex dilemmas of the moral situation, as Henry James observed of this play. In the past

Johan, an innocent youth flattered by Bernick's contrived friendship with him, had taken on the guilt for Bernick's relationship with a woman. Now, wishing to win that woman's daughter and finding his *false* reputation an insuperable obstacle, he wishes to clear his name, which only can be done by also revealing the colossal fraud built up by Bernick upon that initial lie. The men are in conflict over the supreme motives of love and power, for Johan refuses power (a share in the vast new fortune to be made) if this requires renouncing Dina by keeping silent about the past. Bernick, by contrast, had sacrificed love (Lona) for power far back in the past (the pattern will repeat itself in *John Gabriel Borkman*), and it is his desire to hold onto power that drives him to oppose Johan's bid for love.

There follows a finely paced dialogue between Aune, who returns while Johan's threat is still hanging in the air, and Bernick, in which the two men hover over the unmentioned but understood moral abyss that is opening up under them. Bernick then gives way to a frightened but fascinated contemplation of *The Indian Girl* going down, taking with it Johan and the incriminating evidence. The stage darkens with the gathering storm and also metaphorically underscoring the moral journey into darkness. In his realist plays Ibsen extends his actions into a cosmos, as does Shakespeare, but Ibsen's metaphors are also *functional*, as we see in this instance. The gathering storm creates the physical circumstances under which the ship will sink and therefore makes all the more terrible Bernick's decision. Yet this thoroughly *realistic* situation is symbolic; for the ship, whose fatal disrepair ensures that it will not survive the first serious storm, also represents Bernick and his society. But the *symbolic* or *metaphoric* reading is only possible to those who can "see" universals behind particulars, which is itself the program of the cycle. It is sometimes complained that the metaphor of the coffin ship is a too heavy signaling, but I think this complaint derives from detaching the metaphor from the realist context instead of recognizing how natural, integral, and functional a part of that context it actually is.

Thus, the symbolic rhythm of Act IV, opening in darkness and storm with Bernick at his spiritual nadir, and closing with his

resolve to reform, with "the sky clearing," need not embar-
rassedly be played down in a production but, on the contrary,
played up to the hilt. Ibsen's theater is *theater,* a powerful remod-
eling, not a simulation, of our everyday world; and in this play, I
think, the somewhat violent linkage of the particular human
action to the universalizing metaphors is itself an indication of
the gulf between the two which the cycle will bridge.

Let us recapitulate the play's dialectic movement to this point.
In the past, certain actions were committed which scandalously
conflicted with the social mores of the time and even more with
those of the self-ignorant society that, repressing the content of
the scandal (human nature), has since evolved. The pleasurable
life of the past was suppressed and misrepresented to the extent
that Bernick has been able to construct a reputation of considerable virtue; giving him a commanding position in the virtuous
community that savagely would be destroyed if his true past
were known. But the misrepresented figures and actions from
the past now reemerge, to proclaim the truth, threatening to
topple the most able man of the community without at the same
time changing that community's false image of itself.

Bernick's false self must be destroyed to make way for the emergence of his true self, but in such a way that his undoubted abilities and gifts will not be lost to the community. What must be
assured is that the exposure of his guilt will not be the occasion for
an orgy of pharisaic condemnation on the part of his less gifted
fellow citizens. For that is the usual result of the exposure of a
prominent citizen through the revelation of scandal. Instead of
communal heart-searching by the public, there is a nine-days'
wonder of righteous indignation and prurient pleasure, which
leaves the great *communal* lie unaffected. The newspapers have
their week of sensational disclosure; the virtuous public, fam-
ished for scandal, nevertheless professes shock; new hypocrites
emerge to take over the reins from the fallen power by proclaiming
their disapproval—and nothing has been learned by society about
itself. Apollo's command to know ourselves is totally disregarded.

If the communal, as well as the individual, identity is to advance, Ibsen must stage a situation where Bernick is not exposed by others, but by himself. He must make his confession a

thing of individual shame, for it is that, but also make it a challenge instigating self-knowledge in others; just as in *The Eumenides* Orestes' guilt, trial, and acquittal become stages of the community's evolution, too. Those critics who feel that Bernick has not been punished sufficiently, that he has been allowed to get away with too much, misread the play's intention. This is not the old style drama in which villainy is identified, exposed, and punished and in which the innocent suffer unmeritedly; but one in which a representative of our total human spirit learns, fearfully, to know something of itself in the most humiliating and shaming form: And this should be *our* journey to self-knowledge, too.

The dialectic has driven the chief character into an extreme of self-alienation, for the leading pillar of his society recognizes that his actuality, realized in his *actions,* is the antithesis of his *proclaimed* identity. Rescued from moral self-destruction at the last moment, he recoils from this antithetical self. But he must learn to recognize *it,* too, as an essential aspect of his identity. Neither the publicly proclaimed virtuous self nor the privately revealed criminal self is the "true" Bernick identity. The "thesis" of the virtuous identity and the "antithesis" of the villainous one are unsatisfactory extremes to be overcome by a more adequate idea of ethical identity (and a more adequate idea of drama). This can emerge only from the recognition that ethical values cannot be founded on concepts of human identity that actually refuse to acknowledge our total humanity.

We in the audience (at an ideal performance) have experienced an evolution from false to truer consciousness, by which we are brought to see the falsity of the presented appearances of virtue, the superiority of the "pagan" openness, frankness, and generosity of spirit of Johan and Lona, and the increasingly appalling consequences of a way of life not suffused with universal and life-affirming values and drastically severed from its biological nature. (The gods of drama are Apollo *and* Dionysos, the *adelphi* of Delphi.) The portrait is that of a particular and localized society, but, with its archetypal presences and actions, it is an image of our whole humanity, too. Gathered together in the last act, therefore, are not only many plot strands but also many layers of cultural, ethical, and metaphysical implication, shared with the audience, for this first judgment day upon the soul in the cycle.

When Bernick enters, we see that he is *visibly* unwell, indicating how much of his natural self has been violated and distorted by his actions. His worst actions are performed with a horrified consciousness of evil, not with coolly calculated villainy. His associates, less remarkable and less audacious than he, are aware of the shadier side of Bernick's financial dealings, but still smoothly prepare the fraudulent testimonial ceremony staged by the virtuous society. This festival of lies recalls Brand's comment at a similar gathering:

> Jeg ser hva titt meg skar i øyne,
> en løgnerfest til pris for løgne
>
> I see a sight that's often pained my eyes
> A feast of liars celebrating lies

The underlying metaphor of *Pillars of Society*, of false *theatrics*, false role-playing, now is gathered up into a multiple theatric metaphor of the play-within-the-play. Bernick is to pretend ignorance of the torchlight procession in his honor, and for this purpose the window blinds are pulled down. Here, the audience feels a "click" of recognition when *this* task is given to Lona, who in Act I had opened up this window to light. Her exclamation, "I'll ring down the curtain on my brother-in-law, though I'd rather raise it" (Fjelde, 95), extends the metaphor of the theater as does the purpose of this action: that Bernick and his family, when the blinds are raised like a stage curtain, will be seen by the crowd as "a surprised and happy family." As these fraudulent theatrics are being prepared, Johan, Dina, and Olaf break free from this society now stifling in its own lies.

The departure of the lovers is blessed by the watchful, ever-hovering Lona and by her sister-in-law, Martha. This last recruit to the cause of truth and freedom is all the more remarkable, we have noted, because neither she nor Dina, at this moment, knows that Johan is innocent of the crimes attributed to him. It is not with an exonerated Johan that they side but with the apparently *guilty* one, representing a complete reversal of the moral loyalties of the virtuous society. A critic might object that it would be reasonable to suppose that Johan or Lona, "offstage," already has informed the two women of the truth; but this is art and not real life, and Ibsen supplies us an extended dialogue of farewell between the women and Johan that pointedly excludes any reference to his innocence, which shows Lona's surprise at Martha's decision (and, later, Martha will show surprise at Bernick's revealed guilt) and which expresses an explicit rejection of the conventions of the virtuous society by Martha and Dina.

As the lovers depart for the New World, Martha and Lona unite in mutual loss and renewed friendship; a bittersweet redemption of the past and its pain in a reconciliation and happiness that tellingly contrasts with the sham reward and actual anguish with which Bernick's past is being rewarded. Through loss, the "two foster-mothers" have created "new, free life," whereas Bernick, with all his fame and material gains, discovers he has created a "curse" as his son's inheritance. And Olaf's instinctive struggle to escape the curse nearly results in tragedy. But Bernick, we will see, is not ready for tragedy.

He prepares to confront his public triumph with an anguish that shows how his actions have distorted his humanity. His dialogue with Lona now reveals greater self-knowledge together with greater disenchantment with the values of the community he leads. Olaf, he hopes, will somehow free himself from the net of communal lies and guilt, but when Lona reminds him how his son's own heritage will also be a lie, Bernick falls into despair and turns in hatred upon her:

> But someday the curse has to be lifted. And still—all the same—(*In an outburst*) How could you bring all this down on my head! But now it's done. I have to go on now. You are *not* going to crush me!
>
> (Fjelde, 103)

Bernick recognizes at last that the lie he has lived and must continue to live is the curse on his house which even the news, from Lona, that Johan and Dina will not perish with *The Indian Girl* and that Johan has returned the incriminating letters cannot lift. When he declares, "I can't live my life anymore after today" (Fjelde, 104), we see that this despair comes from his new self-knowledge, for his *public* image now is assured. Olaf, alone, he believes, will "redeem everything," and it is only now that he learns that Olaf has stowed away on *The Indian Girl*. In tragedy, the curse on the house would have claimed Olaf as its victim and Bernick would have been spiritually destroyed, but Bernick, as Ibsen has conceived his drama, is not equal to such a tragic conclusion, for his process of self-knowledge and self-examination has come too late for him to perceive and act from the universal forces at work within his life. It is not until *Ghosts* that Ibsen's audience will have been coached to this level of perception.

Shrinking from the flames of the public illuminations that spell out "Long live Karsten Bernick," he sees the flames as "tongues" mocking and reproaching him, so that the community sees its hero, for the first time, in considerable disarray. But now Providence will prove kind to Bernick in a series of miraculous peripeties. Olaf is restored to him, Aune repents, and *The Indian Girl* is saved. Therefore, if he wished, Bernick now could receive the public tribute and retain his secure position in society. But, recognizing the monstrous identity he had uncovered beneath his public persona, Bernick decides to communicate this discovery to the crowd and then embark upon a process of reconciliation with Aune, his family, and, if possible, his society. This closing action is staged against a clearing sky and will receive Lona's benediction, two indications that Ibsen does not intend us to distrust Bernick's motives.

Rørlund has been selected to deliver the encomium to Bernick and, as usual, this beautiful soul manages to glide, with facile incomprehension, over the whole moral minefield that the theater audience now knows lies beneath social life. He takes up, in succession, the "surprise" of this procession for the Bernick family, Bernick's achievement in laying a firm moral foundation for society, his unselfish public spirit, spotless family life, and personal character, his good relations with his workmen, the disinterested-ness of his financial dealings, and the community's good fortune in escaping corrupt influences from outside. Now, he prophesies, the community stands on "the threshold of a new era."

Bernick's response to this eulogy is a careful dismantling of its structure of lies: an act of demolition of the conventional idea of society as the preparation for the building of a better one. It has been objected that Bernick's confession is not total, and some have questioned its sincerity, suggesting that Bernick is merely adopting another moral pose behind which to hide his self-interest; but this is to read into the stage situation the kind of subtle cynicism that fights against theatric art itself. The audience has to trust the presented details if they are to work forcefully and coherently, and to require from the audience, instead, a canny distrust of what it sees is not to elevate its perception. And as there is no reason why Bernick should confess at all except that he is penitent (for there is no evidence against him: Johan has left for America and Lona would keep silent), it is absurd to question Bernick's sincerity.

It is true that Bernick refers to his greatest *contemplated* crime—the willingness to let *The Indian Girl* fatally set sail—only as "much, much to repent of, but that concerns my conscience alone," but surely he is right! The community must be told enough at this moment (when Bernick has only just begun to plumb his own depths) to instigate self-examination on *its* part. Each individual has his and her private world of demons to wrestle with as well as a public self to set in order. And Bernick is announcing only the beginning, not the end, of a process of self-examination. Our guide here must be Lona Hessel, who, while approving of Bernick's confession, will insist that he and the community still have much to learn and do.

The play does not end with firm conclusions, only with proposals—an ethical blueprint. The citizens, and theater audience, now must go home and reflect on the nature of their newly perceived community and its leaders. The wife, Betty will try to win her husband, and the repentant father must win his son, who will be encouraged to determine his own life. The bad ship will be better repaired and the workers, with the new technology, will be reconciled to an understanding boss. All this simply cannot be presented in the theater cynically. The sky clears (and critics who distrust Ibsen's psychology must at least accept his meteorology!), auguring both a safe journey for the lovers and a different kind of journey—to truth and freedom—for the community. If we are dissatisfied with the "positive" ending of the play, we can console ourselves by reflecting that the journey to truth and freedom that follows in the cycle will bring us to grimmer conclusions as the spirit of the cycle becomes more adequate to the insights of tragedy.

Lona now can reveal her Athene-like mission, which was "not hatred then? Not revenge?" as Bernick asks, incredulously. She had returned to the community so that she could see the "hero" of her youth "standing free and true." And, as in *The Eumenides*, the hero's freedom is also the inauguration of a new age for the community. I believe Ibsen's play does lightly draw upon its greater Greek predecessor: Orestes, rescued by Apollo and Athene, and Bernick by Johan and Lona are the very different heroes of very different communities, but ghosts from the earlier play occasionally haunt the text of the later.

Bernick, for all the magnitude of his contemplated crime, is the hero of the play, whose journey into moral darkness brings about the salutary devastation of his once confidently lived but false public and private identity. The *agon* of the central character reveals the nature of the ethical world to others; but Bernick's suffering had been without tragic dignity because, not acting from and holding onto ethical principles (as Helene Alving will), he is not capable of the tragic elevation she attains. For that elevation is the privilege of the fully human only; and Bernick, from the "animal community," is only just discovering his humanity.

The optimism of the play's conclusion springs from the conviction that, the consciousness of virtue being such a sham, it must collapse under the pressure of the spirits of truth and freedom. But our escape from the accumulation of lies and distortions from the past and our recovery of our true and free humanity has only begun. The play proclaims that within the past itself are the forces that can find out and combat the sham and expose the lies. The past recovered and exonerated in this play has been the "local" past of ten years or so within a provincial Norwegian town; a strategy the cycle will keep to. But this local time and space is invested with "archetypal" attributes that bring our larger, cultural past into the drama. It is only in this way, and not as historical costume drama, that the past is built into our present. Not to see the archetypal dimension of the Realist plays is to take away from Ibsen half of his power and beauty and almost all of his intention.

His procedure is far from solemn, as we have seen, for solemnity would be false to the Hellenic spirit. If Apollo, Dionysos, Athene, Orestes, and the Athenian *polis* "play" about the modern characters, they do so "playfully." And with this procedure, it should be noted, Ibsen is doing nothing new in European art but is, instead, retaining one of its most traditional methods, vital to the humanist procedure. In painting, the depiction of classical and biblical figures in the costume and setting of the artist's time is paralleled in the drama. In the medieval plays Christ is born in an English village or crucified by English guild members, and Shakespeare and Racine costumed their ancients, and made them speak, as moderns. Henry Fielding, as well as James Joyce, modeled his novels on classical works. Like many such avant-garde artists, Ibsen's innovation was to find vital new ways of presenting the great traditional themes of art. Ibsen, in my view, would not sacrifice this creative interplay of past and present, which the best art always has sustained, for a narrow concept of "realism."

If we contemplate the overall symbolic action of *Pillars of Society,* the arrival from the past of a dynamic and wise figure who wishes to rescue a hero and his community from the great danger they are in, who watches over his painful process of self-knowledge and finally declares her divine purpose—liberation of the community from a false way of life after the hero acknowledges his errors before a large civic procession—we better will see also the archetypal content of this tale. Like all good stories, *Pillars of Society* exists also on this level—and exists intensely on it. The last words of the play, legislating a new ethical order, are spoken by the "Athene figure" as she corrects her hero's declaration that women are the pillars of society:

> Da har du laert en skrøpelig visdom, svoger. (*Legger hånden vektig på hans skulder*) Nei du; sannhetens og frihetens ånd—det er samfunnets støtter.

> Then it's a pretty flimsy wisdom you've gained, Karsten. (*Sets her hand firmly on his shoulder*) No, my dear—the spirit of truth and the spirit of freedom—those are the pillars of society.

> (Fjelde, 118)

Near the conclusion of *The Eumenides,* Athena tells the community of the new spirits (the Erinyes, who have become the Eumenides) she has persuaded to be a part of the *polis.*

> These blessings I bestow on you, my people, gladly,
> I enthrone these strong, implacable spirits here
> And root them in our soil . . . to rule the lives of men.[10]

Lona teaches a new *wisdom,* which was Athena's special attribute. Her Athena-like quality seems to be reinforced by the gesture of placing her hand, commandingly, on the hero's shoulder as she speaks the words about the new order to come. The sculptural nature of this closing tableau brings to mind the friendly divine-human contacts of Greek literature and art. Lona, of course, is human, but that is how the divine expresses itself in our modern world.

Pillars of Society does not solve the ethical dilemmas it opens up, but it suggests the spirit in which they can be met; and this very opening up of spiritual terrain is a major purpose of the dialectical action. The pragmatist separation of the practical from the spiritual, in which "Providence" is safely distanced and piously invoked to sanction the most dubious enterprises, never has been better exposed and challenged than in this play. At the conclusion, Spirit becomes active within human reality and, in such later figures as Nora Helmer, Osvald and Helene Alving, and Thomas Stockmann, will subject our reality to more searching ethical scrutiny, a process that will recover more and more of the Hellenic sources of our culture.

6

A Doll House, or "The Fortunate Fall"

ADMETUS. *O builded house, how shall I enter you? / How live, with this turn of my fortune? How different now and then.*

CHORUS. *Many are the forms of what is unknown / Much that the gods achieve is surprise.*
What we look for does not come to pass / God finds a way for what none foresaw.
            —Euripides, *Alcestis* (trans. Richmond Lattimore)

At the conclusion of *Pillars of Society,* the chastened hero had advised his fellow citizens to go home and "look deep into" their own hearts, the beginning of a self-examination that needed to be conducted by each household in the community. In *A Doll House* and *Ghosts,* we see such households subjected to the workings of the spirits of truth and freedom upon the subtler deceptions and self-deceptions within the home and family. In these two plays we leave the busy, crowded scenes and the public *personae* of the social actors and their more obviously fraudulent show for a quieter, more private, and more deeply self-searching dialectic. The evolutionary process whereby the "mini-Nora" of the opening scenes becomes the "super-Nora" of the close is not unlike the biological process from grub through chrysalis to butterfly: The dialectic is a painful one and involves the death or discarding of previous selves through three stages of violent change. These are the violent *peripeties*, which lead to their agonizing *anagnoreses*, act by act (a process repeated in the similarly three-act *Ghosts*), until a whole worldview is converted into its opposite. In *Pillars of Society*, the dialectic forced the communal spirit to recognize that what it believed an alien evil was a living presence within the community. In *A Doll House* this aspect of the cycle's dialectic takes a further step. It is conceded by the Helmers that guilt and sorrow are present in society, represented by the disgraced Krogstad and the sick Dr. Rank, but these are quarantined, as it were, from the Helmers's innocence and happiness within the doll home.

This, though a "higher" level of illusion than that held by the virtuous community (for Torvald is no hypocrite: he is walking by the best light he has), is still an error. The Helmers must learn that guilt and sorrow are inextricably built within the reality they share with the rest of humanity. *Sunt lacrymae rerum* (there are tears in the nature of things) could be the Virgilian motto to the play. In *Ghosts,* guilt and sorrow will be the great themes from the beginning. Helene long has recognized these within her home and family but falsely believes that her ethical value—duty—was the "good" that had opposed and defeated the "evil" represented by her husband. But she will come to learn her very loyalty to her principle of duty and her strong-willed resolve that her son will inherit nothing from his father are aberrations that will be terribly punished by the values represented by the dead and scorned husband and father. This is the heart of the Hellenic vision, and its art form is tragedy. The ghosts of the Oedipal and the Orestean plays therefore invade the Alving drawing room. The reception of *Ghosts* by the Norwegian and European publics demonstrated how difficult it was for Ibsen's contemporaries to rise to the level of the Hellenic vision at its most courageous, in spite of the careful preparation represented by the advancing dialectic from *Pillars of Society* to *A Doll House.*

Bernick had been the outstanding man of action of his community, a man with greater capacity for good or evil than his fellows.

The Helmer household, however, is the very essence of the ordinary. Though Kristine Linde confides to Krogstad that she has seen "such incredible things" in the Helmer home, nothing actually occurs that could not be repeated in countless other homes. It is the very ordinariness of the pair, calling to mind Tolstoy's comment that all happy marriages are the same, that makes the play's analysis of marriage so disturbing. Had Torvald been in any way "oppressive," Nora's decision to leave him would not have carried such shock value. The rejection by the wife of the all-too-human husband for not being able to perform the heroic act she romantically had dreamed of is a rejection, at the same time, of the false histrionics of the romantic worldview itself: a more unsettling conclusion, for all parties, than striking a partisan blow for the feminist cause.

Familiarity with the play (for, with *Hedda Gabler,* it is the most performed and studied of Ibsen's plays in America) has served to obscure its strangeness. We need once again to see its nonnaturalistic quality in order to appreciate its full power. There is a strong suggestion of ritual about its hugely coincidental action, set at the time of the death of the old year and the birth of the new, and its *dual* feasts of the pagan *yule* (*jule* from O.N. *jöl*) with its "props" of the tree, the gifts, the feasting, and the tarantella costume and dance; and the Christian adaptation of that feast, with *its* nonmaterial associations of guilt, sorrow, joy-through-sacrifice, and spiritual rebirth. Torvald and Nora celebrate the pagan festival while Christine and Krogstad will find themselves, unexpectedly, celebrating the Christian one. Hardly a coincidence, therefore, is the fact that the pagan pair have pagan names (Torvald is derived from Thor and Nora from Eleonora/Helene), and the Christian pair have the Christian-derived names Kristine and Nils.

Torvald and Nora joyfully anticipate a momentous change in the new year: a material change when Torvald gets his new job at the bank, increases his salary, and fires the disturbing Krogstad. They celebrate *only* the pagan aspects of the season: feasting, dancing, tree, and gifts. We have met this attractive pair before in Ibsen, as Einar and Agnes in *Brand:* at first a similarly pagan and aesthetic pair who will be changed, momentously, by their encounter with the galilean force of the priest, Brand. We met them cheerfully singing and dancing, fearlessly, on the edge of a precipice, careless of their danger: Agnes, the "butterfly," and Einar, her playful protector. This relationship is repeated, in all important respects, by Torvald and Nora. Like Einar, Torvald is notably *aesthetic,* for Ibsen gives him many actions and speeches to establish this. His fastidiousness against everything sordid or ugly is an aesthete's, not a moralist's. But his is a false or inadequate aesthetics that needs to keep the ugly and the sorrowful at a distance, as at most a flattering background of darkness to enhance the sunlit foreground of his own domestic happiness.

To create an attractive home, to raise a family that will go to the "right" school and university, to fill the home with "tastefully, but not extravagantly" selected furniture, pictures, "small art objects, a bookcase with luxuriously bound books," as in Ibsen's informative stage directions to *A Doll House* (and today we would add the television, stereophonic system, gadgetry, and automobile), is the main goal of middle-class endeavor, to which we are enthusiastically exhorted (as in *Love's Comedy*) by all the forces of persuasion in our culture. Ibsen wishes to attack this whole endeavor as a selling of the soul, and those who wish to see him as the sturdy defender of bourgeois values somehow have to account for the fact that no modern writer has done more to demolish them.

The self-deceptions both Nora and Torvald practice are those we have practiced all our lives: although, of course, in dramatic art, these must take on more emphatic expression than in everyday life. Productions should show both Torvald and Nora as attractive, as the kind of young couple upon which society showers its approval. Their joy at the *wonderful* in life being the end of hardship and the arrival of prosperity and happiness is moving and human. That it is a bartering of their souls only will be apparent after their view of the world has totally been shaken. For selling one's soul no longer is a Faustian bargain with a stage devil in tights and tail, but is the often-performed and commended actions of our daily life. This is one of the most unsettling of Ibsen's many inversions: the conventional worldview, which once had been the vantage point from which one could perceive the *satanic,* has *become* the satanic, while the realm of fearful spirits, of the living dead, has become the redemptive vantage point from which to watch and judge conventional "fallen" reality.

The abyss over which the attractive couple dance is, as in *Brand,* the huge domain of unexamined reality which the doll house contrives to shut out. It is life taken on trust: traditional and time-worn beliefs, as in Torvald's confidently expressed moral principles; habits, opinions, beneath which all the unseen ghosts lurk, secretly impelling our actions. It is when the conventional beliefs begin to dissolve that Nora realizes she has no identity at all and that she has been living for years with a stranger. As Jan Kott observes, Ibsen reverses the situation of Euripides' *Alcestis,* in which the husband discovers in the Stranger his lost wife. "In this new recognition scene the wife discovers the Stranger in her own husband."[1] But this perception of the strange within the familiar is mutual, for the wife Torvald thinks he has got back after he has forgiven her will prove to be a total Stranger.

In the house of Admetus the wife was willing to die for her husband; Nora is willing to die to save Torvald; and her forgery in the past, when her husband's life was in danger, had been a form of self-sacrifice which, delivering her into the power of Krogstad, leads to her contemplating suicide to save her husband again.

The doll home will be rocked and finally shattered by three seismic convulsions, one in each act. The evolution of the three shocks makes up a dialectic progress: (1) the *objective,* social shock of Act I, when Nora is forced to recognize, for the first time, the claims of the public/social world she had frivolously disdained; then, (2) the antithesis to this, the *subjective,* inward shock, in Act II, when she begins to fathom something of her own nature and even her affinity with the disgraced Krogstad; and, finally, (3) the *metaphysical* shock of Act III, when her whole idea of the world she thought she inhabited and of her own, and others', identities is shown to be grotesquely false. This last shock brings about the destruction of both objective and subjective conceptions. The three shocks are accompanied by three different conceptions of "the wonderful"; and these conceptions show a progression also, from material (objective) to inward (subjective) and to metaphysical ideas of the *transformation* of reality.

While the structure and rhythm of the play clearly is dialectical, *A Doll House* is subtly and palpably embodied and finely *felt* as a human story, as countless performances have demonstrated. The dialectic, while not probing as deeply as *Ghosts,* goes considerably deeper than that of *Pillars of Society,* for the protagonists have attained a greater degree of human identity than the social hypocrites. The public consciousness of virtue in the earlier play had been a pose it was easy to expose, but the moral posing of Torvald far less obviously contradicts the life he is living, for he carefully limits the amount of reality he is willing to acknowledge. He is much less of a force in the world than Bernick, but his active involvement in both marriage and business brings him out of the circle of moral and aesthetic impotence of Rørlund and Tønneson and into the area of possible suffering—and enlightenment.[2]

It is Nils Krogstad who gives the doll house its three great shocks. At the beginning of the play his situation is seen as the antithesis of that of the doll house, as the moral and aesthetic hideousness which serves to set into even brighter relief the social grace of the Helmers. But the "evil" that he represents, and which the Helmers consider so utterly alien, will be shown to be woven into the fabric of their own lives. In a form of dual dialectic, Krogstad actually will enter the Helmer home, undermine and take control of it, only to be himself *transformed* through the agency of Kristine. The name Krog-stad, with its associations of crookedness (deformity), alerts us to the first presence in the cycle of a recurring "satanic" identity. In the next play, the satanic figure of Jacob Engstrand actually will be physically deformed. Krogstad is given a notably satanic role: threatening the doll pair in their Eden of innocence and bringing them to a fortunate fall or loss of innocence. In this, Krogstad's accomplice will be Krist-ine, once his lover, who decides to *save* the Helmers' marriage by making them confess and confront the

truth to each other. The satanic threat, in other words, is a salutary shock instigating a movement to a more adequate, or whole,
human identity.

For, by attempting to exclude conflict, guilt, and sorrow from
their lives, Torvald and Nora are evading human wholeness for a
doll existence. *Both* need to be shocked into maturity, so the play
is not about a wife's escape from an oppressive marriage but
about the necessary destruction of an illusory idea of life shared
by both husband and wife. If it is Nora who, most profoundly
experiencing terror and loss of identity, is the first to "awaken,"
this destiny still awaits Torvald at the end of the play.

The doll home encloses a *private* realm of fantasies and illusions, held by husband and wife and sustained by the *public*
realm of law and finance; both realms unexamined from the
viewpoint of "the spirit of truth and the spirit of freedom."
Torvald proclaims his home free of all debt and of all taint of
moral guilt: Nora at first frivolously dismisses the claims of the
public realm altogether. Both Torvald and Krogstad are lawyers,
but Torvald, refusing to handle "sordid" cases, decides to leave
law for finance, which he believes to be free from such contact.
Therefore, one of his first actions in taking over the bank is to fire
Krogstad, who, as a *disgraced* lawyer, can handle hardly anything but sordid cases. Torvald's embarrassment at Krogstad's
overfamiliarity with him is part of his *aesthetic* shrinking from all
contact with what is not "clean and decent" (Fjelde, 131). But it
will be through Nora, of all people (the doll apparently most
shielded from ugly reality), that Torvald will be forced to recognize that he is part of the same human and moral reality as
Krogstad. Without Nora's offense, Torvald would have been able
to sever all connection with Krogstad, and the couple would have
remained in their false consciousness of innocence. That is,
Krogstad forces them out of the inadequate fiction, by which
they "read" their lives, by confronting them with realities their
fiction has evaded.

Two plots counterpoint each other in the play. In one, a marriage is dissolved on a journey from innocence, through experience, to estrangement. This is the experience of Torvald and
Nora. In another, a union is cemented as a couple, Krogstad and

Kristine, journey from estrangement to reconciliation and joy. This symmetrical design has led some to complain at Krogstad's last-minute conversion from villainy to repentance or at Nora's belated but swift discovery of will and determination. But this misses the dialectic nature of the play, in which, from the beginning, the reality presented is far more divided than it professes, the innocents being less innocent than they proclaim, the villain being less guilty than he is proclaimed. In Nora's case, in particular, the stages of her evolution are marked by deep spiritual crises that make her final resolution plausible.

The doll home presents itself to us in the most engaging way. The modest tastefulness of the domestic setting reflects the "aesthetic" view of the world within which the Helmers contrive, totally, to live. There are constant references in the text to Torvald's aesthetic nature: his horror at the sordid and ugly, his concern with taste and appearance, his deprecation of Nora's overstepping "the proprieties of art" (Fjelde, 181) in her dancing, and so on. He would be unable to face the death bed even of his best friend because, Rank observes, of his "sharp distaste for anything ugly." Nora herself actually is the creation of Torvald's aesthetic imagination. He advises her on costume, directs the tarantella, and prohibits the macaroons that might spoil the teeth of his connubial doll. Above all, as we will learn, there is the fiction that he has built up around his wife: that she remains his young bride whom he is bringing to his home for the first time to possess her "young and trembling beauty." The very essence of the family, the sexual relationship, is a form of erotically charged fiction. The living reality of Nora has been transformed into a fictional being with no truth, no freedom, other than that which her "author" provides. But Torvald is not the only author in the play. In Act II Nora begins to "rewrite her script," as it were, *romantically,* casting herself and Torvald in more heroic roles, and in Act III when this script fails, she will abandon the script altogether and leave the house in search of a new one.

When the curtain rises, Ibsen has us look at the set for a few moments before we hear the doll home coming to life: for this will be a play in which the Nora who exits the set at the end is radically different from the Nora we are about to see enter. A bell

rings, a door can be heard being unlocked, and then Nora mer-
rily enters with Christmas packages, overtipping the boy who
brings the Christmas tree. The wrapped presents are the *innocuous* seasonal secrets that can be disclosed, joyfully, to the family,
unlike the graver, deadlier secrets that this season also will bring
to light. The first word spoken in the play, Nora's "*Hide* the
yuletree well . . . " (*Gjem juletreet godt*), announces, like a musical motif, the theme of concealment, hiding, disclosure, and revelation. Nora continues, "the children must not see it until it is
decorated." The decoration and the stripping of the tree will be a
metaphoric accompaniment to Nora's own drama and the word
for decorated, *pyntet,* will be used of Nora also in her fancy
dress.

The yuletree, a natural product of the forests, has been prevented from full growth, cut or transplanted, then prettified and
decorated in a domestic environment, like Nora herself. Charming and attractive as the doll home is, it is as much a realm of
falsehood as the hypocritical society of the previous play. Nora is
presented as performing a life of perpetual self-denial; continually lying to Torvald, manipulating him by flattery and flirtation,
and, as in the master-slave relationship, gaining as much from
the role-playing as her husband, for his pose of manly responsibility is at least as arduous (we learn it nearly cost him his life) as
Nora's pose of feminine helplessness.

It is concern with financial responsibility that in fact brings
Torvald onto the stage in response to the word "bought," in order
to lecture Nora on their responsibilities toward the world of public finance and its laws, on which their private world depends.
He believes he can maintain the home free from debt for "something of freedom's lost—and something of beauty, too—from a
home that's founded on borrowing and debt" (Fjelde, 126). But
Torvald's belief that his home is free from debt will prove as
illusory as his belief that it can be free from moral guilt. And the
agent by which he will be forced to acknowledge his implication
in both will be the same man—Krogstad.

For Krogstad has been extending moral as well as financial
credit to the Helmers and now is determined to demand repay-
ment. For years, the misery and disgrace of his home had served

to define the happiness and innocence of theirs. Krogstad had been marked out for social disgrace by a society which fallaciously segregated humanity into good and evil. Krogstad is that which Torvald and Nora must acknowledge in themselves—a much more interesting function than that of villainy. His development, from disgrace, desperate aggression to joy and forgiveness, and the revelation that he is a human being capable of generosity and love, is a demonstration to the audience, as well as to the doll pair, of the falsity of the distinctions we make between innocence and guilt.

Whereas Krogstad represented the *guilt* from which the Helmer home believed itself to be free, Rank was the no less flattering *sorrow* that set the Helmers' lives in attractive relief. When the curtain rises on their story, therefore, the Helmers are about to undertake a journey into both guilt and sorrow, knowledge of which is essential to the tragic vision. But before they embark, the happy and innocent pair exult over the "new life" that they imagine opening up before them: the "safe, secure job with a comfortable salary" which it is a great joy to think of, as Torvald exclaims. Nora responds, "Ah, it is wonderful!" (Å, *det er vidunderlig*). This is the key word in the play, and its use by the poet is the clearest demonstration of the play's dialectical procedure. In Act I the *wonderful* is a material thing: Torvald's new social position and the new freedom and prosperity this will bring. In Act II, the *wonderful* is the imagined inward transformation of the protagonists into the latent heroism Nora always believed underlay the humdrum of their daily lives, waiting to be called upon. Finally, as "the *most wonderful*" (*det vidunderligste*) which has yet to happen to them both, it becomes a project for the future which the separated couple must work to bring into being. At each appearance of the word it is repeated, usually in close triple iteration, and, in its superlative form (*det vidunderligste*), it is thrice repeated in the last lines of the play.

In its first triple appearance, it is *wonderful* that Torvald has the new job, "*really wonderful*" that the bad times are past, and "*wonderfully lovely*" that Nora will not have to work again. Just as she speaks the word for the third time, the doorbell rings to bring in one of the agents through whom none of these wonder-

ful things will come about—Kristine Linde. The coincidence is
not immediately apparent when it first occurs; but the next time
Nora speaks the word the doorbell will ring again to bring in the
other agent of change, Krogstad.

Kristine not only appears fatefully "on cue," but also after that
decade of absence that will be a recurring strategy in the cycle.
The Christian (or galilean) aspects of her character (apart from
her name) are seen in her personal history: of the sacrifice of her
own happiness (and her lover's) for the sake of duty to others.
Her renunciation, with its consequent chastening wisdom, has
made her life into "one endless workday without a rest" (Fjelde,
133), in strong contrast to the erotic playfulness of the Helmer
marriage, which has lured even the sorrowful Dr. Rank into its
carefree fantasy, as friend to Torvald and secret adorer of Nora.

Kristine arrives at the same time as Dr. Rank, both bearers of
sorrow entering together. She brings into the doll house the
bitter experience of loss and loneliness, poverty and hard work.
Nora, on the other hand, declares that her great aim is to attain a
life that is "completely free of sorrow" (*sorgløs*)—another key
word, repeated four times in close juxtaposition, and which is
directly linked to "*the wonderful*":

> . . . for nu er jeg sorgløs. (*springer opp*) Å Gud, et er dog
> deilig å tenke på, Kristine! Sorgløs! Å kunne vaere sorgløs,
> ganske sorgløs! Å kunne leke og tumle seg med bornene;
> å kunne ha det smukt og nydelig i huset, all ting således
> som Torvald setter pris på det! Og tenk, så kommer snart
> våren med blå luft. Så kan vi kanskje få reise litt. Jeg kan
> kanskje få se havet igjen. Å ja, det er riktignok vidunder-
> lig å leve og vaere lykkelig! (*Klocken høres i forstuen*)
> (S.V. II.425)

> . . . for now I am free from sorrow. (*Jumps up*) Oh God,
> it's so lovely to think about it, Kristine! Free from sorrow.
> To be free from sorrow, completely free from sorrow. To
> be able to play and romp with the children and have a
> charming and beautiful home—everything as Torvald
> likes it to be! And think, spring is coming soon with blue

skies. Perhaps we can travel a little. Perhaps I'll get to see
the ocean again. Oh yes, it's so wonderful to live and be
happy! (*The bell is heard in the hallway*)

(My translation)

It is as if Nora, pronouncing "wonderful" again, had uttered
once more a fateful formula, prompting the nemesis of the doorbell, through the man who will acquaint her with deep sorrow—
Nils Krogstad. The emphatic iteration of the word *sorgløs* represents a desire for a life free from tragedy: a natural desire, but
one as unrealistic as Torvald's shrinking from everything sordid
and ugly.

As Krogstad is shown into Torvald's study, another man of
sorrows, Rank, comes onstage. Rank, in fact, is an example of
how sorrow inescapably is woven into life: for he must suffer
from his father's joyful (*lystige*) hedonism. Even hedonism,
therefore, brings about sorrow. "One does not get anything for
nothing," Rank observes. When Rank draws a parallel between
moral and physical corruption, and uses Krogstad to condemn
society as a hospital, Nora dismisses his observations with the
comment, "What do I care about dreary old society?" (Fjelde,
140). She finds it "quite delightful" that Torvald now will have
power over others, so that her frivolous disdain of the social
realm and its obligations is seen as ruthless and dangerous in its
thoughtlessness.

Her children, whose arrival prompts the other characters to
leave, report to their mother that "a big dog" ran after them and
Nora assures them that "big dogs don't bite pretty little doll children." Unfortunately, that is what big dogs often do, and now
Krogstad enters, unseen, as Nora romps and plays with her children in a game of hide-and-seek. The naturalness of Nora's action should not conceal its metaphoric aspect. Hiding, in a more
somber sense, has long been Nora's strategy for evading unwelcome truth. After Krogstad leaves she will seriously, not playfully, hide from her children, who will not appear again in the
play. Also a metaphor, in a play that is so much about *evolution*
(and from the "animal community" of the previous play), might
be Nora's action when she confronts Krogstad: crawling on all

fours from under the table, like an animal from its lair, then rising, first to her knees, then to the fully erect, *human* posture.

This is the first confrontation of the polar opposites of the play's ethical division: the sheltered, protected, innocent denizen of the doll house, the "Victorian" heroine; and, at the other pole, the melodramatic "shady" "Victorian" villain from the realm of social sordidness. In conventional nineteenth-century drama, the two remain "poles apart"; villainy can never be admitted into respectable society, while if the heroine should ever venture into the sordid world, she is lost to her family forever and is doomed to a life of degradation, madness, and death. What is interesting, immensely so, about *A Doll House* is that Ibsen does not just *invert* these ethical terms: He keeps the conventional action *but utterly transforms it.* That is, the guilty secret is discovered, the outraged husband flourishes the incriminating letter, the guilty wife is forced to leave her home and family forever. This is the subject of one of the most famous of Victorian paintings: the triptych, by Augustus Egg, that bore the very Ibsenian title, *Past and Present.* In the first painting of the triptych the husband, holding the letter, exhibits the same grief-stricken but implacable moralism as Torvald, and the wife, utterly crushed, lies on the floor. On the wall are two emblematic pictures: the expulsion from Eden and a shipwreck. In the large mirror over the family hearth can be seen reflected the open door through which the disgraced wife must now pass forever while, to one side, two children watch their house of cards collapse to the floor. Here is the conventional "family tragedy," adorned with little anecdotal, symbolic touches. Ibsen's action also is an expulsion from Eden, a *necessary* one: He, too, uses the imagery of shipwreck, but it is Kristine Linde's highly moral life and marriage that is seen as such. Nora walks through the door, most likely never to return, but it is in order to save herself from the intolerable degradation her marriage has become, and so on. It is not that Ibsen is deliberately "parodying" Egg's famous picture, for he may not have seen it copied or reproduced: It is just that the two artists are looking at the same thing from two entirely different worlds.

In Ibsen's play, "heroine" and "villain" will be drawn closer together, Nora becoming aware that she shares with Krogstad experiences at a depth that she has never shared with her husband. This is not just due to the identity of their *social* offenses—forgery—but also from a disenchanted self-knowledge they both have, in Act II, of their own *inner* depths and weaknesses. Nora's offense, though unthinking, is no less reprehensible than Krogstad's: for thoughtlessness is not a good defense to plead at Ibsen's judgment day on the soul.

Nora's "proudest secret" which had given her marriage a hidden, heroic dimension, now, horrifyingly, is revealing itself, under Krogstad's lawyer-like cross-examination, to be similar to the "sordid" offense that has socially disgraced him; and this is just the beginning of the process of things dialectically turning into their opposites, which is Ibsen's procedure throughout the cycle. It is another irony of the play that it is Torvald's squeamish dismissal of Krogstad from the bank, so as no longer to have to have contact with him, that forces Krogstad into the action that will bring Torvald to see his complete dependence upon him. At the same time, by being willing to push Krogstad back into the social pit from which he has climbed with such difficulty, Torvald reveals the *heartless* nature, at bottom, of his fastidiousness: a heartlessness that goes far to justify Krogstad's blackmail of the pair.

Krogstad's determination to secure the future of his sons is no more ignoble a motive than Nora's past wishes to save her husband's life and to spare her dying father. Thus all the categories of conventional thinking—innocence and guilt, victim and villain—dissolve under Ibsen's gaze. Krogstad's brutal initiation of Nora into the social realities of the law and of the consequences to oneself and one's loved ones of treating the social realm as flippantly as she hitherto has done is the first stage of the education into reality that the spirit must undergo if it is to live in truth and freedom. The secure, materially prosperous, and sorrow-free future she had so joyfully envisaged—the *wonderful*—already is crumbling away as graver ideas of reality take its place.

Pleading Krogstad's case to Torvald, Nora learns that what most offends her husband is not so much Krogstad's crime but his refusal to "take his punishment." Poor Torvald himself is to be terribly punished for this complacent judgment, with its total lack of self-knowledge, when, in the last act, he all too humiliat-

ingly will refuse to take *his* punishment as he desperately prepares to do anything to save his household from scandal. It is not
that Torvald is at all more cowardly than other men and women:
just that his complete and not-uncommon ignorance of his own
human nature has created a lurid, melodramic world of good (us)
and evil (them), the collapse of which totally devastates him. His
desire to protect his home from contact with such as Krogstad is
expressed in the fastidious terms of the aesthete: "I literally feel
physically revolted when I'm anywhere near such a person"
(Fjelde, 152).

In Act II the yule tree stands "stripped of ornament, burned-
down candle-stubs on its ragged branches" (Fjelde, 154). But
Nora sets about repairing the fancy-dress costume in which she
will decorate *herself.* The stripped tree, discarded of its color-
wrapped presents, suggests the abandonment of *one* form of
illusion-decoration—the *wonderful* as the material prosperity so
warmly anticipated in Act I. The fancy-dress costume, on the
other hand, anticipates a new concept of the *wonderful* to be
born out of the *agon* of this act: the new, romantic, and psychological heroism that Nora believes will blossom from the crisis.
The *wonderful* has shifted from the objective world of material
prospects (the tree and *its* secrets) to the secret depths of the
subjective spirit, where an underworld of heroism is ready to
possess the stage. It is only when she sees through this illusion
also that Nora will discard the fancy dress.

The frantic movements of her opening soliloquy, where she
fearfully waits for the menace from the outer world to invade the
home, reveals how much of her earlier, seemingly carefree identity associated with the tree has died. This new nervousness
implies a growing *inwardness* within which there is a ferment-
ing of the spirit that will overflow, wildly, with her unrestrained
rehearsal of the tarantella. The growing agitation of this inward
drama ("inward" but clearly visible to *us* as stage "action") has
fatally disturbed the Edenic innocence of the doll home, which
now seems menaced by an alarming realm of public law and
retribution.

Though, as Kristine comments, Nora is "still a child," we are
made aware of the *latent* maturity of her character. She startles

Kristine by revealing some knowledge of the causes of Rank's inherited disease, and this revelation makes all the more jarring (and dramatically telling) her reversion to childish stratagems when she pleads with Torvald for Krogstad. She possesses a better grasp of realities than she ever allows Torvald to perceive, and this is manifest in her subsequent dialogue with Rank in which, as the conversation grows more somber in subject matter, the room darkens, "accompanying," as it were, the gruesome details of Rank's impending disintegration. She still desperately attempts to evade the sorrow Rank is communicating, but at least she is given a closer glimpse of that darker reality with which the Helmers have been in daily contact without daring "to see." She concedes it is "sorrowful" (*sørgelige*) that the good things of life strike at one's bones, and "most sorrowful of all" (*sørgeligste*) when they strike at the bones of those who did not take part in the pleasure. Thus, it is dawning on her, faintly, that the sorrowful is inescapably built into life, but she then recoils from Rank's account, begs him to talk "cheerfully," and refuses to permit the dying man the small comfort he craves of declaring his love for her.

Why does Ibsen show her so vehement about this? I believe it is because, just now, we are to see her as embarking upon a process of re-creating, "rewriting," reality and Rank's declared love seriously complicates this new fiction. The truly "heroic" nature of the mutual love between herself and Torvald is about to be put to a tremendous test from which it will rise to a sublime level of self-sacrifice. She is not yet certain as to the way this will happen; but she is at least certain that another lover, in the background, would be an appendage that would fit most awkwardly into the romantic plot. The theme of the *ménage a trois*, which is repeated in *Ghosts, Rosmersholm, The Lady from the Sea*, and, in dazzling proliferation, in *Hedda Gabler* (where *every* physically, if not legally, eligible individual seems to constitute one part of at least one, and often more, triangle), continues in the last four plays and clearly represents a thematic intention on Ibsen's part integral to the cycle; for it also was built into the beginning of the cycle with Karsten Bernick, Lona Hessel, and

Betty Hessel. In *A Doll House* Helmer and Rank clearly constitute antithetical views of the world, and it is to Rank's view that Nora, though trying to be loyal to Torvald's, will be led ultimately. But she is not ready yet. After flirting with Rank, therefore, in the famous "stocking scene," she retreats back into the role of scatterbrained charmer, which is so congenial to Torvald's view of things.

She had flirted with Rank in order to enlist his help against Krogstad; but his declaration of love forces her to face the selfish nature of her relationship with him. As her new fiction requires "selfless" love on her's and Torvald's part, nothing could be more unwelcome than the obtrusion of Rank's love to the foreground of the composition. She had been aware of it, "in a way," but, like the Helmers' usual attitude to awkward reality, she had allowed it to stay in the background as an unexamined but pleasing extra dimension to her marriage: just as Rank's suffering, for Torvald, served as a dark background, setting in bright relief his own domestic happiness. In order to return this relationship to the undisturbing background, therefore, Nora refuses Rank's offer of help and faces Krogstad alone. In the ensuing dialogue with Krogstad, Nora reveals to "us" how far she has journeyed from the childish consciousness of Act I. When he asks her if she now has a clear idea of her offense, she replies, "More than you ever could teach me" (Fjelde, 168), implying she has been pondering her predicament in more than its legal terms.

It is during this duologue that the guilty pair, Nora and Krogstad, discover their unexpected affinity. Krogstad probes Nora, guessing she has contemplated suicide, as he once had done, and his relief at hearing that she, too, dared not seems partly due to her not possessing the courage he had lacked:

> KROGSTAD: De flester av oss tenke på det i førstningen. Jeg tenkte også på det; men jeg hadde min sel ikke mot—
> NORA. (*tonløst*) Jeg ikke heller.
> KROGSTAD (*lettet*) Nei, ikke sant; De har ikke mot til det, De heller?
> NORA. Jeg har det ikke; jeg har det ikke.

KROGSTAD. Most of us think about *that* at first. I thought
about it too, but I discovered I hadn't the courage—
NORA. (*lifelessly*) I don't either.
KROGSTAD. (*relieved*) That's true, you haven't the cour-
age? You too?
NORA. I don't have it—I don't have it.

(Fjelde, 169)

Krogstad's "most of us" brings Nora into his world as a social
outcast and, going deeper, with their shared acknowledgment of
cowardice, she is exploring the same humiliating, subjective
self-knowledge he has suffered—a world of which Torvald is
ignorant. But now Krogstad unfolds to Nora his truly "satanic"
plot to gain total power over Torvald and to reduce him to being
his terrified lackey at the bank. Torvald, who has striven so val-
iantly to live freely in social innocence, would then be in a truly
pitiable position, and those who condemn him for his later panic,
for not living up to Nora's romantic idea of him, presumably
themselves possess heroic, Brand-like unconcern as to their own
careers, social standing, and domestic happiness.

It is now that Nora is convinced that she has, deep within her,
the courage for suicide, even after Krogstad's brutal description
of the aftermath of drowning:

Under isen kanskje? Ned i det kolde, kullsorte vann? Og
så til våren flyte opp, stygg, ukennelig, med avfalt hår—

Under the ice maybe? Down in the freezing, coal-black
water? There, till you float up in the spring, ugly, unrecog-
nizable, with your hair falling out—

(Fjelde, 170)

The opposite, that is, of the pretty doll that costume, cosmet-
ics, and Torvald's careful training have made of her. Alcestis-
like, Nora now accepts this death. Her reply, "You don't scare
me," indicates to us how much her consciousness has grown
within this scene alone. Earlier, in this act, she had been unable
to hear the details of Rank's disintegration. Now, as she feels her

husband's life endangered, she finds the courage that eluded her minutes before.

Those who grumble that Nora's transformation in Act III is too sudden to be plausible should at least consider how Ibsen is preparing us for it, subjecting Nora to a series of shocks that forces her to discard her false identity, and an actress would show that the Nora of Act II is very different from the Nora of Act I. This second shock is subjective, psychological, an unnerving exploration of inner depths which has included overcoming the fear of death. Assuming that Torvald shares this deep, heroic love, she sees reality as suddenly, miraculously, transfigured, and this is the new *wonderful* thing which, she tells Kristine, is about to happen. Again, the key word is sounded three times in the typical dialectic exchange of an emerging concept that we find repeated in the cycle:

> NORA. Det er jo det vidunderlige som nu vil skje.
> FRU LINDE. Det vidunderlige?
> NORA. Ja, det vidunderlige. Men det er så forferdelig,
> Kristine; det må ikke skje for noen pris i verden.
> (S.V. II.456)

> NORA. It's the wonderful that is going to happen.
> MRS. LINDE. The wonderful?
> NORA. Yes, the wonderful. But it is so terrifying,
> Kristine; it must not happen for anything in the world.
> (My translation)

This marks the second stage of the evolution of the idea of the *wonderful.* It becomes also the terrifying that must not happen "for anything in the world," a wonderful flowering within the spirit out of the anguish, compared with which all the material blessings envisaged as the wonderful in Act I vanish into insignificance. In a form of epiphany, the rose will bloom on the cross and Love will emerge to transcend all the dangers that beset it. In Nora's new fiction the doll pair will rise to the heroic gestures of mutual self-sacrifice, a bourgeois Tristan and Isolde.

It is in this exaltation of spirit, after Kristine hurries out to *save* her, that Nora frantically dances the *tarantella,* feeling the deadly poison in her blood and striving to expel it. She learned this southern dance on Capri. In Ibsen's symbolic geography the south always represents the pagan, Hellenic values: eros, joy-of-life, the creative spirit, as in Osvald's Paris in *Ghosts,* or the south to which Mrs. Wilton will take young Erhart Borkman. It probably was as much for metaphoric as for medical reasons that the aesthetic Torvald's life had to be saved by a trip to the south, for which he will have to pay by having the spirit of tragedy born in his house, as we will shortly see.

Ibsen further underscores Nora's southern identity when, in another of those triple iterations which perfect Ibsenites have learned to "register," Torvald, in Act III, intoxicated and infatuated, calls her "my lovely little Capri girl, my capricious little Capri girl" (Fjelde, 181), just as her tragic identity is to be revealed. "Capri" is the plural of *capra*—goat—so a dancing Capri girl can be said to be dancing a goat-dance. The word *tragedy* means "goat-ode"—an etymology debated by scholars ever since Aristotle. Many hold that tragedy evolved from choruses of goatskin-clad dancers such as are depicted on Attic vases. Others suggest a goat was the prize offered in such contests. All this is unimportant compared with the fact that the goat is associated with tragedy and with the tragic Nora, the modern Alcestis, who, after "dying" for her husband, returns to leave him forever. The "birth of tragedy" occurs in Ibsen's cycle when Nora descends, in Neapolitan costume, immediately after having spectacularly danced her Capri dance.

For a theme of *A Doll House* is the maturing of our modern spirit, our culture, to the point at which it can arrive at tragic perception: a goal intended from the beginning of the cycle with Lona Hessel's arrival. Ibsen had to train his audience, as well as his dramatic characters, to rise to the level of tragic perception, and the hostile reception of *Ghosts*—the play in which the Greek tragic vision is fully operative—shows how necessary this careful training was.

The *tarantella,* which takes its name from the ancient Greek city in Italy of Taranto, was, according to tradition, the dance which the victim of the tarantula spider's bite had to dance until he or she died or, in another version, the dance that alone could expel the poison from the victim's body. Both motives fit Nora's situation. Her old "doll identity" will die from the poison of knowledge injected into her by Krogstad. At the same time, she will get rid of the poison, at this turning point of the year, to undergo a form of rebirth into a new identity. The dance rehearsal, with its startling release of wild, Dionysian energies—"as if [her] life were at stake"—greatly disturbs the decorous Torvald, for whom it is "pure madness." That is, Nora has far outstepped the bounds of Torvald's limited and careful aestheticism which carefully evades tragic possibility. The terror and the sorrow Nora has absorbed, on the other hand, are the conditions of tragic identity—as they are, according to Aristotle, for tragic experience.

For the acting out of the tragic action of Act III, the round table and its chairs have been moved to the center of the stage. Furthermore, this circular table will remain centerstage for the entire action of the next play, *Ghosts*. In Ibsen's artistic world, where the invisible hand of the dramatist now drags the table to the center, such changes are for more than technical reasons.[3] Two couples will sit at this circular table, one to restore a broken relationship, the other to dissolve an existing one. The created union will be between two people who come to each other in sorrow and guilt, to make the best of two "shipwrecked" lives. Though they discover an undreamt-of joy, this hardly is "the most wonderful thing of all" that Nora will require for a true marriage, which must be made of more heroic stuff. Kristine and Krogstad's union is the Christian or Galilean one of self-sacrifice and mutual forgiveness; and it is this which Kristine, unavailingly, wishes to urge upon the Helmers (as Gregers Werle, another Galilean, as unsuccessfully urges upon the Ekdals).

Krogstad's whole action against the Helmers, hitherto relentless, is reversed through Kristine's influence into his independent determination to save them; but Kristine, whose whole action up to now had been to save the Helmers, now reverses *her* purpose and is determined that the Helmers should confront each other in truth. The *major* peripety for Kristine and Krogstad, however, will be from deep sorrow, which has colored both their lives, to great *joy*. "I can't believe it! I've never been so happy!" exclaims Krogstad; and Kristine will say, after Krogstad leaves to wait for her, "How different now! Someone to work for, to live for—a home to build" (Fjelde, 179–80). All through their dialogue of sorrow and reconciliation can be heard up above the Helmers dancing, and this latter couple, through an even more astonishing series of peripeties, will undergo the opposite *major* peripety as their marriage will be shipwrecked.

Torvald, dragging Nora away from the dancing, is erotically inflamed at the sight of her in her Neapolitan costume. "You still have the tarantella in your blood," he tells her. He confesses to her his personal sexual fantasy: that they are newlyweds and that he is about to enjoy, for the first time, her "young and trembling beauty," establishing the immaturity of Torvald's aestheticism in which his fictional Nora is not allowed to grow up. But Torvald's desire quickly to enjoy his seductively decorated wife (as his most deliciously wrapped Christmas present) will encounter a series of obstacles. First, he is annoyed to discover Kristine waiting for them. "Are you here so late?" he ungallantly asks. Kristine then urges Nora to confess to Torvald, thus unintentionally strengthening Nora's resolve to commit suicide.

Nora, therefore, is far from responsive to Torvald's ardor. Undoubtedly there is a degree of melodramatic "play-acting" in her romantic idea of her impending death sacrifice. And, as a mere fantasy, it hardly is able to cope with the actualities of Torvald's inflamed *eros*. There is a struggle as Nora resists, in an erotically charged scene. "Your trembling young beauty . . . when I saw you turn and sway in the tarantella—my blood was pounding till I couldn't stand it . . . that's why I brought you down here so early—" and, after Nora's rebuff, "Nora, you're teasing me. . . . Aren't I your husband?" (Fjelde, 183).

His passion is interrupted by Rank's entrance enigmatically to announce his own impending death.[4] Beautifully worked into the major peripety of the play is the double shock that will end Torvald's infatuated advances: the *sorrow* in reality, represented by Rank, and the *terror* Torvald will feel at the collapse of his world through Krogstad's menace. These will be absorbed, and reflected upon, by Nora, then "delivered" with brutal swiftness to Torvald. The first, Rank's horrible death, is not sufficient to shock Torvald out of his aesthetic attitude, which still can find something comforting in the prettifying metaphors he uses to avoid facing up to reality. Rank, he muses, is hiding himself away "like a wounded animal." His suffering and loneliness had been "a dark cloud setting off our sunlit happiness" (Fjelde, 186) like an interestingly somber "touch" added to a pleasant picture; and all that Rank's death prompts Torvald to is to fantasize that he might be called on to rescue Nora from some terrible danger. Cruelly, he is given his chance with the opening of Krogstad's letter, and his pose immediately collapses.

But even the shock of Krogstad's letter does not dislodge Torvald from his aesthetic stance. His revulsion from the discovery of Nora's crime is one of recoil from its *ugliness:*

> "Å, denne bunnløse heslighet, som ligger i alt dette. Fy! fy!"
>
> (S.V. II.471)
>
> Oh, the infinite ugliness that lies in it all.
>
> (My translation)

And his overriding concern is to save the *appearance* of their marriage even though its substance has been destroyed. Having lived a prettifying, self-deluding fiction of innocence for the eight years of their marriage, Torvald now is willing to live a hypocritical fiction of innocence without the former happiness:

> Her efter dags gjelder et ikke lenger lykken; det gjelder bare å redde restene, stumpene, skinnet.
>
> (S.V. II.772)
>
> From now on happiness does not matter; all that matters is saving the bits and pieces, the appearance—
>
> (Fjelde, 188)

Such a speech would gain in performance if it were spoken with genuine grief. As author of the fiction of his marriage, Torvald now has to rewrite it, as it were, in a consciously dishonest way: in very poignant contrast to the narration of cloudless happiness he had composed until this revelation. He is like a romantic novelist of innocent love-fictions who, disillusioned, still has to pretend innocence to keep his public. Throughout we have seen Torvald carefully *creating* the terms of his fictive world: never at a loss for moral maxims, pontificating complacently on borrowing money, or on telling lies, or on taking one's punishment manfully—even on eating macaroons or on dancing the *tarantella* with propriety. Torvald, one imagines, could easily have been a popular novelist much commended for the beauty and soundness of his pictures of domestic life. Rørlund would have read him to the ladies' circle in *Pillars*.

There now follows a series of reversals. Just as Torvald is reconciling himself to composing the new fiction of his marriage, he reads Krogstad's second letter and undergoes another reversal from despair to joy. Nora, at the same moment, reverses *her* decision to sacrifice herself to save Torvald and now prepares to sacrifice Torvald to save herself. "I am saved!" Torvald exults, but the dialectic is evolving a more searching definition of salvation. Returning to his aesthetic facility, Torvald now can compose an even more attractive fiction, one that can prettify and neutralize the previous shock. First, "this ugliness all has to go. Let me see— (*Takes a look at the note*) No, I don't want to see it; I want the whole thing to fade like a dream" (Fjelde, 189). As it fades like a dream, a charming new fantasy takes its place. "I'll keep you like a hunted dove I've rescued out of a hawk's claws. I'll bring peace to your poor, shuddering heart" (ibid.). None of this is unattractive, and Torvald's speeches need not be spoken unctuously. So ingrained is his aesthetic vision that he must undergo yet another peripety—the most painful possible—before he is shaken into truer perception.

Nora's final perception—a metaphysical one—also is the most painful possible. We put up with the quotidian, unheroic, unromantic pettiness of bourgeois life because we believe that this merely covers a substratum of true heroism which, if the really great challenge presented itself, would rise to the occasion. Then the world would become numinous, wonderful and terrible at the same time, and all that we believed of the human spirit at its most sublime would become manifest. Such a faith permits us to live in daily inauthenticity and to accept the debilitating process of the world's demands upon us: that we sacrifice something of truth and freedom every day. When Torvald wished he could risk his life to save Nora from some great danger, and when Nora saw the "wonderful" happening when Torvald discovered her secret, *both* were projecting onto the realm of fantasy values they had failed to establish within lived reality.

Nora's love for Torvald therefore was as much an illusion as his for her. Her revulsion, when he fails to step into the romantic role she had assigned him (for she is as much a maker of fictions as her husband), is due to her perception that her whole conception of life (and of Torvald) is grotesquely wrong. Unlike Torvald, she cannot continue to manufacture the fiction. Nora will be shocked to find that, though she was willing to die for her husband, Torvald is not the man she believed she had married. There is no place in her idea of reality for the frightened and selfish human being she finds masquerading as her husband. Therefore, the justification for the marriage vanishes and so does Nora's *identity* as partner to this marriage. It is not that Nora has any very clear idea of or firm grasp upon reality—she admits she has not. It is that the idea of reality she previously lived by has failed her, like a script which the principal actress no longer recognizes or can find interest in. Whatever reality might be "in itself," *this* version of it no longer is actable—or livable. That her expectations of Torvald's heroism were themselves unrealistically romantic only further intensifies her alienation.

However, I share with a number of commentators some uneasiness at Nora's apportioning of blame to her father and husband. "You're to blame that nothing's become of me." This uneasiness can, of course, be attributed to male chauvinist guilt, but I do not think this is so. The Nora we have observed during the play has not seemed a passive creature wholly molded by others. Ibsen has depicted her as willingly playing the doll game to her own advantage. No doubt the nature of society in Ibsen's day made him feel justified in exaggerating on the side of Nora: but in all his later plays, starting with *Ghosts*, the major characters go far beyond apportioning guilt to others for their own errors and shortcomings. This may be how Helene Alving will *begin* her journey to enlightenment, but by the end of the journey she will come to acknowledge tragic *guilt*.

The last shift of the dialectic is not a condemnation of Torvald for lacking romantic heroism anymore than Bernick had been reproached for lacking virtuous innocence: It is a rejection of the worldview that projected heroism onto the plane of romance instead of establishing it in everyday life. Such an authentic heroism would require a journey of *solitary* self-discovery, for neither partner, living in illusion, can be anything but an obstacle to the progress of the other. If, after Nora's leaving the home, Torvald is sufficiently shocked and awakened to embark upon such a journey himself, then an authentic marriage, in truth and freedom, might be possible. Both Nora and Torvald must transform themselves if "the most wonderful thing of all" (*det vidunderligste*) is to happen. Again sounded three times, now in its superlative form, the word is like a summons to both Nora and Torvald to make themselves into free and courageous individuals, architects of new realities. Such a concept of a "true marriage" must remain more of a metaphysical signpost than a concrete prescription, for it is not the job of the poet to redesign the nature of marriage in the modern world. And "marriage," in Ibsen, is always a metaphor for the alliance of forces and powers in our culture whose joining is necessary for human wholeness.

As in *Pillars of Society,* there seems to be a strong emphasis upon *role-playing* in *A Doll House:* of a play-within-the-play, where the characters put on a show for each other but also, unwittingly, for *us* as well. This is evident in Torvald's careful "posing" and Nora's pretenses at childishness with Torvald and Rank. Above all, it is there in the identity Torvald and Nora have created around the Capri costume and the *tarantella,* transforming reality into *picturesque* fantasy. This private theater and its false histrionics must be abandoned for the world of objective reality still waiting to be transformed. Whatever tragic truth Nora will establish in the *everyday* costume (*hverdagskjole*) with which now she replaces the fancy dress, it will not be by means of romantic histrionics. *A Doll House* thus demolishes another form of false consciousness, an Idol of the Mind, from the cycle. Nora's last scene with Torvald establishes that clash of Duty versus Truth, on which the structure of the next play, throughout, will be built.

Nora does not follow Kristine's example, does not leave the doll home to sacrifice herself for others. Hers is the more selfish and ruthless decision to re-create herself in truth, if possible, whatever the consequences: an uncompromising and strong-minded resolve as unsettling as any in the cycle's long line of heroes and heroines, and one which is characteristic of the tragic temperament. If, earlier, Nora, willing to die to save her husband, had been an Alcestis, now she resembles an Antigone, willing to take on all society, if necessary, to hold by her own idea of Right.

But it is with Torvald that the play ends:

> HELMER. Nora,—kan jeg aldri bli mer enn en fremmed for deg?
> NORA. (*tar sin vadsekk*) Akk, Torvald, da måte det vidunderligste skje.
> HELMER. Nevn meg detter vidunderligste!
> NORA. Da måte både du og jeg forvandle oss således at— Å, Torvald, jeg tror ikke lenger på noe vidunderlig.
> HELMER. Men jeg vil tro på det. Nevn det! Forvandle oss således at—?
> NORA. At samliv mellom oss to kunne bli et ekteskap. Farvel (*hun gå ut gjennom forstuen*)
> HELMER. (*synker ned på en stol ved døren og slår hendene for ansiktet*) Nora! Nora! (*ser seg om reiser seg*) Tomt. Hun er ikke mer. (*en håp skyter opp i ham*) Det vidunderligste—?! (*nedenfra høres dronnet av en port som slåss i lås*)

> HELMER. Nora—can I never be more than a stranger to you?
> NORA. (*Picking up the overnight bag*) Ah, Torvald—it would take the greatest miracle of all—
> HELMER. Tell me the greatest miracle!
> NORA. You and I would have to transform ourselves to the point that— Oh, Torvald, I've stopped believing in miracles.
> HELMER. But I'll believe. Tell me! Transform ourselves to the point that—?

NORA. That our living together could be a true marriage. (*She goes out down the hall*).
HELMER (*sinks down on a chair by the door, face buried in his hands*) Nora! Nora! (*Looking about and rising*) Empty. She's gone. (*A sudden hope leaps in him*) The greatest miracle—?
(*From below, the sound of a door slamming shut*).

(Fjelde, 196)

The word *vidunderligste* (most wonderful) is brought out by Nora as a newly evolving concept, different from the "vidunderlig" of her previous identities, in which she no longer believes. In its superlative form it is taken over by Torvald as a disciple might take an idea into his consciousness at the prompting of a master; and it is Torvald who will believe in it and who will speak it out, *in hope,* as the last word of the play. The juxtaposition of budding hope and slammed door, future possibility with finished past, indicates that the spiritual dialectic of the cycle must continue. Both Nora and Torvald must transform themselves, for to see Torvald as the one in need of "reform," to see wrong as that which the *other* sex commits, is to remain in the pharisaic world.

And, indeed, the next twist of the cycle's dialectic spiral will involve a feminine consciousness, Helene Alving, acknowledging guilt and error. Only in the last act of *A Doll House* was the spirit brought to see that guilt and sorrow were within the house itself. In *Ghosts* this long was known before the action of the play commenced, but *now* the dialectic will push forward until the guilt and error are located *within, inside the guilty spirit itself.* Helene Alving will discover a sorrow and terror within reality greater than Nora could imagine and so will attain the desolate distinction of tragedy. And Apollo, whose implacable deity is responsible for the infliction of disease as well as of Light will, as the sun also rises, look down upon a tragic outcome as terrible as anything in Greek drama. Transfixed in Ibsen's cycle, like the damned in the *Inferno,* Helene Alving must scream helplessly down future centuries before the horrible devastation of her son which she has helped to bring about: not with Agavé's excuse of madness but from pious, conscious Duty.

7

The Physician and the Gadfly:
An Enemy of the People

For I do nothing but go about persuading you all, old and young alike, not to take thought for your persons or your properties but first and chiefly to care about the greatest improvement of the soul.

—Socrates, *Apology*

. . . received the decisive thought as to how a philosopher ought to behave towards men from the apology of Socrates: as their physician, as a gadfly on the neck of man.

—Friedrich Nietzsche

Though almost always successful in production, *An Enemy of the People* does not stand high in critical reputation among Ibsen's plays. William Archer dubbed it a *jeu d'esprit,* and most critics concur that it is one of Ibsen's slighter pieces, for all its merits. Although, it is to be hoped, we no longer read the play as covert autobiography, as "Ibsen's reply to his critics," it still often is assumed that the play cost Ibsen less effort and demands less from us than the other plays in the cycle. Considering the very great artistry of the work, this is a surprising judgment, and it suggests that critics are not at ease with the genre of political comedy to which the play belongs. It is the comedy or satyr play that concludes the Hellenic tetralogy that began with *Pillars of Society*.

The Hellenic parallels and echoes in the play are more on the surface than in the earlier plays, as is appropriate to its comedic form. In *Ghosts*, the long, searching dialectic journeyed through darkness to end with the light of the sunrise and with the central consciousness, Helene, brought to a complete reversal of the self-approving idea of past and present with which the play had opened. The joy-of-life and the sunrise, recovered by the agonizing tragic action of *Ghosts,* seems to have set the stage for *An Enemy of the People,* which is notably "sunny" and buoyant in atmosphere. The spirit of this play is not that of painfully uncovering the guilty reality beneath the consciousness of a hard-earned good but, instead, of a zestful, naive, combative individual taking it upon himself to be the champion of truth and freedom. This has so dismayed some Ibsenists that they actually have gone against the whole spirit of the play (and of comedy) to discover sinister and devious motives behind Stockmann's championship of the truth, taking the view of Thomas that Peter and the editors of the *People's Courier* take rather than that of Captain Horster, Katherine, and Petra. This is to choose odd allies indeed and shows to what lengths the critic, anxious to load a clear and coherent artistic structure with a subtle and confusing "ambiguity," will go.

The play contains at least four levels of action, beautifully and seamlessly integrated, and these should create objective subtleties and complexities enough without confusing our attention to the artwork.

1. A quarrel between two brothers for control of the community.

2. A truth-telling patriot of his *polis* increasingly alienating his entire community.

3. A shift from communal integration into a new ethical individualism.

4. The development of the concept of human good from a material and physical value to a spiritual/intellectual value.

Each of these levels of action has its own image cluster and archetypal reference. The cultural and historical archetypes are essential to the play's meaning and action, but they do not proclaim themselves portentously. Indeed, they have not been noticed by critics and therefore do not violate the play as an image of Ibsen's own world. The Hellenic sequence of Hegel's argument in the *Phenomenology* which I claim Ibsen is following, from "society as a community of animals" being forced into ethical reason (*Pillars of Society*), to the conflict between the law of man and the law of woman (*A Doll House*), through the collision between the living and the dead (*Ghosts*), now concludes with the civil war within the *polis* represented by the contest by *two brothers* for the community. Hegel had in mind the contest between Eteocles and Polyneices. In his lectures on fine art and on history Hegel more appropriately traces the decline of the Greek *polis* by drawing upon Aristophanic comedy and the new ethical individualism of Socrates, anticipating, with the latter, the argument of Nietzsche's *The Birth of Tragedy*. And few would deny that the Socratic challenge and its consequences was one of the major "phases" that have gone into making up the identity of our modern, Western spirit and that a psychoanalysis of the *Weltgeist* therefore could not ignore this moment.

In Hegel's argument, too, this phase of our spiritual history involved a shift from the idea of the good life conceived in communal and material-physical terms—the life of the beautiful *polis* and of the athlete-warrior—to that of the spiritual and intellectual individualism of philosophy, a stage preceding the appearance of Christianity. The Christian, dualistic worldview itself, that of the Unhappy Consciousness turning inward and away from the life of the *polis* and its laws and duties, begins with the next play, *The Wild Duck*.

An Enemy of the People is a political comedy whose conclusion is that the *polis* must be surmounted. The play's opening themes and metaphors emphasize materialist ideas of the good life, as in the opening of *A Doll House,* but the play works upon and transforms these until they are converted into emphatically spiritual terms of truth and freedom. The good doctor, who heals sick *bodies* and delights in the spectacle of *physical* appetites and health, gradually becomes the outlawed prophet determined to heal sick *souls* and will set about nourishing the *minds* of intellectually starved street urchins (he decides upon *twelve* such disciples). Beginning with feasting, with a *dining* room in view, the play ends in Stockmann's *study* as he outlines a program of reeducation of his society: a visual progression first noted by Kenneth Burke.

In the major action of the play, the patriot of his beloved community, seeking to proclaim truth, finds himself condemned by that community and branded its enemy. The intensity of Thomas's love for his community (unusual in Ibsen's writing) drives him to intemperate action when he is proclaimed its enemy, but there is no doubt as to that love. If, as I argue, Ibsen is drawing upon Hellenic themes and models for these first four plays, the most appropriate model for the patriot who is proclaimed an enemy of the people is Socrates. *An Enemy of the People,* I believe, draws upon the three archetypal models mentioned above: the fraternal struggle for control of the community, Aristophanic political comedy, and the Socratic challenge to the community.

I noted earlier that an Ibsen character is not a composite of archetypal identities, a mechanical construct; the archetypal identities are raised by the character's *actions in performance.* Stockmann is not Socrates (or Polyneices) in modern dress; he is a modern character whose actions lead him into the Socratic situation, someone who repeats one of the significant, and therefore recurrent, actions of our species. The sum total of all such archetypal actions in the cycle, we might say, makes up the most authentic and adequate portrait of our humanity, creating the supertext that reproaches the "fallen text" (doomed for the Button Molder's ladle) of our everyday lives. If, as I claim, Thomas's dialectical evolution raises the ghosts of Eteocles-Polyneices, then of Socrates, and finally of Christ, this is an evolution marking the progress of the human identity which the cycle is establishing. Though Ibsen's method frequently is playful, this is not an elaborate game, a puzzle to be solved by academics but, as with the method of James Joyce in *Ulysses,* the artist's totally serious creation, through his medium, of the adequate truth of our collective human reality.

Thomas's modern identity is that of the physician-scientist, a figure whose quest for truth in the nineteenth century was both the equivalent, and continuation, of the Hellenic tradition of rational inquiry; as in Socrates' day, changing our concepts of the cosmos we inhabit. The microbial science, employed by Thomas, in its way opened up as vast perspectives as the biological theories of Darwin and the findings of astronomy. The microscope is as much turned toward infinity as the telescope. In the generations presented by the play we can watch the evolution from pre-scientific to post-scientific thought. Old Morten Kiil belongs to a generation to whom microbes are incomprehensible, though he is willing to use the public's apparent acceptance of this "absurdity" as a weapon against the mayor and colleagues who have driven him from power. This later generation of entrepreneurs can appropriate the new science for selfish and limited purposes while refusing to permit to science the one thing it requires to flourish: the dissemination of truth. Thomas therefore allies himself with the younger radicals and liberals who seem to have outgrown the ideology of Peter and his associates but who show that they, too, are interested in truth only for partisan purposes. Therefore Thomas, like Socrates/Plato before him, will set about molding a new generation of minds altogether to create a future in which the truth can flourish.

As far as he can within the repressive "decencies" of nineteenth-century theater, Ibsen recovers much of the Aristophanic political comedy; and there seems a direct "quotation" from *The Clouds*, at the end of which Socrates' house is attacked by a mob (Strepsiades and his slaves), in the last act of Ibsen's play where Stockmann's house was attacked. Ibsen, however, reverses the Aristophanic judgment upon the enemy of the people. There are striking similarities, despite the equally-as-striking differences, between Ibsen's Thomas and Plato's Socrates.[1] Socrates, driven on by his inner voice or *daimon,* generated more and more alarming ideas within his community and demolished accepted ones until he finally was condemned as his people's enemy. Like Thomas, he was notoriously absentminded (Thomas continually is forgetting the name of his own housemaid) and, though poor, enjoyed feasting and company, especially the company of young men who would represent the future of the *polis*. Though more urbane and ironic by far, Socrates was no less outrageous before the public at his trial than is Thomas at the meeting which is virtually *his* trial and condemnation by the community, too.

A comparison between post-Periclean Athens and a nineteenth-century Norwegian community might seem lopsidedly in favor of the former, but it is almost certain that few in Norway, as few in Europe or America today, would have thought the comparison to their disadvantage—another reason why they would need "awakening." The dialectic that drives Thomas into the situation of the Socratic rebel also will be the means for the education of that community to Socratic individualism.

Stockmann begins by detecting the microbes within physical reality undetectable by ordinary seeing, then proceeds to discover the polluted sources of our spiritual life that are undetectable by ordinary thinking. The pollution descending onto the town from the hills will be seen as insignificant compared with the pollution descending from the cultural past. This theme of pollution, so important to *A Doll House* and *Ghosts*, in the form of the disease originating in the past and striking down the present generations, had been a central theme of Greek tragedy: the pollution following upon the curse on the house of Labdacus or of Atreus. But the pollution of *An Enemy of the People* has changed and in precisely the way this theme changed in the minds of Socrates and Plato: not in terms of the doomed and exemplary family but in terms of the entire community and its past—its philosophically unexamined traditions and customs. In *The Republic* and other writings, this led Plato, through the figure of Socrates, to a radical criticism of the entire religious, cultural, and ethical origins and history of the *polis* and with the determination to formulate (with that daring of which the Greeks were capable) new principles of living for the cleansed community. We are the result of that decision.

Peter, as his name suggests, in contrast to his doubting brother, is the rock of orthodoxy on which his community's spirit is *petrified*, representing the established oligarchy and the community's traditions. His aggression against Thomas drives his brother into the ranks of the opposing liberal and democratic forces, and this political version of the Eteocles-Polyneices conflict reaches its climax, visually and thematically, in the comedic struggle by the two brothers for the mayor's hat and stick—the insignia of power in the community. There then occurs the major peripety in the play, after which this *political* phase of the dialectic evolves into the "higher" conflict between the individual and society.

The central and appropriately Hellenic metaphor in the play is that of the baths, and it is to this metaphor that critics of the play often point to justify their low estimate of its poetry. The metaphor, it is claimed, states its themes, makes its neat analogies, and points its lesson so obviously, and by means of such one-to-one correspondences, that it is not, like the best metaphors and symbols, able to have a life of its own, to grow and suffuse the play and to instigate the subtlest and deepest reflection on our part. But this is to do it an injustice and fails also to concede the metaphor's fine appropriateness for a political comedy. As the central object of the communal consciousness, the baths give rise to violent actions and reactions whereby, as in Aristophanic comedy, political factions reveal themselves and their motives. Many of Ibsen's symbols and metaphors have the excellent quality of being clusters of images and meanings while at the same time being palpable, functioning, and consequential *things* in the world of the play. Because, for Ibsen, the natural thing is always the most adequate symbol, his stage world has a double life, revealing that humanity always is engaged simultaneously in acting on one level and in symbol-making on another, so that the symbolic is merely the actual looked at from another perspective. The community in the play not only creates an actual object, the baths; it also creates the metaphor by which, from another perspective, it will be assessed and judged.

The baths began as an *ideal* reality, as the idea which, in his lonely exile in the north, the patriotic Thomas thought up for his community. After some effort, he impressed this idea upon his pragmatic fellow citizens, and it then was appropriated by the oligarchs, who used it for personal profit as well as for public good. However, in spite of the physician's warnings, they bungled the job by cutting costs: They did not lay the pipes carrying the healing waters high enough back into nature (a Romantic subsymbol in itself). The baths now become the focus of a struggle for political power between the oligarchs and the democrats, and when the physician reveals the calamitous defects of the baths, the liberals see the chance for a "revolution" that will sweep the conservatives from power and install themselves. But the baths now are established as the main source of the community's prosperity, and whole streets of "doll houses" have been built whose owners have formed an association with vested interests in hiding the truth of the defects, whatever the cost to human health.

More subtly coercive than the overt tyranny of *Emperor and Galilean,* this world of material interests will prove the major opponent of the spirits of truth and freedom that Thomas serves. Material interests, the tanneries and other agents, also have polluted the pure sources, the springs, that feed into the baths. As Rolf Fjelde has observed, water, in the Bible (and in other mytho-historical sources), is associated with life and with the spirit. The waters that were to bring health bring disease; but, as Thomas ponders their significance, they become a metaphor for spiritual/cultural pollution and now contribute to his awareness of new principles for spiritual health. Pollution is not a matter only of sources infected at a point in space but also of an infection going far back in time. The progress of the metaphor is thus a dialectical spiral: beginning, naively, as an idea waiting for embodiment, then embodied defectively, but thereby revealing the spiritual reality of the community and, but at a higher level, once again becoming an idea, a project for the community as a spiritual, not a physical, healing. Objects are revealed as ideas when subjected to dialectic thought.

Baths were a central institution of Hellenic and Hellenistic culture. In Aristophanes' *The Clouds,* the play in which Socrates is mocked and condemned as an enemy of the community, a (somewhat scabrous) debate on the baths, in which Right (or "Philosophy") attacks and Wrong (or "Sophistry") defends the institution, is an important phase of the ephebe Pheidippides' initiation into the supposed Socratic lore. References to the pub-

lic baths recur in Hellenic and Hellenistic writing, in Aristophanes, Plato, Plutarch, and many others; sufficient to establish
them as central to the culture. Ruins of magnificent baths' structures (frequently named after Herakles) can be found in many
classical sites in the Mediterranean area.

Ibsen certainly was aware of this. In the Athenian and Hellenic Act II of *Emperor and Galilean,* one of the most decisive
anagnorises of the entire drama, Julian's disillusion with Hellenic philosophy is summed up in the episode of the new,
wealthy young students arriving in Athens and being escorted to
the baths to be fought over by the venal philosophers, including
Libanius. The parallel between the philosophers selling corrupted philosophy to the youthful students (in contrast to Socrates, who refused payment) and the community's leaders willing
to peddle poison to invalids arriving to seek health is an example
of how Ibsen's method converts ancient situations to modern
ones, for, of course, Ibsen is a poet, not a pedant. And it is
corrupted *philosophy* (ideas) that, Thomas will come to see, is
the source of the community's real evils.

A consciousness of the good life as *physical* well-being, together with a positive delight in the physical world and its pleasures, are manifest throughout Act I, which opens with Katherine Stockmann offering food to the young man, Billing, who sits
in the dining room. An emphasis upon the physical will be evident in the character of Thomas, too. He takes pleasure in his
new material prosperity, his home comforts of feasting and drinking, which he is eager to share with others. He is excited by the
burgeoning new life he imagines flourishing in his community,
and by the presence of young, healthy life at his dinner table
devouring beef and, later, joining him in a small symposium.
This gregarious, sociable, life-loving aspect of Thomas ensures
that his rebellion against society is of a very different nature than
that of the somberly messianic Gregers Werle of the next play,
who notably is indifferent to all that Thomas takes delight in.

Thomas emphatically is a lover of *this* world, and even as rebel,
it is in an attitude of higher patriotism that he wishes to transform his society. Nothing could be further from the brooding,
introspective, unsociable Gregers, who tries to find in life some

manifestation of his subjective and demanding ideal of authenticity. The inward, individual, subjective alienation that *The Wild Duck* initiates introduces into the cycle forms of inner complexity wholly unlike the objective dramatic characterization of the four plays of the first group.

The opening lines of dialogue repeat the little word "taste" (*smake*) and turn on the themes of food and digestion, which then are continued and amplified when the mayor, Peter Stockmann, enters. With a poor digestion for food or ideas,[2] he nevertheless takes satisfaction in the material well-being of his community; property taxes are lowered, property values are rising, and unemployment is reduced, as we learn from the assenting rhapsodies of Peter and Hovstad, the liberal editor. Like the "wonderful" prospects contemplated by the Helmers in Act I of *A Doll House,* this is an idea of the good life in purely material terms.

The first hint of the fraternal rivalry that is to agitate the first three acts of the play emerges from Peter's tetchy response to Hovstad's praise of Thomas. Conceding, superciliously, that his brother is good at "ideas, unfortunately" (*desverre*), Peter insists that when it comes to practical matters, "another sort of man" is needed. This division between the pragmatist and the idealist views of life is notably different from that of *Pillars of Society,* where the idealist vision, in Rørlund and Tønneson, simply removed itself from any contest. In *this* play, idealism will become militant and effective. Thomas does not impotently invoke a distant Providence; he *embodies* the universal spirit by taking on the kinds of action that have archetypal significance.

The difference between the two brothers is immediately apparent upon Thomas's entrance. His conviviality has swept up the mildly protesting young captain, Horster, and brought him in to feast with the other guests. While Peter fastidiously recoils from the sight of the young men and boys feasting at the table, Thomas hugely enjoys the spectacle, rhapsodizing on the "young men" with their "endless appetites" who need food "for strength" in order to "rake up" (*rote opp*) "the stuff of the future" (*fremtidstoff*). He envisions "a whole new world" springing up, with the younger life superseding the older. Peter indignantly denies his impending redundancy in the progress of humanity, and, though

Thomas makes the more pleasing impression, we will later discover that Peter's shrewder and more cynical reading of the political realities of his society is more accurate than the idealist's. Peter better can manipulate his world, but he can manipulate only a fallen world.

Settling down to the material comforts of toddy, pipe, and smoking cap, Thomas draws his young friends about him in a convivial symposium on the subject of politics. When Captain Horster professes no interest in such things, Billing, the journalist, protests that society, like a ship, needs all hands at the wheel. In the first of the many echoes in this play from Greek drama and from Plato, the captain replies that democracy would be of no use on a ship.[3] This remark, together with his whole character, sets the captain apart from the other male characters in the play as uninvolved in political life. He is thus the opposite of Thomas, yet the dialectic of the play will drive Thomas to adopt Horster's individualism, a development "clinched" when Thomas, in the last act, agrees to live and teach his new ideas in Horster's house.

Horster would appear to have his place in the larger scheme of the cycle, too. He is bound for America, that "freer" realm whose spatial immensities are contrasted with Norwegian-European constrictions, and, of course, he is associated with the sea, another free domain. We hear about the restrictive community from Petra, who enters with the letter Thomas has been awaiting impatiently: for when Katherine expresses uneasiness at Billing's professed "paganism" (he will profess shock at Thomas's "blasphemy" in Act III), Petra deplores, "At home we have to keep quiet and in school we have to stand and lie to the children" (Fjelde, 296). Horster immediately offers Petra his house in which to teach the truth and, though Petra declines, she, too, will finally join Thomas, in Horster's house, for his new educative project.

The highly histrionic nature in which Thomas discloses his first great discovery—the pollution—makes for good comedic theater: But it is also a revelation of his character. He enters the room flourishing the letter for maximum attention, teasing the curiosity of his captive audience to breaking point. Pacing up and down the room before them for full effect, he delays the revelation until he reaches a climax of mystification and suspense in which to drop his bombshell. His public, histrionic character revels in the spotlight which his strutting and posing create. He delights also in his heroic conception of himself: the hero of the community who, like a Theseus, will rescue his people from the danger threatening them and receive their adulation. To some stern critics indifferent to human praise, this vanity is sufficient to indict his whole moral character and his motives. Such a view reveals an unawareness of the nature of dramatic art. Vivid dramatic characters, especially those in political comedies, cannot be saints devoid of all human frailties, and Thomas's histrionically manifest love of public praise, his frank enjoyment of the affection and esteem of his fellow citizens, is the condition of his whole public-spirited civic identity, which, for all its (forgivable) vanities, *will* be capable of heroism at the crucial moment.

One critic has declared that Thomas goes too far, loses the audience's sympathy, and comes to embody a negative rebellion like Coriolanus's.[4] Considering Ibsen shows Thomas alienating only the most contemptible people in the play, while gaining and keeping the attachment of the best (Petra, Katherine, and Horster), one only can marvel at this judgment. It quite patently is to run counter to the play's meaning to develop sinister traits in Thomas and it also is to lose sight of the nature of a dramatic art in which the audience in the theater can only respond to what is mimetically presented. When an accomplished dramatist wishes us to note hypocrisy or sinister intention in a character, he indicates this *clearly* to *us,* however much the other stage characters may be fooled. There is no artistic merit in leaving out these essential indicators; in the artist sitting back, secretly, and seeing if we will "get" what he has cunningly "planted" in the text. Ibsen is playing a bigger and more honest game than this. He gives Thomas the failings of a *good* man who earns our good-natured laughter at his confusions. Thomas's relish at the prospect of greatly stirring up the town, of vindicating his earlier, disregarded advice and, later, his pugnacity when attacked, insulted, and silenced, are shrewd strokes by Ibsen in his portrait of the type that would become a brave social rebel.

In Act II the "simple" problem perceived by the physician, the

overcoming of a physical and medical danger, will become increasingly a political and ethical problem: already we see the
process whereby the "quantitative" physical situation dialectically changes into a "qualitative" nonphysical one. A succession
of disturbing visitors gradually will impress upon Thomas the
nature of the reality he confronts.

The first of these visitors is Morten Kiil. His pre-scientific
mind cannot believe in the existence of microbes, but he decides
he can use this absurd but accepted belief as a weapon against
the oligarchs. Kiil is only the first of those who reveal that they
wish to *use* the truth instead of serving it, who, in fact, wish to
make *selective* truth serve their partisan ends—which is the condition of political life. And this will be the major distinction between Thomas, who genuinely wishes to serve the truth, and his
opponents. As Socrates discovered, service to the truth is not
considered a civic virtue.

It is the self-server, Hovstad, who begins the process of transforming the physical pollution into a political metaphor:

> HOVSTAD. You said yesterday that the polluted water
> came from the impurities of the soil.
> DR. STOCKMANN. Yes, beyond a doubt it comes from that
> poisoned swamp up at Mølledal.
> HOVSTAD. If you'll pardon me, Doctor, I think it comes
> from another swamp altogether.
> DR. STOCKMANN. What sort?
> HOVSTAD. The swamp where our whole community lies
> rotting.
> DR. STOCKMANN. What the deuce is that supposed to
> mean, Mr. Hovstad?
>
> (Fjelde, 306)

Thomas is puzzled by Hovstad's method of twisting the language of fact into that of political metaphor. It is not the scientific
way he, Stockmann, has so far used language. But as his own
awareness of the political and ethical implications of the social
situation widens and deepens, so Thomas, too, begins to use not
the scientist's language of fact but the transformed language

necessary to express his new awareness. This development within Thomas's *language* indicates the development of his own consciousness. And it is a development that is taken up by the consciousness of the whole cycle, for in the next play, *The Wild Duck,* the language of visionary metaphor will be taken to an extreme by Gregers Werle. Visual, verbal, and conceptual language evolves in the course of the Realist Cycle's progress.

The evolution of Thomas's language follows the phases of his gradual alienation from his community, but Thomas never *breaks* with that community, as Gregers does. In Thomas's speech, metaphor is a weapon to be used against the social order, with which he remains actively engaged and on which he hopes to effect reform: It is not the language of an alternative world of the brooding spirit into which the Unhappy Consciousness (Hegel's "unglückliches Bewusstsein") retreats because it has lost all hope of effecting change within the world. This latter is the condition of consciousness, the Ekdal's, upon which another aspect of the unhappy consciousness, Gregers Werle, works. He transforms the objective world into a private allegory, constructing parables in which amazingly clever dogs come to the rescue of wounded wild ducks at the bottom of swamps; where families like the Ekdals, indifferent to the "claim of the ideal," are suffering from "marsh gas"; where one cannot be sure an attic is not really "the depths of the sea"; and where the missionary spirit is fated to be "thirteenth at table." The *physician* of this play, Dr. Relling, also speaks an ambiguous language: one of lies and deception which reconciles a fallen humanity to its unfreedom and untruth.

Hovstad's translation of literal fact into political metaphor, however, is limited to his narrow range of political interests, which are those of partisan power only. Thomas is perplexed by Hovstad's reasoning: that the oligarchs responsible for building the baths and benefiting the community now can be dispensed with and thrown out of office. His mounting bewilderment and indignation is interrupted by the arrival of Aslaksen to pledge the support of another large body of partisans: the home owners' association. The appearance of this succession of visitors is a demonstration of political realities as much as it is an advancement of the plot, showing how the practical world *uses* ideas and betrays them for its partisan interests.

"We" in the theater quickly detect the high degree of opportunism behind their professions of support, for Ibsen, as we noted, clearly indicates devious motives when he intends them, so that the violent peripety of Act III, when Thomas is hurled from his seeming pinnacle of victory over his brother to seemingly total defeat, already is prepared for. We also see the *necessity* for this later defeat and disillusion, for Thomas cannot be an effective force for change in his community all the time he so idealistically and naively misunderstands it.

A visit from Peter soon ends Thomas's perplexity as to why Hovstad and Aslaksen think he will need their help in simply proclaiming the truth, and partially opens his eyes as to the nature of the society he belongs to. Peter acts both from personal vanity, fearing the truth would uncover his own ineptitude, and from group loyalty, threatening his political control and that of his associates. The verbal formula which the mayor adroitly uses to justify denying the incontrovertible evidence is, "I am unable to persuade myself . . .," which neatly removes the doctor's statement from the objective realm of science, where Peter would be vulnerable, to that of subjective opinion. Thus smoothly disposing of the objective and scientific validity of Thomas's account, Peter can enlarge on the economic and political consequences of its disclosure. Peter's idea of his community is frozen into its past. Any development, any life, within the community alarms him. "The public is best served by the good old time-tested ideas it's always had" (Fjelde, 317). Thomas's disclosure that the *People's Courier* already knows and will publish the truth enrages Peter to the point that he accuses his brother of being "an enemy of society" (*samfundets fiende*), which, intriguingly, "echoes" the title and thematic phrase of the first play, *Samfundets støtter*.

The quarrel between the two brothers almost becomes one of physical violence and Thomas is prevented from assaulting his brother only by the desperate intervention of Katherine, who "throws herself between them" (Fjelde, 321).[5] When Peter leaves, Thomas's family divides over the ethical issue of having the "might" or having the "right" on one's side—an issue which opens up the major argument of *The Republic*.[6]

If the truth is to be told, it must reach the people, but in the modern world the conduits of information, the press, are polluted by party and financial interests, which bend the truth for factional purposes: the most fundamental problem of democracy. The shabbiness and evident poverty of the offices of the *People's Courier* rub in the close relationship between information and economics. This is the Grub Street of the modern age, and in this act (III) we will see a number of mendacious versions of reality, in manuscript, and will contrast their reception with that of Thomas's truth-telling article: the various manuscripts presented, flourished, concealed, and rejected supplying a clear visual commentary on the action.

The journalists excitedly talk of "revolution" when discussing the doctor's article, but from the beginning we can see that their concept of the campaign is unscrupulous and self-serving. They can, they declare, make *something* of the situation, *whatever* the outcome, for their interest is in damaging their enemies by any means and helping their friends. By contrast, Thomas, far more naive than they, manifestly is a good man lost in this political swamp. His pagan-warrior temperament and love of esteem are the all-too-human qualities of the heroic identity. Both as a patriot and as a physician, he understandably is outraged by Peter's attempt to force him to suppress the truth and harm his community and its visitors. Those ready to criticize the vehemence of his reaction should pause for a moment and consider what Peter and his associates are willing to enforce: the dispensing of infected water to the unfortunate sick who come and pay them for help. Hippocrates himself would have reacted as Thomas does.

Furthermore, his brother's charge that he is society's enemy has struck deep and the wound is festering. He now resolves directly to contest the control of the community with his brother, to wrest power from him. Though, of course, there is no actual military assault upon the enemy as in *The Seven Against Thebes* and as narrated in *Antigone,* Ibsen nevertheless does give to Thomas the *imagery* of such an assault: of anchoring in the bay of the town and firing shot after shot at the enemy's fortifications:

> I'm going to drop anchor right here at the *Courier* and rake them with broadsides: a fresh article everyday. . . . I'll smash them into the ground and shatter them! I'll wreck their defences in the eyes of every fair-minded man. (Fjelde, 327)

While this is a reference to the piratical origins of the Stockmann family, it also supplies an imagery of war to the intellectual conflict, suggesting that intellectual battle is a sublimation of physical battle.[7] Continuing in the metaphoric vein, Thomas declares, "the whole society . . . has to be purged and disinfected." Thus he takes up Hovstad's metaphor and will act upon it in earnest. The journalists, at least, do not see anything in Stockmann's words to suggest any dubious motive; on the contrary, they call him the "people's friend," and it is not until their own interests are jeopardized, when they patently are in the wrong, that they reverse this term and call him "the people's enemy" (*folkefiende*). There is no reason why we should follow them! On Stockmann's jubilant exit the journalists reveal their cynical opportunism. Hovstad's comment is:

> Han kan bli en ubetalelig nyttig mann for oss.
> (S.V. II.581)

> He can be an exceptionally useful man for us.
> (Fjelde, 329)

Thomas, that is, is to serve their interests, in which the cause of truth and freedom will rank very low. Billing, for example, is secretly applying for public office while proclaiming revolution; both journalists have designs on Petra and her inheritance from Morten Kiil; and on this "cue" Petra enters to return the piously fraudulent English fiction the journalists intend publishing—the second of the visible documents in this act. Petra now learns, with dismay, that the paper prints popular falsehoods in order to build up a readership for its "radical" truths. To damage his rival's chances with Petra, Hovstad attributes all this to Billing (who has left the office) and also reveals that Billing is applying for the public position. But Hovstad also betrays himself and, with Petra's indignant rejection of him, his last *practical* reason for loyalty to the Stockmann family evaporates.

With Peter's entrance we witness the political mastery of the mayor; his easy assumption of authority, the cool politeness that expresses his contempt for his opponents while urbanely seeming to befriend them, his thorough understanding of their opportunism. Though intellectually obtuse compared to his brother, Peter far exceeds him in the corrupt skills of politics. Thomas, by contrast, though as incapable as Socrates of manipulating others, clearly is on the side of the angels of truth and freedom. Peter, adroitly demonstrating how the interests of the paper's readers will be hurt by Thomas's disclosures, quickly pricks the revolutionary balloon so enthusiastically inflated by the journalists. The scene now is set for the major peripety and anagnorisis of the play, that reversal-and-recognition commended by Aristotle as the most perfect of dramatic devices, and used so skillfully by Ibsen in this first group in the cycle. While the great peripeties of *Ghosts,* climaxing in the overwhelming final one, are all crises of *tragic* perception, the superb peripety of Act III of this play is a masterpiece of comedic art. Furthermore, the anagnorisis it begets in Thomas changes the whole direction of his quest, and with this change the conflict of the two brothers for the control of the community changes into the Socratic conflict of the individual with his entire society: one of the clearest instances in the cycle when we perceive a qualitative change that signals a dialectical "leap."

Thomas's exuberant entry to argue against the public demonstration in his honor that he believes his friends to be planning, the increasing embarrassment of the turncoats, Katherine's scolding entry, and the shock of the discovery of the mayoral hat and stick build up to the fine comedy of Thomas's assumption of these insignia of power and his "dismissal" of his outraged brother from public office. This is the climax of the *fraternal* conflict, and Thomas's apparent victory is a delusion that epitomizes his whole misunderstanding of the workings of society. With his perception (*anagnorisis*), this delusion vanishes in a flash and with it vanishes Thomas's reason for contesting the control of the community against his brother. Ibsen presents the anagnorisis as an act of *perception:*

DR. STOCKMANN. (*ser seg om*) Hva skal detter her si?
(S.V. II.592)

DR. STOCKMANN. (*looking about*) What's going on here?
(Fjelde, 343)

The *anagnorisis* could not be more emphatically registered: It is as clear as Helene Alving's "Now I see how it all fits together." Furthermore, Ibsen presents Thomas's perception as total within a few pages of dialogue. The Thomas we will meet in Act IV will be an utterly changed man brimming with new discoveries and seeking disciples. (Katherine's conversion to his cause, at the end of Act III, is a good augury for his future success.)

Until now, Thomas had acted under what one might term the conventional Hellenic ideal of the community: of serving it, embellishing it with his patriotic love, as Pericles had exhorted his fellow citizens to do. But from now on Thomas, like Socrates in the past, will reject the conventional idea of the community and will set about formulating a *new* concept of the individual's role within society. In the next act we will see that Thomas's notoriously illiberal and antidemocratic opinions are almost direct quotations from Plato's *Republic,* the work in which Plato, through Socrates, attacks the democratic ideal of Athens.

The public meeting takes place in Captain Horster's house, indicating that Thomas is being driven to the apolitical individualism that the young captain represents. The confrontation between Thomas and the community is extreme and Thomas's opponents are depicted as only pusillanimous and unreasonable. Unlike another dialectical dramatist, Bernard Shaw, in *St. Joan,* Ibsen is not interested, in this play, in being fair to his protagonist's opponents or in building up any intellectual challenge they may represent. Shaw wished to underline the *rationality* of the historical dialectic whereby, over the centuries, Joan becomes successively divine warrior, heretic, and saint, and for this purpose he is careful to make Joan's most formidable opponents humane, decent, reasonable, and intelligent men. In *An Enemy of the People* Ibsen is writing a parable in which the hero evolves before our eyes from ardent patriot to ardent rebel. It is not necessary to understand the rationality of the townspeople's behavior or greatly to humanize them. The political comedy need only identify, in Aristophanic fashion, the obvious self-interests of the citizens who set themselves against truth and freedom.

Spoiling for a fight, the crowd entering Horster's house lives up to Plato's account of the citizenry as a mob: a realm of unruly passions, not of reason. This act has been read as Ibsen's way of letting off steam against the liberal press that joined in the hysterical attack upon *Ghosts* and upon Ibsen himself: But this extreme confrontation of the individual and the mob is essential both to the design of the play and of the evolution of the cycle. We are presented with humanity in its public, political aspect, the opposite of the heroic individualism that Thomas will advocate, and the language of this act is that of a hortatory rhetoric that does not permit the multilayered ironies of the dialogue of the rest of the play. The noisy crowd, the unruly drunkard continually being ejected and returning, and the physical violence are Aristophanic qualities and, if Ibsen is indeed getting back at his enemies, this would be part of the Aristophanic *form:* recalling the famous *parabases* where the poet proceeded directly to attack his opponents, as in *The Clouds*, where he reproaches his public for preferring inferior dramatists.

Stockmann, it must be conceded, goes on too much and is highly intemperate in what he says and how he says it (an Aristophanic trait in itself), but this is needed, dramatically, to goad the crowd to violence. Socrates, too, at his trial, so offended his audience that more voted for his death than, earlier, found him guilty. Thomas's extremism begets extremism, which turns his public address into his trial. And, again, we must remember the situation. The community that Thomas loves is willing to lure the sick to infected baths and to hide from these unfortunates the terrible danger they will be in. The critic who reproaches Thomas for his anger needs to come up with a convincing alternative of medical ethics.

Thomas's illiberal speeches have been seen as Nietzschean

and proto-fascist, a questionable conjunction in itself. In fact, all his main points are to be found in Plato's *Republic:* a work which also has been assailed as proto-fascist by those forgetting the circumstances of near despair at the situation of Athens in which Plato wrote. As Walter Kaufmann remarks in a preface to a work by the no less illiberal Kierkegaard, it is in the nature of great books like *The Republic* or the *Commedia* to give offense.[8]

Thomas, of course, has opinions of his own not to be found in Plato, but he repeats many of Plato's arguments, examples, and images. One of the most offensive of his proposals, eugenics, not only is Platonic but draws upon exactly the same example of animal breeding: that of dogs and hens (*Republic* V:459). Plato and Stockmann share the same disillusion with man as a political animal. For both, the stupidity of the oligarchical authorities will ensure their demise; for both, the real menace was the masses, the mob, and its party leaders. For Plato, democracy was an evil surpassed only by the tyranny which was its inevitable successor. And both men come up with the same solution: the rule of the elite, of the enlightened minority. (In *The Republic* these will be specially trained: Thomas proposes to train his own elite.) For both men, this elite is not that of the aristocracy but can emerge from anywhere in society. The crowd's angry response to Stockmann's version of this proposal, "So, only the accomplished [should] rule" (Fjelde, 358), is the natural democratic response to his Platonic argument.

Thomas's speech develops the following major parallels with Plato's argument in *The Republic* (I am quoting from the Bollingen Series edition):

(a) The majority is never right (Fjelde, 356; *Republic* VI.490–94).
(b) The accomplished minority is right and should rule (Fjelde, 358; *Republic* VI.501, 502–6).
(c) The aristocracy is not this accomplished minority (Fjelde, 356; Plato insists his Guardians can come from any class).
(d) Truths become old and thus untruths (Fjelde, 356). For Plato (Book III) the old truths by which the *polis*

defined itself are no longer true and must be supplanted by philosophic truth.

(e) The masses are not a people but only the material for a people (Fjelde, 358; in *Republic* Book VIII, Plato insists that the true state has to be carefully *created* out of the masses.)

(f) Good breeding and fine culture are essential to create adequate citizens. Example, dogs and hens (Fjelde, 359; *Republic* V.459). Plato advocates eugenics and sets about reforming the cultural education of the young for his ideal republic. Book III discusses the new education, cultural and physical.

Thomas's revulsion from democracy has major variations of its own for, of course, the play is not *reproducing* the past. An archetypal action in the modern world will be in modern terms. If, in George Santayana's phrase, those who cannot learn from history are condemned to repeat it, it also is true that those who act significantly in the present will reenact the significant past. The portrait of humanity Ibsen is painting in the cycle is made up of its memorable identities, those that escape the Button Molder's ladle.

Summing up the situation of the enlightened individual confronted by the multitude, Plato describes him as one of:

> a small band who have come to understand the madness of the multitude sufficiently and have seen that there is nothing, if I may say so, sound or right in any present politics, and that there is no ally with whose aid the champion of justice could escape destruction, but that he would be as a man fallen among wild beasts. (*Republic* 498)

This idea of the apolitical individual set upon by the mob is developed more memorably in Book VII, in the famous allegory of the Cave. Here, the prisoner who has escaped from the Cave and its darkness into the light of truth and freedom returns to rescue his former fellow prisoners: But living in the light has made him unaccustomed to the darkness and so, when he returns, would he not provoke laughter, and would it not be said of him that he has returned from his journey aloft with his eyes ruined and that it was not worth while even to attempt the ascent? And if it were possible to lay hands on and to kill the man who tried release them and lead them up, would they not kill him? (*Republic* 496)

Plato, of course, was not spinning a fancy, for the speaker of these lines, Socrates, was executed by the Athenian multitude, long before *The Republic* was written. Much of Stockmann's clumsy behavior at the meeting, his intemperate language provoking laughter and outrage, is that of a man newly dazzled by the light and now stumbling awkwardly in the medium of ideas he has not fully adjusted to his new perception. His recent long exile in the north can be seen as equivalent to exile from the Cave, making him unacquainted with the nature of his society. It possibly is only a coincidence that the audience in Horster's old-fashioned and dark room have the lights that illuminate the room *behind* them, like the Cave's prisoners, and that they stare in front at the opposite wall. Knowing Ibsen's *galskap* (playfulness), the idea should not simply be dismissed. Certainly, Plato's parable, the most famous of all metaphors employing darkness, light, and the ascent to enlightenment and the sunlight, is close in spirit to Ibsen's own light metaphors. The condition of being the prisoner in the Cave, fearful of the light, informs Helene Alving's speech on ghosts (*gengangere*), which concludes:

> Og å er vi så gudsjammerlig lysredde alle sammen.
> (S.V. II:512)

> And there we are, the lot of us, so miserably afraid of the light.
> (Fjelde, 236)

Helene's tragic *agon* had resurrected the painful family tragedies of Greek drama; of the Orestes story, of Oedipus, and of *The Bacchae;* Thomas's comedic *agon* has resurrected Aristophanic political comedy. The stages of his evolution, from the Eteocles-

Polyneices fraternal conflict through political comedy to Socratic individualism, create as significant a spiritual movement as any in the cycle. But his evolution does not halt with the Socratic identity. His last words in Act IV are:

> Jeg er ikke så godslig som en viss person; jeg sier ikke jeg tilgir eder; ti I vet ikke hva I gjør.
>
> (S.V. II.610)

> I'm not as meek as one certain person; I'm not saying, "I forgive them, because they know not what they do."
>
> (Fjelde, 365)

This is the first indication of the increasingly messianic role that Thomas playfully adopts but also that he has thrust upon him. In the *Phenomenology* the birth of the Christian spirit arises from the death of the *polis* within the unhappy and alienated Roman world. This will be the phase of spirit explored in *The Wild Duck,* but Act V of *An Enemy of the People* (and only this act) acts out a "lighter" version of the Christian themes.

Act V is the Scene of the Tempters, or satanic couriers. The new "project" of this act will be *education,* and we note that the scene has shifted to Thomas's *study* with its desk and bookcases. The conflict between the traditional education of the *polis* and the new education introduced by Socrates had been the main subject of Aristophanes' *The Clouds,* in which Socrates' house, like Stockmann's, was attacked. Socrates and his disciples were to embark upon a new process of education which was to change our cultural identity—not an insignificant event for Ibsen's art to take note of. There are two forms of evolution present in *An Enemy of the People* and in the cycle: the random, undirected nature of evolution by natural selection which, for our species, is over; and cultural/spiritual evolution, a very recent development in the world, in which the human spirit is able to shape itself, careful to lose nothing of value. In Act IV Thomas had discussed this cultural evolution in terms of eugenics, but in Act V he will develop the alternative Platonic concept of *intellectual* discipleship.

Thomas's very house undergoes a reversal: Beginning as the

hospitable and convivial center drawing to it the brightest young spirits of the town, it now has become the besieged house with broken windows from which Thomas and his family will be evicted. Act V opens with Thomas collecting the stones thrown at the house to serve as "holy relics" (*heligdom*) for his sons to contemplate.[9]

The spiritual ills to which the physician and gadfly must now address himself are summed up in the *leitmotiv* "dare not" (*tør ikke*), which surfaces continually in the dialogue as an example of the widespread thralldom to party and group interests that has imprisoned the entire community. Contemplating exile (as Socrates had been urged to do by his friends), Thomas declares that the town will have "driven out a patriot," but before he makes a decision whether or not to leave, the tempters arrive. Peter is the first, bringing with him his brother's dismissal but also the offer of reinstatement after a decent interval if Thomas will retract his accusation and tactfully leave the town for a while. In angry response, Thomas repeats the word *fanden* (the devil) four times, and this repetition will continue throughout the act. On the last iteration of the word to Peter, the "satanic" Morten Kiil appears. Kiil, "the Badger," was "hounded out" of the town council "like a dog." Like other of Ibsen's "satanic" figures, Krogstad, Engstrand, Relling, and Brendel, he suffers some form of social disgrace or ostracism.

The satanic dimensions to Kiil's identity are light but seriously inform the temptation scene in which Stockmann takes on more and more of the Christ identity, not simply likening himself to Christ but actually performing Christ's *actions*.[10] Kiil urges Thomas to make him "clean" by denying the truth about the tanneries, where he, his father, and grandfather have been like "three murdering angels" poisoning the streams that brought the healing waters. But Kiil is concerned only with *external* cleanliness of reputation. Tempted by the prospect of controlling the baths through the shares that Kiil has bought with Katherine's inheritance, Thomas tells him, "When I look at you I could be seeing the devil himself!" (Fjelde, 378).

As he hesitates, two other tempters appear, Hovstad and Aslaksen, who are willing to add to the financial power Kiil offers, the power of public opinion through the press. If Thomas accepted, he would be the virtual monarch of this kingdom of lies, controlling its wealth and its information. Again using the oaths of the devil, he grabs an umbrella and drives out these traders of the spirit, like Christ cleansing the temple, as Dr. Einar Haugen has observed.[11] He now sends a note to Kiil, the word "No" written three times, recalling Christ's threefold rejection of Satan's temptation. Dismissing the idea of exile (as Socrates had done), he decides to stay in his community and to live in Horster's house, where he and Petra will found a school. "I need at least twelve boys to begin with" (Fjelde, 385), he observes, neatly combining the Socratic and messianic roles. Summing up this day of the tempters, he comments:

> Well, if I haven't been visited today by all the devil's couriers, I don't know what! But now I shall sharpen my pen against them until it becomes an awl; I will dip it in venom and gall; I shall hurl my inkstand at their skulls.
>
> (My translation)

The playful references to Christ and Luther in this passage have the buoyant openness appropriate to a comedy where the alerted audience is meant to enjoy, immediately, the archetypal overtones it sees emerging through the realist art. These archetypes are not random or arbitrary and are not present to "inflate" the realism. They occur because these archetypes alone can embody Ibsen's great action. I am convinced Ibsen would not have developed his realist art at all if it could not have embodied at least the same dimensions of reality as the method of *Brand, Peer Gynt,* and *Emperor and Galilean. An Enemy of the People* is an engrossing modern human story also and can be (and is) enjoyed on that level alone. Similarly, Leopold Bloom is a convincing modern Dubliner, but the reader gains more from *Ulysses* when he is aware of the parallels with *The Odyssey* and the other sources Joyce drew upon.

I am not claiming that Thomas *becomes* the archetypes his actions raise, any more than the medium at a séance does. The history of our species might seem, as Hegel wrote, a slaughterbench to which humanity is dragged, but it also is a history of human actions and identities which are worth preserving from the carnage and carrying into whatever future we permit ourselves. I am writing these words in Beirut after a brutal invasion and within a seemingly incessant and horrible civil war, and I am more than ever conscious of how the human spirit needs to rise to the rational, the universal, to a concern with preserving, like the precious heirlooms of refugees, the memory of its best identity. To deride this humanist endeavor is a treason of the clerks which hardly is forgivable. The "third empire of spirit" does not seem such an abstraction in this time and place but, rather, an urgent necessity.

8

The Turning Point in
The Lady from the Sea

*Every human being is a miniature world. The entire past has helped
in his formation, the qualities of innumerable generations slumber
as aptitudes in the fructified eggshell to which he owes his existence. All of us contain infinite possibilities although few of them
have the opportunity of real expansion. Most of us live and die
without suspecting that we are more than the ego that we ourselves
know, that the personality which discloses itself is only a fragment.
It is pure chance that informs certain people that their natures can
sink to depths at which they are horrified, or can rise to heights
which they would have considered unattainable.*
—Sigurd Ibsen, *Human Quintessence*, 191

Though the seas threaten, they are merciful.
—Shakespeare, *The Tempest*

In an earlier study of *Rosmersholm*,[1] I suggested that the ensemble of characters of that play (or of any Ibsen play) actually was
the collective image of a single mind whose "characters" were
separately individualized aspects, or forces, of one spiritual/
cultural *gestalt*. In one sense, to state that a play such as *The
Lady from the Sea* depicts the separated, individualized forces of
a single mind, as a psychomachia, is to state a truism, though

one often forgotten in the interpretation of fiction. For each character on the stage is both an aspect and a product of the single creative mind of the poet, Ibsen. It is within *his* mind, now opened up as a stage space, that these forces and forms have been conjured to life and endowed with interest and significance, then placed in a world in which they live and move and have their being. A dramatic poet who intends to people a stage is certain to be aware that he is calling into aesthetic life shapes which, though independently embodied before his eyes as actors and actresses, nevertheless have their origins in his imagination. Each individual, Hegel remarked in the *Philosophy of Mind,* is an individual world soul, and Sigurd Ibsen echoes this idea when he writes, "Every human being is a miniature world. The entire past has helped in his formation, the qualities of innumerable generations slumber as aptitudes in the fructified eggshell to which he owes his existence."

At first glance, *The Lady from the Sea* is an oddity in Ibsen's Realistic Cycle. One of its levels seems to be that of melodramatic romance or romantic (and Romantic) melodrama, with the Flying Dutchman theme retaining perhaps too much of its Romantic resonance to suit a Realist dramaturgy. But the play explores depths and indicates a degree of *loss* (for humanity) that goes far beyond romance or melodrama. The sea depths and mountain heights that make up the "scenography" of the play are not examples of the *picturesque* but are metaphors charting a soul-territory that encompasses a history stretching back to the origins of life itself.

At the nethermost depth is the id-like seabed with its endlessly shifting and mysterious forms, like the lower sea depths of Julian's tranced vision in *Emperor and Galilean:* "the dark and slimy seabed in all its ghastly nakedness." Yet, just as Julian's vision is completed by the ethereal "infinite arch of the sky" where "the invisible took on form and the silence became sound," so the scenography of *The Lady from the Sea* is completed by the most impressive and beautiful landscape yet presented in the cycle. The "life" of the seabed is a metaphor for the most "primitive" or primordial stages of our physical and psychic life and (as Sigurd Ibsen observed) perhaps filled with infinitely richer possibilities (whose processes we recapitulate in our individual lives) than we later have realized. From these origins came the first sea forms and the evolutionary process whose land development Ellida, at one point, regrets.

The play's overall metaphor of a fundamental opposition between sea and land is maintained throughout, in structure, texture, actions, dialogue, and stage scene. Action and dialogue exhibit a continuous ebb and flow as if responsive to powerful gravitational pulls, and the theme of a fearsome pull or attraction working on individuals is dominant. This same rhythm is established between the character-pairs themselves, as well as between themselves and their world. Most unusually for Ibsen, the play contains, as well as its major plot, the triangle Wangel-Ellida-Stranger, the further triangle Arnholm-Ellida-Wangel, and then two other subplots, Arnholm-Boletta and Lyngstrand-Hilde. In each of the couples, one partner is associated with the mystery of the sea or with the wider world beyond the confines of the little community, to which the other partner is attracted. The scene constantly before us is a visual movement from a solid foreground of land, through the fjord and its islands, to the distant (unglimpsed) sea, so the pattern of couples, if set out in order, creates a similar land-to-sea, sea-to-land movement (see diagram).

Sea Partner		*Land Partner*
—————————	Sea realm	—————————
(Sea) Stranger		Ellida
—————————	Social realm	—————————
(Ship) Ellida		Wangel
(Shipwreck) Lyngstrand		Hilde
(Island) Arnholm		Boletta
—————————	Carp pond Confinement	—————————

From Boletta and Arnholm to Ellida and the Stranger, we find a greater and greater progression to sea-commitment or sea-attachment. Rolf Fjelde has indicated how the names of Lyngstrand and Arnholm epitomize their sea-situations. The name Arnholm, the most land-based, is derived from *arne*—hearth and *holm*—a small island on a lake or river. Lyngstrand has suffered actual shipwreck and this, Fjelde notes, seems reflected in "his very name, combining *lyng* and *strande,* [which] signifies someone stranded or wrecked in the heather." He notes that the young would-be sculptor, "like a fish out of water . . . gasps for air."[2]

At the furthest limit of this progression, passing beyond the bounds of social or even, perhaps, human order is the Stranger-Ellida alliance. Ellida's pagan name is that of a viking *ship*. The Stranger is "like the sea itself," and the terror and attraction he exercises over Ellida is exercised, in turn, and closer to the land-realm, by Ellida over Wangel. This pattern of a landlocked creature attracted by a sea creature is continued further within the social realm by Hilde's malicious fascination with the world of death, which the sea-submerged Lyngstrand is soon to enter. At its most modest and land-centered is Boletta's attraction to the world outside, which Arnholm both represents (he lives on the sea coast) and offers an escape into. In each case, the "sea-lure" is from the confined to the unconfined and, in Ellida's case, from the limited to the limitless.

The theme of the Flying Dutchman, searching for the one heroine who would utterly pledge herself to him in sacrifice and join him in "the depths of the sea," already had put in a nominal appearance in the first play of this group, *The Wild Duck.* In the present play the legendary, Vanderdecken aspects of the Stranger are even more striking than his Merman qualities, for he apparently travels the world, like the Dutchman, seeking his true partner. In strong contrast to this highly Romantic (Wagnerian) situation is the prosaic little fjord town with its multiple discontents and very human history, shut in from the sea by the fjord and from the wider earthly terrain by the towering mountains. A thematic interplay between the limited and the illimitable seems, visually, to be established.

It is possible for us, contemplating this town through its representative family, the Wangels, to see in it a psychological, social, cultural, and epistemological condition which, for the time being, I merely will name "Kantian," waiting until later to elaborate on this: a contrast between consciousness of the limitless and of the humanly limited, between the categories of human knowing and actually unknowable reality (the thing in itself); of *phenomena* and *noumena,* of the lure of an *absolute freedom,* which at once terrifies and attracts and which will be relinquished for a *freedom with responsibility.*

The cast of main characters is supplemented by many others: townspeople who appear onstage at significant moments, and the tourists, who also contribute to the total metaphor of restlessness, yearning, that the play develops. Most interpretations (and many productions) ignore these minor characters and concentrate on the central drama of Wangel, Ellida, and the Stranger. This will produce a clear foreground drama but only a blurred background. By widening the focus we will find that the background is integral to the total design of the composition. In a play in which, as Sandra Saari has indicated, there is so much emphasis on art and on *seeing,* it is important that *we* see the whole in breadth as well as in depth. This inevitably will involve us in very extended analysis, but this is preferable to pronouncing on the play's meaning without any close attention to the text. And as I believe the play comes to a very startling and unsettling conclusion (the intimation of the extinction of our species), such an analysis is called for.

Serenely to ignore those aspects of the play inconvenient to realistic explanation would be to ignore too much to offer an interpretation at all: though brave attempts have been made to fly swiftly over the territory passing judgment on the fauna from above. To *enter* the territory is to encounter, head-on, a strange menagerie for which our realistic guides have not prepared us. For example, there is the Lyngstrand plot. He was the sole witness to the Stranger's response to the newspaper report of Ellida's wedding and was shipwrecked with the Stranger, who is presumed to be drowned; but then Lyngstrand arrives, a perfect stranger, at Ellida's house to agitate her with the history of this encounter and with her guilty memory of the Stranger, just at the time when the Stranger himself is approaching the town to confront Ellida. The story that Lyngstrand tells Ellida, too, of the Stranger aboard ship just happening to light upon those newspapers (surely very provincial ones) that carried news of the Wangel marriage, the Stranger's curious howl and his whispered accusation, of the subsequent wreck and the Stranger's disappearance in the sea, and Lyngstrand's emergence from his sea-immersion with the resolve to become a sculptor and to sculpt the Stranger and his faithless lover, is not the kind of story we expect from a drama of realism.

The reader reluctant to see a Hegelian underpinning to Ibsen's cycle must nevertheless concede that the title of the sequence in the *Phenomenology* to which, according to my argument, *The Lady from the Sea* should correspond, *Absolute Freedom and Terror,* does recall the action of the play. The spiritual world of Hegel's analysis was exemplified for him in the Romantic movement, the French Revolution, and the Idealist movement, beginning with Kant, in German thought. It was the period when art and literature explored the sublime, mysterious, and even horrendous (*gruefulle*) in Nature and the human spirit, tracing, also, psychic yearnings and longings and recording social and cultural alienation. All these are, I am convinced, reflected in the details of scene, character, action, and dialogue of Ibsen's play. If the unbiased reader were to indicate the most *Romantic* of the plays in the cycle, he would choose this play. By so choosing, he or she would already concede much of my argument. The quality in the play of educated and refined people gazing at a mysterious, sometimes frightening, often symbol-laden landscape was beautifully rendered by the Romantic Dresden painter Caspar David Friedrich, whose close association with the Norwegian landscape painter J. C. Dahl would almost certainly have made him familiar to Ibsen.[3] The Friedrich paintings seem the visual equivalents of the post-Kantian perception of the world: in itself unknowable but capable of being beautifully and profoundly experienced through the shaping categories of human consciousness.

Hegel's analysis of this phase (period) of human evolution traces that movement of the European spirit in which the whole fabric of society and of the individual's very identity as a social being threatened to dissolve violently when confronted with the lure of a terrifying yet attractive absolute freedom. At first individual consciousness is confronted with a universal consciousness, and the universal will becomes "a single individual will to which universal law and work stand opposed."[4] Absolute freedom can achieve nothing positive, "either universal works of language or of reality, either of laws and general institutions of *conscious* freedom, or of deeds and works of a freedom that *wills* them," because it cannot divide itself into stable, separate spheres, as in a social fabric. It maintains the absoluteness of freedom by refusing to participate in the complexity of social organization. "Universal freedom, therefore, can produce only a *negative* action; it is merely the fury of destruction" (359).

The individual self-consciousness, defining itself in terms of absolute freedom, becomes a self without content, "a negation, moreover, of the individual as a being *existing* in the universal" (360). Absolute freedom

> becomes explicitly objective to itself, and self-consciousness learns what absolute freedom is. *In itself*, it is just this abstract self-consciousness, which effaces all distinction and all continuance of distinction within it. It is as such that it is objective to itself; the *terror* of death is the vision of the negative nature of itself. (361)

But, after this terrifying encounter with the annihilation of the self, the spirit returns, though transformed by its experience, to a world of duties and responsibilities. "These individuals who have felt the fear of death, of their absolute master, again submit to negation and distinctions, arrange themselves in the various spheres [i.e., organized society] and return to an apportioned and limited task, but thereby to their substantial reality" (361). The human spirit has felt itself to be a universal will, an absolute freedom, located in the individual. It also has experienced itself as the ground of all being, as the formal *a priori* of Kantian philosophy (362). In the moral sphere, the categorical imperative is legislated by the universal will within each individual as a rational being; epistemologically, the rational individual, through the *a priori* categories, is the creator of the world. Of the "moral outcome" of the experience of absolute freedom and terror, J. N. Findlay writes in the edition of the *Phenomenology* I am citing:

> Absolute freedom has as its positive outcome a purely formal moral will, universal as much as individual. The Kantian Categorical Imperative is the other side of revolutionary destruction. (568)

Hegel's packed and succinct dialectic is a very different thing from Ibsen's expansive, richly embodied dramatic action, so that it in no way takes from the originality of the poet to claim that his play explores a profound division within the human spirit philosophically explored by Hegel.

The metaphors Ibsen has devised for this play do point to the dialectic extremes of Hegel's account of the violently alienated, then reconciled, human spirit. The confrontation of an individual (Ellida), alienated from the social sphere by a disturbing presence (the Stranger) who offers a form of absolute freedom, threatening the existence of the individual but also terrifyingly attracting her; the fear of annihilation she undergoes and her subsequent return to a "sphere of duties" is simply too emphatic to deny; and this a version of Hegel's "story." Hegel's story ended with the establishment of the Kantian Categorical Imperative. An interpreter of *The Lady from the Sea* who, I imagine, would be most reluctant to concede Hegelian underpinnings to Ibsen's text nevertheless, in his account of the play, is drawn to note how *its* whole action, too, ends with "a kind of popular paraphrase of the Categorical Imperative."[5]

The plot and structure of the play, when compared to the taut plots of the plays that precede and succeed it, *Rosmersholm* and *Hedda Gabler,* is expansive to an extreme. It is leisurely in the pace with which it unfolds its multiple plots and puzzling in its presentation of the differing discontents of the women, Ellida, Bolette, and Hilde, who are variations on the same theme. Two excellent accounts of the play, by Rolf Fjelde and by Sandra Saari, while offering equally penetrating and compelling interpretations, come to diametrically opposite conclusions as to the play's ultimate judgment upon its action.[6] Fjelde sees Ellida's dismissal of the Stranger as a positive victory for the human world of love and of *true* freedom; Saari sees the same action as Ellida's defeat, her betrayal of the value represented by the Stranger as she surrenders to the "monocular" vision of "Christian bourgeois domesticity."

Saari notes the significance of the metaphors of *seeing* and of *art* in the play. When the curtain rises, we are confronted by an impressive Romantic backdrop of fjord and mountains, as in *Love's Comedy;* in the foreground is a canvas upon an easel which re-creates the background scene. Ballestad's painting is an artificial re-creation of a theatrical backdrop, which is itself an artificial re-creation of a possible landscape in the world outside the theater; but, in the Kantian worldview, we ourselves create, in terms of time and space and the categories, the world we "see"; we all are artists, if not very good ones, in a sense. Furthermore, different phases of spirit, or different historical periods, create different worlds: Pericles' contemporaries inhabited a different cosmos from that of the contemporaries of Jesus, or those of Dante or of Galileo. It was in the Romantic, post-Kantian period that this was most explicitly acknowledged; that "my shaping power of Imagination," in Coleridge's words, was the creator of the reality I found myself in. And, we will see, the dialogue of our play continually reverts to concepts of *gestälten,* of individuals shaping others in their own terms or of creating *bilder*—images, more or less distorting, of the world. The extraordinary consistency with which Ibsen inhabits each of the different worlds of the cycle, giving each play its own language as well as its own distinct scene, is the result, I believe, of his seeing each as a complete worldview.

Appropriate to the worldview I have called Kantian is the strange dual reality of the play in which the world we ordinarily inhabit and "know" is challenged by another order entirely, not subject to our categories of thinking. The Stranger is a character of many names and habitations, and of at least two radically different physical appearances, past and present. His constant quality, however, is his sea-identity epitomized in his *eyes,* which, when fixed upon mere human perception, attract and terrify. Though constant in their immediately recognizable spell, they also have the uncanny property of changing color according to changes in the natural world—the sea (the one world, in Ibsen's day, not radically changed by man, as Albert Bermel has observed in a study of *The Wild Duck*).[7] That is, unlike our human vision, the Stranger's may see, without distorting, all shifting forms of reality "in itself."

The Kantian dualism between how we inescapably only can shape the manifold of "reality" from our categories, and the nature of reality "in itself"—forever unknowable—is only one of the very drastic dualisms of the Kantian worldview which are reflected in this most dualistic of Ibsen's plays. Ibsen also contrasts the characters' strong sense of limitation, of being bounded and confined, yet aware of the boundless and limitless surrounding them. The alienated consciousness of defined and restricted social organization and responsibility finds itself, in Ellida, lured by an invitation to an absolute freedom destructive of all social organization. It is possible to come to completely opposite judgments upon the Stranger because of his fundamentally ambiguous nature. He threatens the destruction of loyalties and responsibilities established in communal and familial life, yet he also is associated with a freedom toward which the community, however fearfully, is strongly responsive.

Saari, noting Ibsen's use of the term *Gestalt*, suggestively cites the Gestaltist drawings in which the figure and the background shift indefinitely. Jean Paris, in *Painting and Linguistics*, cites "some unusual objects whose characteristic is to forbid the formation of *one single* hypothesis,"[8] such as the Necker cube "or Mach's coupled rectangles, seen in perspective, whose borderline seems to protrude as well as to recede . . . or the conflicting perspectives of Hogarth's *Fisherman* or Escher's etchings"[9] and other such examples. In language, too, Paris notes, this characteristic, revealed by Chomskyan analysis, confirms "the necessity to consider the linguistic process at two levels. This necessity, so often unnoticed, and totally ignored by structuralism, appears only when our immediate expectation of a meaning is deceived, deviated, and has to vacillate between conflicting possibilities."[10] In Ibsen's play, this fundamental ambiguity of evidence constantly is referred to, summed up in the phrase "sign against sign" (*tegn imot tegn*). It is likely that Ibsen, himself a painter, was familiar with this form of visual ambiguity and with its linguistic equivalents. Not the least of the difficulties in interpreting this play, therefore, is that it presents two contradictory perspectives upon the same event, each of which is equally plausible. As Paris comments, citing the work of the Russian Formalist school:

> In this respect, ambiguous objects are the threshold of aesthetics, for not only do they reveal our vision as essentially *dynamic,* but they help us elucidate its functioning. In no way, indeed, can we get rid of the *signifier,* not even by means of a previous hypothesis. The figure resists, like a painting, all reduction. One interpretation prevails only to yield at once to the other, and as no external criteria can specify which is the 'correct' one, the perceptual system confirms them both and never comes practically to any conclusion. We are thus condemned to endure these oscillations, to remain trapped in a paradoxical perplexity, "like a trial judge, getting incompatible evidence from two witnesses and accepting both stories," would have to admit that "two things that cannot possibly occur together" do nevertheless occur together, each one asserting itself in turn without being able to triumph definitively.[11]

Belonging to no human community, the Stranger nevertheless visits such communities and the result of such visits, we might infer from the example we witness, his effect upon Ellida, is to agitate that community at its center and, on his withdrawal, to give rise to a profoundly ambiguous attitude, both of loss and of gain. It is the Stranger's influence that lures Ellida's consciousness close to insanity, yet it is the Stranger's visit that forces Wangel to the action that rescues Ellida from insanity. Throughout, the play seems to employ an *objective* ambiguity that makes contrary interpretations of its details equally valid.

The scenography of the play, for four of its five acts, is an out-of-doors, an *alfresco* setting, suggesting the play is dramatizing a cultural/spiritual condition different from the earlier plays, all confined to interiors. That the spiritual condition of *The Lady from the Sea* is more "advanced" than any hitherto depicted also can be gathered from Ibsen's own remarkable notes and jottings on the play, notes which show him to be speculating on future prospects for our species, while contrasting this limitless prospect with the painful consciousness of finitude, limitation:

> Life is apparently a happy, easy and lively thing up there in the shadow of the mountains and in the monotony of this seclusion. Then the suggestion is thrown up that this kind of life is a life of shadows. No initiative; no fight for liberty. Only longings and desires. This is how life is lived in the brief light summer. And afterwards—into the darkness. Then longings are roused for the life of the great world outside. But what would be gained from that? With changed surroundings and with one's mind developed, there is an increase in one's cravings and desires. A man or a woman who has reached the top, desires the secrets of the future, a share in the life of the future, and communication with distant planets. Everywhere limitation. From this comes melancholy like a subdued song of mourning over the whole of human existence and all the activities of men. One bright summer day with a great darkness thereafter— that is all.[12]

This note recalls the speeches of certain of Chekov's characters—Vershinin, for instance—speculating on the future and on the universal condition of the race. It is a good indication of Ibsen's conception of drama that he prefers to *act out* rather than *speak out* such an insight; that we should glimpse this condition *behind* the speeches and actions of characters who are not conscious of it. Other notes, just as remarkable, wonder whether human evolution has not taken a wrong path and whether sea life or the ability to fly were missed biological opportunities; or if, in the future, men will build cities on the sea, moving them north and south to suit the climate, "and we will not be there to enjoy it!

Will not 'experience' it!" Here, at least, Ibsen's thoughts seem close to that of his son in *Human Quintessence*.

This contrast between the limited and the unlimited, of wondrous developments not to be experienced by the present generation; a sense that human existence is a "life of shadows" with the darkness closing in; the yearning to possess knowledge transcending the categories of our understanding, yet the awareness that we never can do so, is an idea of reality that might be prompted by the Kantian revolution in thought, which Hegel saw as "the last stage in history, our world, our own time."[13] It is in this age, Hegel wrote, that the problem of the relation of Freedom and the Will is most urgently and acutely raised: in France, bringing about a revolution; in Germany, culminating in Idealist philosophy. Only after experiencing the terror caused by the rage for absolute freedom threatening to destroy the whole social fabric could individuals relinquish their longing for such a freedom, to settle down to the task of uniting in freedom with responsibility in a world of apportioned duties, ranks, and orders. Hegel's attitude to the Kantian solution, however, is itself very ambiguous.

It is this momentous and highly ambiguous drama of the spirit which I believe is reexperienced in the action of *The Lady from the Sea*. The community depicted in the play *is* one animated by yearning, by longing for release from confinement and finitude. It is restless, discontented (Boletta), unhappily malicious (Hilde), or, like Ellida, subject to extreme disorder. Surrounding this community is the huge natural world stretching beyond the mountain peaks into infinity, and this world soon will be subject to cold and darkness, suggestive, like Ibsen's note to the play already quoted, of extinction. Before the dark and cold arrive, however, the Stranger will appear with his offer of an absolute release from this and all forms of limitation. Those who "see the Stranger"—Ellida, Wangel, Lyngstrand, and Hilde—are all to be deeply changed by the encounter. Furthermore, Ellida, Lyngstrand, and, in *The Master Builder*, Hilde all will be animated by the idea of *a betrayal of a promise made in the past*.

The topography of the play moves from the "height" of Dr. Wangel's garden, which commands a view of the fjord below, to the greater height of the *Utsikten* locale of Act II, then back to the Wangel home. In all the acts, with the exception of IV, the magnificent natural scene and its vistas supplies something like a "cosmic commentary" on the action. One meaning of the play seems to be that human life itself, in the entirety of its history, is but one stage in an evolutionary process; it is as if the human species has evolved to the point where it can "see" or "confront" its world of sea and mountain, giving it shape and form without comprehending its mystery, before the darkness and cold arrive. Yet, perhaps, in the figure of the Stranger, this mysterious "in-itself" returns the human gaze, luring the human watcher beyond the categories of human understanding. As Rolf Fjelde notes, the sea and the Stranger are both associated with mental/spiritual qualities and faculties beyond human reason:

> Significantly, all the paranormal experiences recounted in the play—telepathy, clairvoyance, precognition, bodily materialization, psychic possession—are associated with the sea. They constitute submerged potentialities in the total field of being that practical land mentality denies.[14]

The society shown in the play has few material problems to solve and has the time to develop, modestly, the arts, by which to render reality. *All* the major arts are represented by the play: poetry (quoted), music, sculpture, dance, painting, and architecture (Ellida's summerhouse), and this emphatic presence of the arts suggests humanity's constant endeavor to impose *form* upon finally unknowable reality. Almost all the consciousnesses of the play are to a degree *artistic*—wishing to be the shapers of others' lives or of their own—and they talk of this *shaping*. They set great store by *images* within the mind or impressed upon the mind; of acquiring new images and of discarding old. They are conscious of the darkness and cold soon to come, and wish their lives to take on significant form in the face of this. Hugo von Hoffmansthal, describing "the Ibsenist creature" as "the artistic ego," dwelt particularly on this play.[15]

Ranged against the spirit of transcendental yearning is the

spirit of compromise, of *acclimatization* on the part of a species learning to adapt to its given environment. When Ellida accepts Wangel's offer and returns to his world, the comedic sense that she has escaped a danger is offset by a tragic sense of a vital challenge having been evaded. "The sea lanes soon will be locked in ice," quotes Ballestad, as if the last possibility of escape, before the closing darkness and cold, has been shut off.

Before the dark and cold arrive, Time is not an urgent matter, and the play unfolds with a leisureliness and an amplitude unique in the cycle. But, with the arrival of the Stranger, Time suddenly concentrates, first to twenty-four fateful hours, then to mere minutes of unavoidable decision, punctuated by the warning ship's bell.

The stage background, we saw, reveals the natural world at its most beautiful, but this sublime natural world is seen only through the frame of trees of Wangel's garden—apart from the *Utsikten* scene of Act II. It is therefore an *enclosed*, an *unfree*, vision of natural freedom. In the foreground is the social world at its most decorous and pleasing: the "spacious veranda to the left" and the garden, with the flagpole and, to the far right, the pretty summerhouse to enclose the restless presence of Ellida. Ballestad's unfinished painting suggests the human spirit "at play." The attractive figure of a young girl carrying "a large vase of flowers" adds to the civilized pleasantness of the scene, which later will be played off against our awareness of the melancholy, the longings, and unsatisfied desires at the heart of this attractive world. As in the paintings of Friedrich where the elegantly dressed ladies, artists, and friends confront superb natural vistas, the scene will come to seem suffused with inner sadness, with a sense of finitude before the mystery.

Bolette is engaged upon a *private* ritual, the secret mourning of her dead mother: Ballestad is engaged upon a *public* ritual, raising the flag to welcome visitors. "Are you expecting visitors/strangers (*fremmede*) today?" he asks, in the first words spoken in the play. Bolette applies this designation (visitor) to her old schoolmaster, Arnholm, but the words already sound a *leitmotiv* of the play—the arrival of a Stranger: already, we see, the language of the play can admit of two meanings, a friend and a stranger. And that other

Stranger is, at this moment, on his way to the Wangel house as his ship approaches the little community.

The private ritual, enacted by the girls in memory of their mother, contains a world of personal reference and significance from which Ellida is content to be excluded, for hers is a spirit that cannot enter into and adapt itself to the world she inhabits, seeing it as wholly alien to her. Though the word is overworked, it is apparent that she is *alienated* from the complex of loyalties, memories, and duties by which her surrounding human world is sustained.

Sharing the stage with Bolette is Ballestad, an artist whose talents have dispersed into a multitude of social trades and functions, and he lacks the capacity to integrate this multiple activity into a single activity or art. He complains he cannot find a suitable model for the mermaid he wishes to place within his painted landscape, whereas, as Sandra Saari has pointed out, he has a model, close at hand every day, in Ellida, who actually suggested the subject of the mermaid for the picture. Another artist now appears onstage, the young sculptor Lyngstrand, who, the opposite of Ballestad, has the single-minded capacity for seeing, close at hand, the obvious model for his artwork: the sculptural group of the drowned sailor returning to his faithless wife. In contrast to the versatile but dispersed Ballestad, Lyngstrand has only one art form and one subject for that art form, to which he devotes all his creative imagination. This is to be as inadequate as Ballestad for the opposite reason. Ballestad's painting is all background with the foreground figure missing, recording the *natural* scene but unable to give it compelling human content. Lyngstrand's artistic conception, on the other hand, is only all intense foreground, the drowned sailor standing over the faithless "wife." The subjective power of this conception will move and disturb Ellida; but it is inadequate art, for its subjectively intense image (somewhat like Ibsen's youthful *Catiline*) is incapable of being placed within a larger, more objective perspective. Ibsen's own play, among other things, will integrate Ballestad's "background" with Lyngstrand's "foreground," teaching *us* that both are equally important for an adequate interpretation of the play.

Wangel cannot break his daughters' attachment to their past

and only ineffectually protests over the rite that excludes Ellida. His character throughout is notably bourgeois. Unable to come to a firm decision, his time is spent shuttling inconclusively between the world of his wife and the world of his daughters, between the veranda and the summerhouse. Wangel, it is true, is good, thoughtful, selfless, and humane: but he also is irresolute, weak-willed, and reluctant to face up to unwelcome reality. His evasion of unpleasant truth is shown in his frequent drinking, his constant prescribing of drugs for Ellida to induce artificial calm, and his inability, until pushed to an extreme situation by Ellida, to take any decisive action. When he conceals from Lyngstrand the truth of his situation (that the young man is dying), this is from one point of view kindly consideration but from another a cowardly evasion. As with so much in the play, if one looks hard at a detail, it becomes, like the Necker cube or the Escher engraving, another thing altogether.

In leisurely exposition with Arnholm, Wangel reveals his alarm over Ellida's condition. We learn that she once lived in a lighthouse (*fyrtarnet*) at *Skioldviken* and would visit Arnholm, who lived in "a priest's house" (*prestegård*). These two domiciles are arrestingly different: one isolated from the human community and turned from the land toward the sea; the other emphatically *within* the community, ministering to it, turned from the world of nature and supplying the community with a traditional relation to infinity. Because of her name, Ellida was called "the pagan" by "an old priest": The details, here, look back to the conflict of *Rosmersholm*, where "that enchanting mermaid" Rebekka West, from the pagan north of Finnmark, also entered a priest's house—the house of Rosmer. Both "Skioldviken," and "Bratthammer," where Ellida and the Stranger first united, carry associations of viking (and therefore pagan) warriorship (shield and hammer).

Ellida's first words, on entering, are to Wangel, "Thank God to see you again!" We later learn that when Wangel is not present *physically* she cannot recall his image; whereas the image of the Stranger as he was at Bratthammer, long ago, remains fixed and clear in her mind. Similarly, Ellida is unable to see the meaning behind the girls' memorial rite, which is performed before her eyes, whereas her response to Lyngstrand's account of his *intended* sculpture, a thing that does not yet exist, will be, "Yes, I can see it, *lys levende*" (lit. "alive as light"). Neither Ellida nor Wangel knows much of each others' pasts; Wangel because Ellida has kept from him her most momentous experience; Ellida because she has been unable to enter with any interest into Wangel's world and its past. When Arnholm expresses his incredulity that Ellida would have settled down as Wangel's wife, Ellida concedes that, in the past, she too never could imagine such a marriage because, though Wangel is "good," "honest," and "genuinely kind to everyone," he and Ellida are "*himmelvidt forsjellig*"—heavenwide in difference.

This implication that her marriage is a violation of her past self now is reinforced by her confession to Arnholm of a passionate though incomprehensible love affair at Skioldviken: a confession broken off with the reappearance of Lyngstrand, "on cue," to bring his story of her old lover, the shipwrecked Stranger. The great coincidence of this on-cue entrance alerts us to see in Lyngstrand the "artistic emissary" of the Stranger, who will create the powerful image in Ellida's imagination that will "color" the way she actually will "see" the Stranger. And Lyngstrand is fated to die soon after this mission is accomplished.

As Ellida receives Lyngstrand's image of his projected sculpture, she leans back in her chair, eyes closed, actually re-creating in herself the figure of the sleeping wife over whom, in Lyngstrand's projected sculpture, the drowned sailor menacingly hovers. It is Lyngstrand who will call the Stranger "the avenger, drowned, and yet coming back from the sea" (Fjelde, 613). Yet, on his appearance, the Stranger does not threaten, does not behave like an "avenger," although Ellida will react as if this description were accurate. She will "see" the Stranger through the image Lyngstrand, in an overwrought way, has created of him.

When Lyngstrand exits, Arnholm, believing her evident agitation to be due to her discovery of her exclusion from the children's rite, is astonished to discover that it was Lyngstrand's relating of "this nonsense about a dead man" that has so disturbed her. In Ellida, two levels of reality intersect: the everyday and given world, from whose rites she is content to be excluded, and, hidden from this, a fantastic and fearful world on which her inner life feeds but from which her conscious self recoils.

Act II, set in the Prospect (*Utsikten*) park, only recently won for the community from the natural terrain, as the text underscores (Fjelde, 620), and from which the landscape displays its greatest vistas free from all domestic "framing," is, visually, the most *restless* of the acts. This restlessness thus is seen as an aspect of the "world" of the play, not merely of one of its households. It opens with young couples from the town and foreign tourists clambering after their guide, Ballestad, whose visual identity is submerged beneath the tourists' shawls and traveling bags that he is carrying. His very voice is dispersed into the alien languages of English and German: a comedic image of the "disintegrated self." The tourists have stopped in the little town on their way to see the midnight sun and, on this Prospect point, they are able to contemplate the world at its most beautiful before the impending winter darkness.

The *human/social* celebration of beauty also is sounded by four-part singing in the distance, establishing the human harmony achieved within this natural world. There will be a similar musical accompaniment, counterpointing the Stranger's bid for Ellida, in Act V. After the tourists leave, other "couples" appear: Hilde and Lyngstrand, Bolette and Arnholm. Hilde is presented as the most *energetic* in the group, briskly climbing the slope on the right and emerging first; already the modern young Valkyrie who will appear in "mountain climbing clothes" (*fjelluniform*) and wearing a seaman's hat (combining the challenge of mountain and sea, Prospect and Stranger?) in the divided household of Solness, holding *him* to a promise made, like Ellida's, back in the past.

Hilde is fascinated with Lyngstrand's "condition," for she learns that he is wholly unaware of his imminent death, which will bring to nothing all his ambitious plans for the future; and this fascination, which repels Bolette, suggests the dark and perverse nature of her trapped, civilized spirit.[16] Her civilized perversity, though different from her stepmother's more *natural* strangeness, draws her to Ellida, of whose history she diligently has ferreted out lurid details: that Ellida's mother was insane, for example. Wondering why her father "dragged" Ellida into his house (the word suggests the mermaid transplanted to an alien environment), Hilde speculates that Ellida, too, will go mad. After this prognosis, Ellida enters, accompanied by Wangel, Arnholm, and Lyngstrand.

In the first of a series of *false* diagnoses, Wangel tells Ellida he is confident he has "seen to the bottom" of her distress: that he has allowed his memory of his dead wife, shared with his daughters, to frustrate his marriage with Ellida. But it is the opposite that is true, for it is not Wangel's but Ellida's past which divides them, and now she reveals the full story, made more disturbing by Lyngstrand, of her nonlegal marriage to the young sailor: a commitment of her *will* made in freedom outside the bounds of communal sanctions, not only beyond law and order but also beyond conventional ideas of rational experience. Reading the supertext of this story, we could see this "marriage" as the human spirit's commitment to the idea, incapable of actual embodiment, of "absolute freedom" itself. This idea, according to Hegel, animated the French Revolution, and the revolutionary nature of the Stranger is reinforced by his "regicidal" "necessary and right" killing of his captain, a murder that Ellida quite equably accepts, in contrast to the horrified Wangel.

The Stranger's name, Freeman (*Friman*), also reinforces his revolutionary connotations, for this name is no more a coincidence than the name of the ship Billy Budd must leave, *The Rights of Man,* in Melville's sea story. Since his "marriage" with Ellida the Stranger has traveled the entire globe, like the Flying Dutchman, but also perhaps like the spirit of absolute freedom itself. He still exerts a strong fascination over Ellida, a fascination she terms *grufulle*—dread-full—a word that will undergo an astonishing sequence of repetitions in a later scene in the play. In the present scene the word receives one of Ibsen's significant triple iterations.

Ellida began *seeing* the Stranger at just the time, she learns from Lyngstrand, that the Stranger had learned of her marriage to Wangel. His image is never full-face, never looking at her, but simply being there as an inescapable fact—as Wangel, when absent, is not. In Ellida's divided spirit, therefore, Wangel exists only in the directly perceptible objective world, whereas the Stranger exists also in her subjective and imaginative world. The child she bore from Wangel, she insists, had the Stranger's eyes (his vision?), with their uncanny facility of reflecting the changing colors of the sea. Of this "psychic bigamy" Fjelde writes: "Either his presence was so powerful in her thoughts, or his claim was so ruthlessly bent on possession, that the body that lay with hers at the conception was not her lawful husband's but another that acknowledges no law."[17]

There is a sense that this is true of all lovemaking, in which the immediately perceptible, civilized, contemporary, and "tamed" identities of the lovers are only the surfaces of different, primitive, biological identities responsive to no man-made laws or customs and going back to the original life impulse itself at the very beginning of evolution. It especially is during sexual passion that one can be aware of how tenuous is one's possession of the human, rational, and civilized aspects of one's identity and of how strong is the pull of the mysterious, libidinal, unbidden, and overpowering force of the life impulse itself. Such moments can achieve a "devastation" of everyday identities, and one can imagine never returning from these depths back to the decorous cultural identities of our particular place and time. Ellida, it seems, *does* find the hold of the "land-world" upon her to be of this tenuous nature when confronted with the powerful pull backward (what she will call the *undertow*) into a dread-full, nonhuman recidivism.[18]

But is it recidivism? In this play the undertow, with so much else, is ambiguously presented as greater and more mysterious than the merely subhuman. Unlike the troll-recidivisms of *Brand* and *Peer Gynt,* commitment to the Stranger requires an act of will and of courage and decisive choice, more like Julian's abandonment of the known world of faith and learning for the *mystery* of Ephesus. A reading of the play is possible in which the land world of the little community might reveal a closer resemblance to the troll world. For Ellida's whole account of her past, in which we receive *our* first "image" of her relationship with the Stranger, is amplified, or underscored, by the immense scenic background of mountains and of the fjord's extension to the still-unglimpsed sea:

the two forms of Romantic reaching for the infinite, upward and downward, the unattainable extremes between which life on this planet exists. Such a scenography seems to make the Stranger an aspect, or agent, of this infinity.

The scenic details of Act III make a metaphoric "frame" for the conflict to come. In the foreground is the "damp and marshy" corner of Wangel's garden, overshadowed by large old trees. To the right, the opposite side of the stage from which the Stranger will enter, is the stagnant carp pond with its old, canny, mysterious carp gliding in the murky waters: an emblem, in its contrast with the open sea, of the tamed human/social mind with *its* trapped and artificially evolved instincts. The time is "almost evening" (so that it *will* be evening by the time the Stranger arrives) and thus is a time of deepening shadows. The immediate setting is closed in and gloomy, but, in the background, there remains visible through the "domestic" frame of trees the great panorama of mountain and fjord: a constant visual reminder of the lure of the infinite which the Stranger will represent. This, the most secretive part of the Wangel estate and, with its carp pond, the "deepest," is the only setting in which the Stranger will make his two appearances. It is as if what the Stranger represents emerges only when consciousness confronts its most brooding depths and is most aware of its trapped condition. (I realize that this "as if" presents a hostage to the hostile critic prepared to pounce; but this procedure seems appropriate to an art as richly suggestive as that of *The Lady from the Sea,* and one as deliberately ambiguous. In Ibsen's "text" the *visual* image is as important as the verbal; and a Romantic *and* domestic, peopled landscape already involves a very complex interplay of meanings calling for interpretation.)

Before the confrontation between Ellida and the Stranger, Ibsen presents the discontents of the society, in the duologue between the other couple, Arnholm and Bolette. Arnholm proclaims that the little modern community depicted in the play has become a "turning point" (*knutepunkt*) for "the world's life" (*verdenslivet*), an idea that Bolette only half rejects as she describes the trapped condition of the community for whom there is "not a word of truth" in the description: "What good is it to us if the great, strange world goes by on its way up to see the midnight sun? We never go along. We never see the midnight sun. Oh no, we live our snug little lives out here, in our fish pond" (Fjelde, 635).

Despite Bolette's protest, the idea is sounded of the world of this play as a turning point for the world's life, a phrase which opens up perspectives vaster than the local time and place reveal. My own reading of the cycle is that, since *Pillars,* it has been advancing, dialectically, up to this turning point, *The Lady from the Sea,* and that the rest of the cycle will lead away from it, as if Ellida's decision is irreversible for the species. Not only spatially, but temporally, this is a turning point: the last journey to see the midnight sun, after which the cold and darkness will arrive. The long, slow movement of the play will arrive at a sudden crisis, a turning point, when time will shrink to a few fateful minutes of decision. What will be required of Ellida is an act of *will.* What keeps Bolette confined and landlocked is her father's "lack of will." The word Ibsen uses for "will" is *fremferd,* a word implying the taking of a step forward, which is in assonance with the word for the Stranger, *fremmede.* The Stranger, I suggest, is associated with the Will and its capacity for decisive choice; acting as a challenge to a human society that has turned its back upon this choice.

When she enters, Ellida shows that she is "nervously animated" as if already sensing the Stranger's imminent appearance. (The unerring speed of the Stranger, arriving at the house only minutes after the steamer docks, adds to his more-than-natural aspect.) It is now, when the Stranger has landed and is making his way to the house, that Ellida muses on the evolutionary mistake made by mankind in leaving the sea. Hers is not a longing for *regression* but for an alternative and superior evolutionary course to the one we have taken, one in which "we would have become something much different and more advanced than we are now. Both better—and happier" (Fjelde, 639).[19] She implores Arnholm to search for her husband because, "now I cannot see him"; nor can she even remember how he looks. The Stranger's approach, that is, seems completely to have obliterated the image of Wangel.

It is in this condition that Ellida now stands "staring down into the pond" as into the depths of her own psyche, and "intermittently speaks in broken whispers" (Fjelde, 640) as the Stranger, unseen by her, enters from the left of the stage. Ellida, whispering to herself, is the very image of an intense *self*-communing into which the Stranger enters. Responding immediately to his soft utterance of her name, she cries out, "Oh, my love—you've come at last!" Which part of her consciousness is speaking to which object of her love is made deliberately ambiguous, in another instance of speech and situation having two contradictory readings. Similarly ambiguous is her simultaneous attraction and repulsion before the Stranger.

While she is terrified of him, and while Wangel will strike up a protective posture between the Stranger and Ellida, it is worth noting that the Stranger himself never threatens. He remains gently firm, relying upon Ellida's own unforced accord. It is the Stranger's *eyes* that cause terror in Ellida, perhaps because eye contact prevents evasion, enforces recognition of guilt and betrayal, and directly challenges the Will. When she tells him that she neither can nor will join him, adding, "*more quietly*," "nor dare to," he steps over the garden fence, trying to assuage her mounting terror by repeating, "Don't be afraid. Don't be afraid." All she can reply is, "Don't look at me like that!" as if she cannot face the truth his stare represents. Whether the eyes are terrifying "in themselves," as possessing some superhuman quality, or terrifying because of what Ellida sees in them, is not clear to us; but we note that in these scenes (in Acts III and V) the Stranger's presence is much stronger and calmer than that of Ellida and of Wangel, who now enters to threaten the Stranger with the law. Wangel, that is, does not draw strength from his own person but from the forces of a well-regulated, bourgeois society that has policemen and magistrates to take Wangel's side. Ellida, at least, rejects this idea, insisting that Freeman/ Johnston "belongs to the open sea." Wangel, however, totally fails to comprehend what the Stranger's nature is.

"Just think—we saw the American," Lyngstrand exclaims on entering, and Hilde chimes in, "Yes, I saw him too" (Fjelde, 647). Contact with the Stranger drastically changed Lyngstrand's life as much as it had Ellida's, firing him to render in the most land-bound of media, the sculptor's stone, the nature of the Stranger's sea-derived pull upon Ellida's spirit. I believe Hilde's meeting with the Stranger will be as decisive and that it is this that turns her into the strangely independent and homeless character, wearing a seaman's hat, who, like the Stranger, startlingly will call upon a married household with the claim that a promise made "exactly ten years ago to the day"—the perennial Ibsen decade—be honored at once.

It was Lyngstrand who planted in Ellida's mind the terrifying image of the vengeful drowned sailor, which then colored her perception of him. "We," as audience, need not share this perception of him, for in none of his speeches or actions is he menacing. What the Stranger represents is a concept, absolute freedom, which will be variously perceived by different individuals. He recognizes no distinctions, laws, social forms, or institutions. He calmly steps across Wangel's garden fence as if it were merely a physical obstacle and not a declaration of ownership; and he sees Wangel himself, as legal husband to Ellida, as no more than such an impediment. He invites Ellida to share in this rejection of the organized world for a life subject to no constraints.

If humanity, as Ellida speculated, had followed a different evolutionary course while remaining in the sea, it might have developed at the highest possible level free from all the land-derived limitations as to property, nationality, obligation, contract, physical institutions, and so on; limitations essential to our human identity. Thus we *can* speculate whether the Stranger is, in fact, a representative of this alternative and higher species, observing the land-species at *its* highest level of development, then taking on human form to contact one of these humans (Ellida) at the point where the land and the sea meet (Skioldviken), drawing her to him in an alliance. As in science fiction, his human disguise is wholly convincing except for one telltale feature—the eyes. Speculating on this *level*—and the play, as well as Ibsen's notes to the play, invites us to do so—a poet might imagine all such fabled sightings of mer-folk (including the Flying Dutchman) as deriving from such "close encounters": that, as a species, we continuously are being watched and, occasionally, invited to join this alluring but terrifying alternative to our human identity, in which absolute freedom might be a possible form of existence. One must not be too insistent here, but it does seem a possible dimension which this very strange play opens up on the text and, consequently, onto the whole cycle. In this reading, our humanity, the image of which the cycle as a whole presents, would be a diversion, or accident within biological nature (as Sigurd Ibsen suggested), and by no means the highest form it might have taken. There seem to be lines of convergence here between Ibsen and the Bernard Shaw of *Back to Methuselah*.

Act IV presents the only interior scene in the play, Dr. Wangel's conservatory; and it is a highly ambiguous setting. As a *conservatory* whose rear glass doors and windows look onto the garden but not onto the distant fjord and peaks, it is a place given to artificially tending and *conserving* life in the harsh northern climate. We notice the *potted* plants, a large flower stand, and "a blossoming rose-tree." These, like the carp in the pond, seem to stand for life forms transplanted from their *natural* environments and bred in an artificial one, and thus are as unable to stand exposure to Nature as the little society is unable to live the life of the Stranger, whose element, the sea, already has doomed Lyngstrand. The conservatory, then, would be something of an inverted carp pond with the good doctor ministering to its sanatorium existence: an idea that goes back to Dr. Rank's sardonic comment on society in *A Doll House,* and all the way forward to the antagonism between the "natural" Ulfheim and the Manager of the Spa in *When We Dead Awaken*. The beauty of the blossoming rose tree reminds us that such unnatural, artificial human life, like a succession of brilliant human epochs (e.g., that set out in Lewis Mumford's *The City in History*), can develop an exotic beauty of its own.

In this emphatically artificial setting the dialogue will be about *art*. Outside, in the garden, visible from the conservatory, Hilde is standing beside Ballestad, watching him at work on a painting. Inside, in a curious inversion of this observer-artist relationship, Lyngstrand, the artist, is watching Bolette embroider. Lyngstrand develops the theme of one person so merging into another that the wife takes on the characteristics and even the talents and skills of the husband. Thus he sees the husband as a kind of artist (not unlike Torvald Helmer) "shaping" another human being. He now asks of Bolette that she should subordinate her identity to his art, to "think of" him when he is absent, to hold his image in her consciousness, so that he in turn can possess in *his* mind the image of a young girl containing the image of him! Thus he wishes to repeat the Stranger's relationship with Ellida, exacting from Bolette a promise that she be loyal to an image of the past, whatever the changing circumstances for her in the future. And by later agreeing to marry Arnholm, and in the same terms of contract and mutual convenience as Ellida made to Wangel, Bolette similarly will (reasonably) betray her promise to Lyngstrand. Bolette's situation, therefore, between Lyngstrand and Arnholm, re-creates Ellida's between the Stranger and Wangel.

In his discussion with Arnholm of Ellida's condition, Wangel confesses, "Behind all her moods there's something concealed (*dulgt*) that it is impossible for me to discover," adding that he believes Ellida was born this way, as one of the "sea people" who should not be *transplanted (omplantet)* so far inland. In a setting of transplanted flowers and plants, this makes Ellida similar to an exotic blossom (the rose tree?) transplanted to a clime where her original nature must be altered (cultivated) if she is to survive. The unhappiness of the Wangel marriage shows that this acclimatization has not taken place. As ever, the metaphor is ambiguous. One might lament the loss of the natural and instinctual and free, but the hothouse life of civilizations, past and present, for all its discontents, has a beauty and fascination rivaling the natural world.

Wangel reproaches himself for not having tried to *shape* Ellida's nature after he had transplanted her. "I should have done my best toward helping her mind develop and grow. But unhappily nothing came of it. I hadn't the willpower for it. I wanted her just as she was" (Fjelde, 657). Part of Ellida's fascination for Wangel is that she *is* out of place, has not successfully been transplanted. Later in this act Wangel will bring up the idea of moving her back to Skioldviken as if to her native soil. The cultivated, bourgeois, modern spirit, therefore, is fascinated with the free, untamed, exotic, and unassimilable. This particularly was true of the Romantic period, whose dialectic I claim the play is dramatizing. Like the bourgeois of the romantic period, Wangel is divided between two worlds: that of Ellida and all that, in her, attracts and terrifies him; and that of his daughters and the social world in which they must find their futures. Much of the Romantic movement was an attempt to return humanity to the natural, instinctual, and limitless at a time when the human spirit was being shaped and confined by the terms of modern middle-class life.

Wangel feels he has much to atone for: He is the guilty horticulturalist, as it were, who has removed a rare specimen from its native soil and ever since has sought to maintain its life with artificial remedies (the drugs). It is what Ellida has in common with the Stranger that attracts and frightens Wangel, for Ellida and the Stranger seem mutually to have established terms of communication beyond ordinary human categories. "I neither believe nor disbelieve," he says of the strange power the Stranger seems to exert over Ellida; and though he fiercely rejects the idea that his and Ellida's child inherited the Stranger's eyes, he is notably evasive when Arnhold probes him as to the nature of these eyes (Fjelde, 658). From his hesitations, it is clear that he did notice *something* that he is reluctant to admit. Similarly, when faced with startling evidence of the Stranger's implication in Ellida's subjective life, he only halfheartedly puts forward more commonsensical explanations of the strange events (Fjelde, 658–59). What is at issue for the theater audience here is *not* to decide whether the Stranger is a supernatural creature, but to keep in suspension two ways of looking at an object or of grasping reality, where our normal, everyday perception of reality finds itself shifting to a wholly different form of perceiving. In *The Master Builder* this is how Hilde Wangel will invite Solness to perceive his *past*.

Arnholm's response to this conflict of normal versus paranormal explanation and evidence is, as Rolf Fjelde has noted, a quotation from *Emperor and Galilean*, a play which similarly sought to transcend the terms of ordinary consciousness: "So— signs against signs" (*tegn imot tegn*). Julian, faced with signs against signs, chose disastrously, turning away from the mystery and the empire of the spirit for the empire of the world. Is this Ellida's final action as she renounces the Stranger and the mystery he represents to choose Wangel, just as Svanhild in *Love's Comedy*, as Sandra Saari notes, renounces Falk for the bourgeois safety of Guldstad? Shaw seemed to recall both plays in his *Candida*.

Ellida, frightened now of the sea for the first time, begs Wangel not to leave her, as if Wangel's world might dissolve without his reassuring presence. Wangel makes much of the fact that the "image" of the Stranger, which Ellida had been carrying within her since their meeting a decade earlier, is different from the Stranger as he appeared before her the day previously. One cannot see why Wangel attaches so much significance to this. The Stranger normally would change in ten years and, to the maturer woman, the figure of the youthful sailor actually would be less authoritative than the more mature figure who now appeared before her. Furthermore, the most important thing, the Stranger's *eyes*, remained the same, and Ellida quickly recognized them. But Wangel attempts to persuade Ellida that the *idea* of reality represented by the Stranger has been superseded by a more *adequate* one. A "new image in you now, shaped out of reality" (*virkelighetsbilde*) (Fjelde, 661) has "blocked the light from" or "is eclipsing (*skygge for*) the old one." The old one, Wangel insists, is made up of "sick fantasies," but, as Saari argues, this is *his* interpretation of the old reality, not Ibsen's. "It's a good thing the reality came" (Fjelde, 661), he assures Ellida, but she, instead of being impressed by this, is moved by the *old reality* and, in a reversal of roles, now becomes the stronger partner of their duologue, forcing unwelcome truth upon the resisting Wangel. Speaking from the point of view of that past she had shared with the Stranger, she pronounces that, in their marriage, she and Wangel have been "lying" to each other; that her marriage was vitiated from the beginning by the fact that she sold herself and that Wangel bought her. The marriage is described as a "contract" (*handelen*) of mutual convenience only, and not as an act of the free *will*.[20]

The marriage was a *contract* only because Ellida did not assent to it from her own free will but from contingent and constraining circumstances which had no *universal* validity. With the Stranger, one form of freedom, a true marriage, might have been possible. The freedom offered by the Stranger "terrifies and attracts" just as the idea of absolute freedom terrified and attracted human reason in the time of Kantian philosophy. It is now, in fact, as the idea of the terrifying attraction is voiced, that the duologue of Ellida and Wangel enters upon an astonishing *eleven* repetitions of the word "dread-full" (*grufulle*). We watch, and hear, the pair contemplating the vast, unknown, horrifying yet tempting and luring presence of the Stranger and all he seems to represent; the repetitions of the word like a horrified circling about a "dread-full" center; fearfully exploring beyond conventional categories of thought and experience.

The dread that Ellida feels for the Stranger, Wangel feels toward Ellida. "You, too, both terrify—and attract," he tells her. "You have for me this same horrifying spell, Ellida, this attraction." The word for attract—*dragende*—applied by Ellida to the Stranger and by Wangel to Ellida conveys the idea of a primal, gravitational pull, operating below human comprehension, like mesmeric animal magnetism. This pull, Ellida insists, is not from without but from within her own spirit and she is uncertain she wishes to resist it even though, if Wangel does not release her, it could drag her into insanity, below—or beyond—the realm of reason. Wangel offers to "dissolve the contract," after the Stranger leaves, an action that Ellida declares will be "too late." It seems, in the argument of the play, that if the possibility of choosing absolute freedom is not permitted to the human will, then it will remain a lure pulling the human imagination beyond all *conditional* terms of freedom.

If the temptation to absolute freedom could *freely* and unconditionally be confronted and rejected, then there *might* exist for the individual a world of conditional freedom he or she could accept (freedom with responsibility) within which to function without a sense of deep loss. This is the ambiguous conclusion the dialectic of the play will reach. Ellida has hitherto had no inkling that such a realm of free responsibilities, originating in *love,* really is waiting for her, and she is startled to hear that Hilde long has been waiting for "one expression of love" from her. From now on, in the play's dialectic, the value of *love* will be pitted against the value of *freedom*. Love *is* the value that recognizes and accepts freedom only within responsibility, which allows a marriage to transcend the condition of a contract.[21]

The conflict between Wangel's world, with its value of love, and the Stranger's world, with its value of freedom, becomes the major action of Act V. The conflict will be richly amplified, beyond the struggle within Ellida herself, to become a metaphor for the human community on this planet. While the Stranger offers *his* temptation, music will sound from the *community,* signifying the harmonious human order Ellida will have to forfeit if she joins the Stranger; while, from the Stranger's side, the ship's bell will clang imperiously, summoning her to a decisive commitment of her *will.*

Again, the setting is the corner of the garden by the carp pond, in deepening twilight, indicating the darkness soon to come which will be acknowledged at the end of the act. That the Stranger appears only at twilight, apart from reinforcing his "mysterious" aspect, might also indicate that he arrives only at the *end* of an era, at a moment of cultural closure, as Ibsen believed his own age to be.[22] Arnholm, Bolette, Lyngstrand, and Hilde are in a boat on the carp pond, and there is an intriguing image of their poling off out of sight as Ballestad appears, carrying a music score and French horn and waving and calling to them. "Their answers are heard farther and farther off in the distance" (Fjelde, 670), thus drifting away from Ballestad on the shore. His shouted words to them—"What did you say—? Yes, that's right—for the English steamer. It is the last time (he) will come here this year. If you wish to enjoy the sounds/tones (*tonene*) you should not put it off too long"—are highly ambiguous. The "he" (*han*) is the ship, which, in Norwegian, takes the masculine form as a pronoun; but the pronoun "he" equally could apply to the Stranger, leaving on this ship, whose last words to Ellida *will* be accompanied by music.

The ambiguity in the use of this little pronoun will be exploited richly in the following dialogue. Ballestad announces to Wangel, "Tonight we will honor the (*englanderen*) English ship." *Englanderen,* however, primarily means Englishman, and Ellida's startled response, "Englanderen! Er han alt i sikte?" (The English—! Is he already in sight?), sustains the ambiguity. The

Stranger's name, Johnston, is English (or, strictly, Scots)[23] and one of his domiciles is Halifax. To Ellida's question Ballestad replies, "Not yet. But he makes his way in between the islands. Before you know it, he is right upon us," a statement which carries more dramatic weight if we see it applying to the Stranger as well as to the ship, making much more of Ellida's tense, "Yes,—that's how it is."

It is not only the dramatist who is maintaining the ambiguity. Ellida is also: She is able to talk about the Stranger to Ballestad, and relieve the pressure on her spirit because Ballestad assumes she is talking of the ship. Wangel, however, seems to understand the ambiguity when he reassures Ellida, "Tonight is the last voyage. Then he will come no more."

This identification of the Stranger with the ship, together with the ship's uncanny way of suddenly appearing without warning, might well be references to the Flying Dutchman legend. Not only does Vanderdecken's ship, in Wagner's version, instantly appear; but its crew is a ghost crew and the Dutchman is the only living creature on it, so that he and the ship are the same thing. If we see Wangel's reassurance to Ellida as applying to the Stranger, then Ballestad's response, "It's a sad thought, Doctor. But all the more reason to do him honor," would suggest that this confined and limited little community with its modest arts and music, waiting for the cold and darkness to descend, is paying homage to a value (absolute freedom) it nevertheless is content to relinquish. Ballestad follows up the thought of losing the ship/ Stranger with the reflection, "Ah, me! These delightful summer days will soon be over. The sea-lanes will soon be locked in ice— as the old tragedy has it" (Fjelde, 671), and he continues that it is hard for the little community to reconcile itself with "the dark times" (*mørketime*) that are approaching. We can respond to this unsentimentally because Ballestad's rhetorical flourishes are what the "finer" characters, Ellida and Wangel, cannot permit themselves. What is comedic pathos in Ballestad is "filled out" by the reflectiveness of the others. Thus the words do carry the sense of some value irretrievably lost.

Ellida is attracted, fearfully, to the unknown and limitless offered by the Stranger, because nothing ties her to "this place."

She owns (*eier*) neither the children nor their thoughts and finds "here" no "binding force, no support, no help, no attracting pull [*dragning*] toward everything that should have been our common inmost possessions." She longs to return to "the man I betrayed [*sviktet*]—he to whom I should have held unshakably fast, as he did to me." The Stranger's coming, "for the last and only time," is to invite her to "live my life again—to live my own true life—the life that terrifies and attracts—and I cannot let go—not of my own free will" (Fjelde, 672).

Ellida's situation is paralleled, in diminished form, by Bolette's relationship with Arnholm. He, too, has held within his mind an image of Bolette yearning for him (as Lyngstrand also wishes), and, though he discovers this is not the case, the image persists, coloring his vision of her—another instance of the human consciousness, as artist, shaping its reality and being shaped in turn by the reality it transforms: a thoroughly Hegelian situation, which will become a major theme of the last, retrospective, play in the cycle, *When We Dead Awaken*. We observed how the Stranger-Ellida relationship is paralleled in progressively diminished form by the other partners in this multipartnered play; and Arnholm, though far from being a power to terrify and attract, *does* represent for Bolette an unknown world, yet to be explored, a future of possibilities denied by the constraining community. Arnholm has implanted in *her* consciousness an image of this liberation, and so powerful is this image's effect upon her that, when he attaches to it the condition of marriage, from which she at first recoils, it persists as a lure. Both Arnholm and Bolette are agitated by such inner pictures, and Bolette finally will join Arnholm in an anticipation of that "freedom with responsibility" with which Ellida, finally, will join Wangel.

Bolette had been able to make the leap after she had rejected the idea of accepting Arnholm's offer of financial freedom while owning no responsibility to *his* feelings of love for her. Ellida's renunciation of the absolute freedom offered by the Stranger when she detects the full extent and depth of Wangel's love for her is a similar acceptance of responsibility. Love, self-sacrificing in the manner of Arnholm and Wangel, is a distinctly Christian value. It is both a strength and a weakness, and by succumbing

to the love value, Ellida renounces, I think, the truth and freedom offered by the Stranger.

Before presenting this major confrontation, Ibsen gives us the
curious scene of Lyngstrand and Hilde each creating pictures of
reality. Lyngstrand confides to her that he now carries within
him the image of Bolette carrying *his* image. He foresees that
Hilde, when she is Bolette's age, will have gained Bolette's appearance and temperament, "as if you and she had grown
together—in one form [*gestalt*], so to speak" (Fjelde, 681). But
Hilde is a match for him in this facility of image-making and
creates one of her own: of herself, dressed completely in black, as
a young grieving *bride,* an image that looks forward not only to
the death of Lyngstrand but also, I believe, to that of Halvard
Solness. The image also parallels Ellida's situation. In a sense
she has been the "bride" of the Stranger and when she rejects
him, she will say, "To me you've become as a dead man," which
would make her the bride of the dead. The two aspects of Ellida's
situation, therefore, are paralleled by the two daughters whose
futures will be the opposite of each other: Bolette settling for
domestic responsibility with Arnholm, like Ellida with Wangel;
and Hilde *forever* leaving home for a dangerous adventuring, as
Ellida might have done with the Stranger. Are these two futures
contained, in the next two plays, in Hedda's marriage with the
pedantic Tesman and Hilde's dangerous alliance with the master
builder? Are there *two* turning points in this play?

Lyngstrand points to the suddenly apparent English ship, so
that when Ellida and Wangel now enter, disputing whether or
not the ship *has* arrived, we note that Ellida, correctly, has di-
vined the presence of the ship in spite of Wangel's confident and
authoritative "No, Ellida, I tell you—you're wrong," adding,
"Isn't that true, Mr. Lyngstrand? (He) is not in sight yet?"
(Fjelde, 682).

Ballestad observes that the ship/Stranger—"he"—"comes as a
thief in the night." This arresting phrase, as Dr. Einar Haugen
reminded me, is taken from a fine passage in Paul's First Epistle
to the Thessalonians, who had asked him about the "times and
seasons" of the messiah's coming. There is no telling when the
Lord will come, says Paul:

For yourselves know perfectly that the day of the Lord
so cometh as a thief in the night.

For they shall say, Peace and Safety; then sudden destruction cometh upon them as travail upon a woman
with child; and they shall not escape.

But ye, brethren, are not in darkness that that day shall
overtake you as a thief . . .

Ye are all children of the light and the children of the
day: we are not of the night nor of the darkness.

Therefore, let us not sleep, as do others; but let us watch
and be sober.   (1 Thess. 5:2–6)

Paul's injunction is that his little community remain in a state
of perpetual preparedness, living every hour ready for the great
awakening and liberation that will be the coming of the messiah;
if we do so, we remain children of the light. By associating the
Stranger with this theme, Ibsen would seem to be investing him
with a power of spiritual liberation. In *this* interpretation of an
admittedly ambiguous text, Ellida, by choosing to remain with
the little community and its compromise with freedom, is not a
child of the day and of the light and will share her community's
descent into darkness.

The Stranger arrives, in deepening twilight, in the dark and
beshadowed corner of the garden, and we have one of the richest
of all Ibsen's stage actions, where sight and sound, image and
melody, unite. From far out on the fjord, music is played to honor
the ship/Stranger and, as Ellida agonizes and hesitates, the brief
and pregnant time is sharply punctuated with the imperative
sounds of the ship's bell, increasing the *audience*'s sense of the
almost unbearable urgency of the encounter. Against the harmony of the music the ship's bell cuts across like shocks to the
nerves, suggesting a *summons*.

Wangel fears that Ellida now is slipping from him into "the
boundless, the infinite, the unattainable" (Fjelde, 685), for even
if she stayed unwillingly with him, she would enter a state of
consciousness resembling insanity. As the Stranger's power over
her increases (he employs no force or menace; he merely lets her
free will find its course), he asks, "Don't you feel, as I do, that we

belong together?" (Fjelde, 684), not because of any binding promises, "which bind no one," but because of a "deeper necessity": "I don't let you go because I can't." He tells her, "I can see it and I can hear it in you, Ellida—it will be me that you choose in the end" (Fjelde, 684). The Stranger is not conceived by Ibsen to be subject to human error so that this statement *might* imply that—whatever her decision—Ellida ultimately *will* join him.

Against the Stranger's quiet assurance Wangel, at first, can only bluster, even threatening to call the police. In response, the Stranger asserts his identity as representative of freedom. "I will live and die a free man" (*For jeg vil leve og dø som en fri mann*), and, at this point Ellida, too, insists to Wangel that *she* is a free spirit: "You can hold me back here. You have the power and means to. And that is what you want to do. But my mind (*sinn*)— all my thoughts—all my luring (*dragende*) longings and desires— these you cannot bind. They will go on craving/aspiring [*hige*] and hunting [*jage*] out into the unknown that I was formed for [*skapt for*] and that you have locked from me."

In desperation, Wangel offers the example of his own love and suffering. He concedes "in quiet pain" that Ellida is slipping from him; that her craving for the limitless [*grenseløs*] and infinite [*endeløs*] and unattainable [*uoppnåelige*] will drive her into "pitch darkness." In the clash here between freedom and love, we should watch closely the nature of Ellida's decision, for on this will depend our interpretation of the play's conclusion. Remarkably, the situation re-creates details of Peer Gynt's encounter with the Great Bøyg, which occurred in "pitch darkness." Ellida senses "black soundless wings hovering over" her, just as Peer's struggle with the Bøyg was accompanied by "the sound of wing strokes of great birds." Peer's imminent collapse was averted by the sound of bells, representing love, rung by Solveig and Aase, just as the sound of the ship's bell punctuates Ellida's struggle.

Who is Ellida's Bøyg, the Stranger or Wangel? Again, "the signs conflict" (as Maximus saw in the séance sequence of *Emperor and Galilean*). The Bøyg was a "will-devourer" and thus would seem to be the Stranger's opponent, yet it was defeated by love, which is the value Wangel offers. But Solveig's love was a challenge to Peer to attain a "project of the will" on the heights, whereas Wangel's love is an invitation to a retreat from the heights to responsible domesticity. *Tegn imot tegn*—sign against sign. Wangel, driven by the Stranger's challenge, at last offers Ellida full freedom to choose her own path, announcing, "our contract's dissolved . . . you can choose in freedom—on your own responsibility" (Fjelde, 685). Confronted with this, and with the spectacle of Wangel's anguished love, Ellida declares, "This transforms everything." If this solution is authentic, then Ellida is saved from the destructive temptation to an impossible absolute freedom by discovering in the moral/social world awaiting her the Kantian resolution of freedom with responsibility, in which her highest (i.e., her rational) self can find free fulfillment in chosen duty.

Ellida rejects the Stranger as the ship's bell cuts across the harmony of the social music for the last time. Remaining calm, the Stranger concedes, "There is something here that is stronger than my will," and Ellida responds:

> Deres vilje mekter ikke et fnugg over meg lenger. For meg er De en død mann,—som er kommet hjem fra havet. Og som går dit igjen. Men jeg gruer ikke lenger for Dem. Og jeg drages ikke heller.
>
> (S.V. III.233)

> Your will hasn't a shred of influence over me now. For me, you are a dead man who came home from the sea. And who has gone back there again. I no longer dread you nor am I attracted to you.
>
> (My translation)

That is, the dread and attraction have not passed from the Stranger: It is only that Ellida no longer feels them. Ellida's rejection of the Stranger therefore *could* signal *her* failure, not the Stranger's.

With no expression of regret, the Stranger now rejects Ellida, as if she had failed a crucial test. His curt and untranslatable "Farvel frue," and his use, for the first time, of the formal "De," subtly expresses his rejection of her.

> Fra nu av er De ikke annet—enn at overstått skibbrud i mitt liv.
>
> (S.V. III.233)
>
> From now on you're nothing more than a shipwreck in my life that I've survived.
>
> (My translation)

He implies that she is the ship (as her name suggests) that has been wrecked by her decision, and that *his* life, like the Flying Dutchman's, will involve other encounters.

If we take our viewpoint on the action from the Stranger, Ellida has failed to rise to the challenge of the freedom he offers, ensnared by the compromise plausibly proffered by Wangel. From the opposite viewpoint, Ellida's bourgeois social/moral identity has been rescued and reinforced by an act of self-renouncing love on Wangel's part. Perhaps *both* viewpoints are valid, and Ibsen's text presents, consciously, "two incompatible, mutually destructive points of view," which Paul de Man believed to be true of all texts, presenting "an insurmountable obstacle in the way of any reading or understanding."[24] In the case of Ibsen's text, however, this fundamental ambiguity is an artistic strategy. I shall attempt to offer an interpretation of the play's conclusion, noting its ambiguity, but opting for the predominance of one meaning over another.

Absolute freedom cannot be lived in human terms, so far as humanity is at present constituted, so that compromise is essential for human life in society. Yet absolute freedom remains an inexpungible lure for human consciousness and will survive the "shipwreck" of one cultural *gestalt* after another in the history of our species. Each cultural epoch is a limiting form of consciousness; but the highest levels of consciousness, such as that of art, religion, science, and philosophy, must try to transcend all forms and comprehend the Absolute behind them all. Within her cultural *gestalt* Ellida was the most responsive (because the most alienated?) level of consciousness, yet she proved incapable of meeting the Stranger's challenge and therefore shares in the doom of her society.

It is the Stranger who pronounces the last words on their relationship as the heroine declines from the bold pagan connotations of her name, *Ellida,* to a mere *"frue."* Like Svanhild, in *Love's Comedy,* the heroine has failed to live up to the heroic associations of her name and returns to the undistinguished clay of ordinary humanity. The Stranger, on the other hand, continues to search for a more heroic consciousness.[25]

The Stranger's visit has not been fruitless, nevertheless. It has saved the Wangel marriage by forcing Wangel "in the deepest necessity and danger" to "risk much" and grant Ellida freedom to choose. Without this, the marriage would have collapsed or would have continued in deep misery. Now, for the first time, Ellida and Wangel agree to share each other's *pasts.* That is, not only will Ellida now share the Wangel memory of the dead wife and the history of the family toward which she has hitherto been indifferent: Wangel also will share in Ellida's past, which contains her history of attraction/fear toward the Stranger, her longing for the sea, and her craving for the infinite. The joining of these two opposite pasts, the infinite and the intimate, will create a more adequate image of reality (*virkelighetsbilde*). Thus, the intense, *subjective* drama of Ellida, whose emblem was Lyngstrand's sculptural pair of drowned sailor and sleeping wife, unnaturally separated from the surrounding world, now finds a place within that world; while the discontented objective world, whose emblem was Ballestad's scene without a central figure, now possesses that figure in the form of the acclimatized mermaid. Ellida's integration into her community is a matter for rejoicing by that community, which now becomes united with its deepest levels of consciousness.

This highly dialectical conclusion, of antitheses synthesizing, leads to the comedic dénouement; but it is elegiac comedy. Young people from the town enter with Arnholm, Bolette, Lyngstrand, and Hilde and gather to watch the ship bearing the Stranger sail away. Arnholm comments, "Nu seiler engelskmannen"—"Now the Englishman is leaving," and the group searches for a vantage point from which to follow the ship's departure. This wistful viewing of "the last voyage of the year" is accompanied by Ballestad's reflection, "Soon are all the sea-lanes closed, as the poet says. It's sad, Mrs. Wangel." The closing of the sea-lanes by the gathering ice suggests, metaphorically, the closing off of this community from the world, the ending of an epoch. Act V began "in deepening twilight," and the now-gathering darkness would increase the elegiac quality of the comedic ending as Ellida announces she will stay "on firm land" and be a creature *shaped* by the land environment (*fastlandsskapning*).

The mermaid takes her place in the foreground by obeying Ballestad's advice to *acclimatize,* though the cost of that adaptation might be hinted at in the fact that Ballestad never can bring out the word without stammering. The great steamer "glides silently over the fjord" and the music that had been playing in its honor now can be heard retreating closer to the shore: a "closing in" spiritually as well as seasonally at this summer's end. The "happy" ending, with its final reminder of the *harmony* (the music) attained by the community within nature, can justify Rolf Fjelde's account of Ellida's decision as "positive." But the sadness beneath the comedy and the elegiac tone speak also of an irretrievable *loss,* justifying Sandra Saari's description of the play as "a troll comedy and a creative human tragedy."

Such a troll comedy might be all our species is capable of. In his letters to Georg Brandes, this is how Ibsen seemed to view post-revolutionary Europe, "living on nothing but the crumbs of the revolutionary table of last century," a diet on which Europe has been "chewing . . . long enough."[26] Of the *conditional* freedom Ellida accepts, one might recall Ibsen's admonition, "Anyone who stops in the struggle for freedom and says, 'Now I have it' shows that he has lost it. It is exactly this tendency to stop dead when a certain amount of liberty has been acquired that is characteristic of the political state."[27] This political state—or organized society—should, Ibsen declared, be abolished, for "the state is the curse of the individual."[28] The concluding words of this letter are worth quoting again, keeping in mind the Stranger's last words to Ellida: "There are actually moments when the whole history of the world reminds one of a sinking ship; the only thing to do is to save oneself."[29]

Halfway through the cycle, Ellida's decision might be seen as a turning point (*knutepunkt*) deciding the nature of the dramatic actions that will follow. Humanity chooses to remain earthbound, to reject the lure of absolute freedom, and to remain *this* side of the third empire of spirit and, in the plays that follow, will be concerned to summon up its entire achievement rather than to undertake any significant advance.

I already have suggested that in the two daughters, Bolette and Hilde, the future course of the cycle might be prefigured, with Bolette married to her schoolmaster evolving into Hedda married to her scholar. *Hedda Gabler* depicts a bourgeois world stifling in its mediocrity. Hedda, who, like Ellida, rejected a "wild" lover for a staid husband and regrets her "cowardice," yearns futilely for some transcendent gesture or value in her world. Hilde, on the other hand, boldly sets out, breaking all social conventions, to attempt to establish in the world the heroism of her imaginings.

Whether or not Ibsen really envisaged any future for our species beyond this summing up of its spiritual content, this is the *scale* of the argument, and of the reflection it should beget in us, that Ibsen's supertext lures us to. We encounter this same daring, speculative, cosmic scale of thinking in Sigurd Ibsen's *Human Quintessence,* and it is not difficult to imagine that father and son, in their intellectual and imaginative life, their shared solitude within the world, had much in common and that neither would have found the immensity of their imaginations very adequately reflected in more conventional accounts of Ibsen's realist art.

9

The Demons of
John Gabriel Borkman

His eyes, the lights of his large soul, contract or else expand
Contracted, they behold the secrets of the infinite mountains,
The veins of gold and silver and the hidden things of Vala.
                    —William Blake, *Vala, or The Four Zoas*

The Mineral Kingdom has nothing in itself either amiable or
attractive; its riches, enclosed in the breast of the earth, seem to
have been removed from the gaze of man in order not to tempt his
cupidity; they are there like a reserve to serve one day as a
supplement to the true wealth which is more within his grasp,
and for which he loses taste according to the extent of his corrup-
tion. Then he is compelled to call in industry, to struggle, and to
labor to alleviate his miseries; he searches the entrails of earth;
he goes seeking to its center, at the risk of his life and at the
expense of his health, for imaginary goods in place of the real
good which the earth offers of herself if he knew how to enjoy it.
He flies from the sun and the day, which he is no longer worthy
to see.
                    —Jean-Jacques Rousseau, quoted by Jacques Derrida,
                                    Of Grammatology

Historicism, for Hegel, reduces all history to tragedy, by conceiv-
ing the monuments of past cultures as empty tombs, irretrievably
different from present needs and concerns.
                    —Charles Altieri, *Act and Quality*

In *John Gabriel Borkman,* a dead and discredited world order seeks to live again in the present, to leave its tomb and take possession of youthful life. The elder trio of the play, Borkman and Gunhild and Ella Rentheim, in terms of the present needs and concerns of the world, died many years ago and have been discarded, whereas the younger trio, Fanny Wilton, Erhart, and Frida Foldal, will escape the dance of death of the elders to travel south to light and warmth. It is by taking possession of the spirit of the young man, Erhart Borkman, that the ghostly trio seeks to ensure their continuation in the world. As one of the trio, Gunhild proclaims:

> Erhart has an obligation, before all else, to achieve a bril-
> liance of such height and scope [*å lyser så høyt å så vidt
> utover*] that not one person in this country will still recall
> the shadow his father cast over me—and over my son.
> (Fjelde, 949)

Ella Rentheim, who professes she wishes to "open a path for Erhart to be happy here on earth" (Fjelde, 949), nevertheless arrives on the scene with the demand that the young man per-petuate *her* life on earth, by taking the name Rentheim. Even Borkman, the most self-sufficient of the trio, will urge Erhart to join him and to "win this new life" (Fjelde, 1004). It is possible, and indeed usual, to read this drama as a study in the aberrant psychology of a Norwegian family—which seems an odd reason for assembling all the machinery of an elaborate dramatic perfor-mance. It also is possible, by paying attention to the supertext, to read the play as an archetypal conflict between the past and the present, between one worldview, about to pass away, and an-other coming into uncertain existence. This is the reading I shall try to establish.

One way the supertext reveals itself is through the imagery of the play. Each Ibsen play, like each Shakespearean play, has a special, predominant imagery deriving from and controlled by the "concept" the play is enacting.[1] As we have seen from the previous analyses in this book, this imagery is both verbal and visual, and it is in the very nature of imagery to point beyond the immediately presented situation to the larger "argument" of the play. As I noted of *An Enemy of the People,* many of Ibsen's metaphors and symbols, in the Realist tradition, are also functioning *things:* and this will be true of *John Gabriel Borkman.* But as the cycle evolved, so the *language* of the cycle became increasingly suffused with an imagery from a reality not immediately present onstage: Indeed we saw this process within Thomas Stockmann's language and noted how, in *The Wild Duck,* this image-filled language became a predominant mode of discourse. If we return to Gunhild's speech just quoted, we will see how it establishes a linguistic pattern in which one ghostly world impinges upon the immediate and "real."

> Erhart får først og fremst se til at han kan komme til å lyse så høyt og så vidt utover at ikke noe menneske i landet lenger skimter den skyggen som hans far kastet over meg—og over min sønn.

To the literalist, the only explanation for this language in Gunhild, Ella, Borkman, and Mrs. Wilton is that these everyday people happen to have very strange linguistic habits. To *shine* so high and so widely *utover* (out over) so that a past shadow that was "cast over" Gunhild and her son will be forgotten is to behave like the sun or like a god of light. If one were to rewrite this speech from the literalist point of view, Gunhild would say, "Erhart has a duty to restore the name of Borkman, which his father disgraced." This eminently conveys the literal meaning, so that the fact that Ibsen did not write this means that he wishes to convey more than a literal meaning. Nor is this an isolated instance. For Gunhild, Erhart's mission is the *oppreisning* of the Borkman name and the full restoration of that name's honor. *Oppreisning* implies not only restitution and restoration but also resurrection: And the idea of young Erhart resurrecting a dead and discredited world and, by his brilliant and far-shining light, dispelling the shadows of the past (there is an emphatic darkness-light imagery throughout the play) suggests an archetypal as well as a realistic action taking place. This has some resemblance to the northern mythic anticipation, unfulfilled, of the regeneration of the ruined northern world by the beautiful young god Baldr, who would restore a world freed from the guilt of the elder gods.

Spiritual vampirism, whereby the archetypal presences of the past seek for a modern (young) humanity who would return them to the world of the living, had been a notable aspect of Romantic literature and art, which often sought to repeople the modern world with figures from the mythic past. This also had been an endeavor of the theater of the time, from Goethe and Schiller to Richard Wagner. The most extravagant of all such forms of spiritual vampirism in art had been the music-dramas of Wagner. It is the very theme of *The Flying Dutchman,* which Ibsen, in *The Lady from the Sea,* expanded to create a parable of our total biological history and destiny. This theme grows into the sublimely monstrous pantomime of the Ring Cycle, where a unique modern theater, Bayreuth, was created so that the modern German spirit could relive the mythic realities of the Nibelung and Eddic worlds: worlds inhabited by spirits, gods, dwarfs, giants, monsters, and heroes who were to be the agents of the cultural transformation of Germany. Thus the old gods and ghosts were made to walk again in order that they might repossess the modern spirit.

This theme appears also in Ibsen's early work and remained, though greatly amplified in scale and wealth of reference, in all his subsequent writing. Ibsen's historical and mythic dramas were attempts to revive the past within the present. In the modern plays, beginning with *Love's Comedy,* the relationship between the past and the present within modern humanity was more intricately explored and his attitude toward the past became more ambivalent. The past not only is a liberating perspective (e.g., of past greatness) upon the alienated and restrictive present; it also is the repository of a multitude of ghosts that inhibit the spirit's struggle for truth and freedom. In Marx's apothegm, "The tradition of all the dead generations weighs like a nightmare on the brain of the living." Jan Kott has indicated the similarity between these words and those of Helene Alving on the ghosts that haunt the present.[2] In every age we find that certain cultural themes exist on both a sublime and a banal plane. *Hamlet* coexisted with the crassest revenge melodramas. *John Gabriel Borkman* and *Dracula* belong to the same culture.

The dual nature of the spiritual past can be seen in the two trios in *John Gabriel Borkman*. Erhart's inversion of his father's history of renouncing love for power breaks with the self-condemning *coldness* of the Borkman spirit and links itself to the life-affirming forces represented by Mrs. Wilton: But, at the same time, Erhart's decision commits him to a lifestyle totally lacking the visionary, if perverse, grandeur of his father's spirit. Where Borkman draws the two women, Ella and Gunhild, into his drama and up to the heights, where he dies, Erhart is a somewhat weak and passive companion to Mrs. Wilton and Frida. The alternative *ideas of life* represented by the two trios goes beyond moral/psychological explanation and judgment to set up the terms for an archetypal drama in which much larger forces are engaged in conflict.

Silence and sound are telling theatric devices in Ibsen's theater, and in this play are used for powerful effect. The superbly uncanny sound of the unseen Borkman pacing over the world of Gunhild and her twin sister, which the audience hears without comprehending, then forgets to hear, suddenly to be startled into an awareness of its grim significance, is indicated by a rich contrast of silence and sound:

> GUNHILD. Always hearing his footsteps up there. From early morning until far into the night. And so loud, as if they were here in this room!
> ELLA. Yes, it's strange how the sound carries.
> GUNHILD. Often I have the feeling that I have a sick wolf pacing his cage up in the salon. Right over my head. (*Listens, then whispers.*) Hear that, Ella! Back and forth—back and forth, the wolf pacing.
>
> (Fjelde, 951)

Set in winter, in a world of snow, *John Gabriel Borkman* is the most "northern" in atmosphere of the last four plays in the cycle, recollecting, as we will see, figures from northern myth and legend. One of the many manifestations of the god Odin/Wotan, and one of the most typical, is that of the *wolf*. The manner in which Ibsen introduces Borkman's wolf-identity causes the audience to "register" it with maximum force. And this is only one of a number of such "northern" attributes given to Borkman and the other major characters. It was the caged wolf, Fenris, whose release would lead to the destruction of the northern gods and their world, to be superseded by Baldr the beautiful, and by the creation of a beautiful, warm, and fertile world—according to the Sybil's song that concludes the *Elder Edda*.

Another important detail of northern mythology worked into the play is that of the *gold-hoard* and the buried *metals*. In its imagery, this is the most "metallic" of Ibsen's plays. Act I opens with the metallic sound of sleigh bells, and closes with the swelling sound of the piano hammers striking the metallic strings. Deep within Borkman's mind, we will learn, is the sound of ghostly hammers striking at and releasing the metal ores within the mines, a sound that secretly punctuates the silence of his lonely exile. In the last act, just before he dies, Borkman not only sees his ghostly metallic kingdom come to life; he *hears* the thousands of hammers and machines creating a new world out of the liberated metals.

In *The Ibsen Cycle* I argued that *John Gabriel Borkman*'s action paralleled one phase of the sequence "Religion" that is the culmination of the *Phenomenology*. At this level, consciousness (Spirit—*Geist*) returns, at a "higher" level, to its earliest mythopoeic and religious awareness. That is, the modern mind must now stage a dramatic sequence in which it relives its gradual evolution, via art and religion, to full philosophic consciousness. It is only after we have relived the long dialectic that took us through the evolution of Hellenic and Christian cultures, culminating in the phase *Absolute Freedom and Terror (The Lady from the Sea)*, where modern Christian Europe was challenged by a renascent paganism and even a form of *militant* Hellenism (*Hedda Gabler*), that the modern consciousness, free of any constraining and limiting cultural context, can relive its highest spiritual conceptions.

For Hegel, this does not involve an abstract and detached survey. The last section of the *Phenomenology* is the most extraordinary of that most extraordinary work, for Hegel actually relives, mimes again, the ecstatic religious spirit and its experience. He reexperiences the worship of God as Light (*Bygmester Solness, The Master Builder*); the pantheistic world where plants and animals take on spiritual form (*Little Eyolf*); the religion of the worship of mineral forms (*John Gabriel Borkman*); and that of the artificer, working upon mineral forms until he evolves into the Spirit as Sculptor for the religion of the Hellenic spirit (*When We Dead Awaken*). Beyond this sequence, Hegel proceeds to modern theology, the death of God, "The Golgotha of the Absolute Spirit," and the philosophic consciousness which is a "realm of spirits."[3]

The "mineral phase" is divided into two activities. In one, the artificer creates riddling "ambiguous beings," half animal, half human, "a riddle to themselves." The second movement is dark, interior, worshipping the inward being of the minerals themselves. "And as yet this inner being is still simple darkness, the unmoved, the black formless stone."[4]

> Both representations contain inwardness and existence—the two moments of spirit: and both kinds of manifestation contain both moments at once in a relation of opposition, the self both as inward and as outward. Both have to be united. The soul of the statue in human form does not yet come out of the inner being, is not yet speech, objective existence of self which is inherently internal.[5]

It is only when the two sequences are joined, we see, that the statue can be given "speech" as the free human being. Passing through the "moments" of Hellenic religion, then Christianity, the dialectic arrives at a form of Christianized Hellenism or Hellenic Christianity—which reminds us of the goal of Ibsen's art—the third empire of spirit.

John Gabriel Borkman resembles the phase of the obscure, interior being of spirit, finding its symbol in the dark minerals, whereas Rubek, as the sculptor of the perfect human body, "Resurrection Day" in *When We Dead Awaken,* takes up the identity of Spirit as Artist. Hegel's metaphor for this sequence is taken from Egyptian religion (though the "dark stone"—the Kaaba of

Mecca—is both pre-Islamic and Islamic). Ibsen has employed this whole Religion sequence before, but *in reverse,* in Peer Gynt's retrogressive journey through modern consciousness, in Act IV, through Islamic (the Prophet), Christian, briefly Hellenic, then Egyptian roles, drawing upon the same metaphors as Hegel repeatedly used: the Memnon statue and its singing, and the Sphinx.

To link the northern cult of mineral forms to that of Hegel's "Egyptian" sequence is perfectly consistent, for, as I have noted, Hegel's uncited examples are ahistorical metaphors for moments within the spirit's evolution and therefore can be replaced by other metaphors from other cultures—as Hegel indeed did by linking Egyptian forms with the Kaaba.

The last four plays of Ibsen's cycle, like the final sequence in Hegel's *Phenomenology,* represent the modern spirit at its highest level of reflection upon the past spiritual forms, or dramas, that have gone into the creation of our modern identities. These reflective actions are *tragic* because these past forms must concede their necessary death. However imposing, "the monuments of past cultures are empty tombs" so that we each carry a necropolis within. But reflection brings life back momentarily to this necropolis and becomes the means by which we rediscover the depths of our identity.

The play strains the Realist method to the utmost. The appearances of the characters in the play have an "apparitional" quality enhanced by the pattern of very startling entrances and exits of each act. Each entrance by Ella, Gunhild, or Borkman is utterly *unprecedented,* as if, for all of them, there is a startling coming-to-life after long entombment. The play opens with Ella's unprecedented invasion of Gunhild's living room, from which, at the end of the act, she will as consequentially exit to enter, also for the first time, Borkman's upper salon. Then Gunhild, again without precedent, will dramatically enter the salon, after which Ella brings off the feat of getting Borkman, for the first time in eight years, to exit from his salon. He descends to Gunhild's room, which he has never before entered, terrifying the maid and startling his son. At the end of this act, he abruptly leaves the house, to the consternation of Ella. In the final act there is a general exodus, when *all* the characters leave the house, either to follow Borkman up to his Valhallah or Pisgah height where he will glimpse his ghostly empire or aborted promised land; or to follow Mrs. Wilton south, to warmth and a new life free of the fierce rivalries of Power, Love, and Honor that had sustained yet destroyed the older generation. This pattern of sudden, unprecedented appearances, of *invasions* by the main characters, of hostile and defensive territories which become scenes of intense conflict, creates a fierce, sagalike atmosphere and rhythm to the play (unlike any other in the cycle) which resembles that of *The Vikings at Helgeland.*

Against the impressive but cold trinity of Love (Ella), Honor (Gunhild), and Power (Borkman), Fanny Wilton establishes a contrary realm of values. She makes a striking *visual* contrast to the trio of the "grim and grizzled," as Henry James termed them. She is extremely attractive, with a ripe (*yppig*) figure, full red lips, playful and mischievous eyes, and rich, dark hair. The word *yppig,* as well as meaning "buxom," can be applied to vegetation with the meaning of lush and luxuriant; and to the earth, meaning fertile and rich (*life* rather than lifeless metals). Her link with vegetation and the natural forces, a Demeter-identity, is visually reinforced on her first entrance, when a lamp is lit for her in the rear garden room, adding a rich, green dimension to the hitherto cold and gray scene: a detail which a production can make vividly suggestive. As the garden room is never used in the play, the *only* function for this stage direction must be to link Mrs. Wilton to the *southern* values of life and warmth to which she later will draw Erhart and Frida, and it sets these values against the snow-covered world of the elder trio.

If Borkman has attributes of the northern god, Odin/Wotan, so Mrs. Wilton would seem to possess attributes of southern earth goddesses who were accompanied by young, subordinate male consorts, the role played by Erhart. It is only *after* Mrs. Wilton enters, establishing her forceful presence, that Erhart enters and adds his youthful and apparently subordinate presence to hers. In her richly furnished sleigh with its chiming silver bells, she will take her youthful companions south for sensuous self-fulfillment; whereas Borkman will draw *his* two gray-haired

companions-in-sorrow up to the cold of the hilltop for his visionary self-justification and their final reconciliation over his corpse.
Such a symmetrical contrast of the two trios has the formal quality of a dance: a dance of death versus a dance of life counterpointing each other. On one side, we feel the pull of earthly life
with its seductive beauty and its invitation to sensuous and sexual fulfillment. In the *other* direction we feel the equally as imperative pull of a visionary and spiritual force with *its* lure to
earth transcendence or transformation. There is no right and
wrong way here, but an imaginative presentation of the paradox
of human dualism, with its long duologue, over thousands of
years and many cultures, between the flesh and the spirit.

The comparative lack of specific social and familial *detail,* encountered again in the next and last play, *When We Dead
Awaken,* partly accounts, I think, for the often stark and melodramatic nature of the characters' speeches and gestures. They
communicate at a level of hortatory injunction that would be
impossible within the context of an intimately shared familial
consciousness:

> GUNHILD (*in passionate agitation*) You want to leave me!
> To be out with those strangers! With—with—no, I won't
> even think of it.
> ERHART. There are so many shimmering lights down
> there. And young, happy faces. And there's music there,
> Mother!
> GUNHILD (*pointing to the ceiling*) Upstairs there's music,
> too, Erhart.
> ERHART. Yes, it's that music *there*—that's what's hounding
> me out of this house.
> ELLA. Can't you allow your father a little chance to forget
> himself?
> ERHART. Yes, I can. I can allow it a thousand times over—if
> I don't have to hear it myself.
> GUNHILD (*looks reprovingly at him*) Be strong, Erhart!
> Strong, my son! Don't ever forget you have a great mission!
> (Fjelde, 965–66)

It is a testimony to the power of the play that it is able to survive passages such as these. The heavily handled references to the music (Saint-Saëns *The Dance of Death*) are bathetic. Gunhild's solemn upward pointing toward what even she must recognize as hardly an inducement to a young man to stay at home, Ella's inconsequential piece of pious solicitude, and Gunhild's grotesque invocation of Erhart's "mission" all create a pattern of exaggerated gestures and responses not rooted in any plausible human situation. Ibsen, I am convinced, intentionally makes the situation grotesque (for this is not the only such sequence), and this is typical of the bold stylistic incongruities he creates for this play; but even so, one cannot help but sympathize with the dilemma of the actors who have to speak lines of such emphasis with so little basis of support from a firmly established and plausible reality. The grotesquerie of the characters is, on the *psychological* level, not as interesting as that of Strindberg's *The Dance of Death,* whose characters have shifts of mood, startling surprises to spring on each other (and on us), abrupt relapses, and sudden new surges of sardonic energy in a rhythm psychologically more convincing than that of Ibsen's play. Ibsen's characters in *John Gabriel Borkman* are "mythic-grotesque," incongruous in the *scale* of their gesturing (Jan Kott has compared the play with *King Lear*), as if the heroic mode of *The Vikings at Helgeland* was transposed, almost without change, to a modern bourgeois household where this mode can be both mocked and honored. These are the awkward conditions the author accepts in order to rise to the thrillingly authentic heights of the last act, for only such odd instruments as these will be capable of the final, grave harmonies.

As a strictly realistic play, *John Gabriel Borkman* would merely be freakish; but the fact that the play is a strong contender for the title "Ibsen's greatest play" (Kott calls it "Ibsen's last masterpiece")[6] suggests that the play's real achievement is established on another plane than that of realistic plausibility. In fact, it is filled with incongruities, making it one of Ibsen's most unsettling dramas and one of the most difficult to grasp, as the very diverse judgments of the critics reveal. This is odd, for the dramatic *structure* has a classic symmetry and simplicity. The governing metaphor is that of a dead or frozen world reawakening to a last burst of life, a final summing up of itself before the total darkness descends. The spiritual condition depicted is fixed and static to an extraordinary degree: the husband and wife frozen for years in postures of noncommunication and into agonized waiting, he for his reinstatement to power, she for the restoration of a shattered honor, through the redemptive action of her son. Also waiting, and fixed, is Ella Rentheim, living for the moment when she can accuse and condemn her betrayer and reclaim the young object of her love, Erhart. Frozen thus, the characters suddenly come violently to life, like a statuary endowed with movement but fitting only awkwardly into a world of warm-blooded humanity. Their gestures are over-life-size, so that their evolution to the statuesque tableau of the closing scene seems a return their natural condition.

This somewhat marmoreal aspect of the elder protagonists seems a conscious intention on Ibsen's part, just as the fluid, painterly rhythms of the sea plays, *The Lady from the Sea* and *Little Eyolf,* seem formal choices. But for all the sculptural rigidity of the elder group the action of *John Gabriel Borkman,* once the curtain rises, is one of extraordinary mobility and rapidity: of sudden, unexpected, and fateful entrances and exits, of people hurrying to and from the house, upstairs and downstairs, in and out—a whirl of movement, like flurrying snow—quite unlike the rhythms of the other plays in this last group. There is an incongruity, therefore, between the fixed and frozen reality on which the elder trio broods and the rapid burst of life that will lead to the revaluation of that frozen past.

The northern and sagalike nature of the action is apparent in the bitter rivalry of the twin sisters, who fought in the past over Borkman and now resume the fight in order to possess his son, recalling the Hjordis-Dagny rivalry, adapted from the *Volsunga Saga,* of *The Vikings at Helgeland.* The northern, Nibelung themes of the fraudulent possession of gold, and of the buried gold-hoards, of the multiple betrayals involving the sacrifice of *love* and the consequent blighting of all life, are as prominent in this play as in Richard Wagner's adaptation of the mythic sources for the *Ring* cycle. The metallic sounds which Borkman continuously hears remind one of the startling score of *Das*

Rheingold, with *its* metallic hammering in the Alberich scenes. The conflict between Borkman and Hinkel resembles that between Wotan and Alberich. Like Wotan, Borkman had tried to bring a great empire into being by means of fraudulently obtained gold; like Wotan, he sacrificed love (Freia in the *Ring* cycle) to obtain power, but was to see his entire dream of empire, and its power, collapse. The twin sisters, Ella and Gunhild, have their equivalents in Freia and in Wotan's intensely jealous wife, Fricka, who, like the Greek Hera, was concerned above all with family honor. (Wagner was aware of, and developed, the Greek parallels to his northern pantheon, just as his cycle was to be a northern equivalent of the Aeschylean tetralogies.)

Behind the modern story of the defeated industrialist, therefore, is a historic, cultural, and archetypal past built, layer after layer, into the modern structure and texture. In Wagner's *Ring,* love is twice bartered, or betrayed, for gold-power, by Alberich as well as by his rival, Wotan, just as in Ibsen's play Ella is cynically bartered by Borkman. When Freia is taken from the gods in exchange for gold, they become old and gray, and the earth sinks into lifelessness. Ella will describe the death of love in herself in similarly mythopoeic and universal terms:

> ELLA. You're the guilty one. You put to death all the natural joy in me.
> BORKMAN (*anxiously*) Don't say that, Ella.
> ELLA. All the joy a woman should know, at least. From the time your image began to fade in me, I've lived as if under an eclipse. Through all those years it's grown harder and harder—and finally impossible—for me to love any living creature. Not people, nor animals, nor plants.
> (Fjelde, 987)

These words, which could have been spoken by the forsaken Freia or the desolate Demeter, are typical of the *universalizing* phrasing of the three main characters: of their depicting themselves and their situations in more than human terms. Here the imagery is of an *eclipse* and the loss of love toward *all life* and, a little later in the dialogue, of the world itself having become a *sterile desert.* If we refuse to grant that Ibsen, by this imagery, is building up a poetic/metaphoric structure extending beyond the presented realistic events, then we are denying to Ibsen the very conditions of his art. We should, rather, respond to the tantalizing oddity of "From the time your image began to fade in me . . ." and innumerable other such expressions, and then seek to establish an adequate poetic dimension to the realistic situation that better can account for such a language.

Such mythopoeic expressions and presences in the cycle are not evoked to add an exotic "spicing" to the realism. The supertext they draw upon and establish is an intellectually responsible one, lifting the action from the particular to the universal. In this play, with its highly poetic presentation of the unpoetic matters of finance and industry, theft and fraud, Ibsen most likely is pondering the deeper instinctual and spiritual origins of such a startling phenomenon in Western history as the total transformation, within so short a period, of our civilization by modern industrial capitalism, long recognized as a predominantly *northern* phenomenon. In *Brand,* Ibsen had deplored this development in the lines given to Brand describing the debasement of our modern humanity and our world by "Britain's smoke clouds," a development Brand feared would create a humanity unequal to its spiritual past. Commentators like Max Weber and R. H. Tawney have seen this development as rooted in the northern Protestant *ethos.* Ibsen would be likely to note the *continuity* in the northern consciousness from the earliest, mythopoeic times of the theme of the transformation of the world through metallic power. What is of particular interest is that Rousseau, describing this development, depicts it in terms of the loss of the natural and instinctual world closely resembling that of the northern mythopoeic account cited above. Of the man who turns from nature to the mineral world, Rousseau writes:

> He buries himself alive, and does well, not being worthy of living in the light of day. There quarries, pits, forges, furnaces, a battery of anvils, hammers, smoke and fire, succeed to the fair images of his rustic labors. The wan faces of the unhappy people who languish in the poisonous va-

pors of mines, of black forgemen, of hideous cyclops, are the spectacle which the working of the mine substitutes, in the heart [womb] of the earth for that of green fields and flowers, the azure sky, amorous shepherds and robust laborers upon its surface.[7]

Many myths and legends of the north describe the buried treasure whose possession confers power: of dwarfs who are miners and fashioners of metallic—especially gold—objects; of the false acquisition of gold and its powers, leading to the destruction of the possessor. In *The Perfect Wagnerite*, Bernard Shaw demonstrated how the overtly mythic and archetypal *The Ring of the Nibelungs* also was an allegory of the rise of modern industrial capitalism, and that Wagner's gods and heroes represented powers within the contemporary world. I am suggesting that *John Gabriel Borkman* reverses this; that its modern identities contain mythic and archetypal origins from which the modern identities evolved.

Ibsen gives Borkman and his obsession with the buried metals under the earth that same combination of the visionary and the unscrupulous that Wagner gave to his Wotan. Whereas Alberich had used the gold merely for greedy self-interest, without any higher purpose or vision, in the way that Borkman laments his contemporaries have done, Wotan, like Borkman, had wanted to use the power conferred by the gold for a transformation of the world. Borkman's heartrending lament over the debasement of his projected empire might well be the older, godlike vision bewailing the debasement of the metallic powers by the forces of modern industrial capitalism.

The northern pagan world heroized and spiritualized metallic forces, and its legends reveal a fascination with treasure hoards, with the reward to heroes of metallic weapons and ornaments which also were buried with dead heroes and kings. Such metallic objects were the symbols of honor and were avidly sought after. Yet these metallic powers also could be treacherous, especially to the discoverer of the buried hoards, which often had monstrous guardians. Such hoards carried a "curse" that was visited upon the discoverer, and Wagner's *Ring* cycle draws upon this tradition. The fascination with metals continues through the medieval world, in the alchemist's dream of absolute power over metallic forces, and into the period of industrial technology which was transforming the world Ibsen inhabited. If this is the theme of the drama, it is not a negligible one.

As the curtain rises we see that the stage is arranged to simulate an old-fashioned, fadedly elegant living room, which, we learn, is in a house on the Rentheim estate near the capital city. The rear of the stage is a glass wall looking into a garden room, just now darkened and obscure, and through the windows and glass door we can see a snowstorm whirling continuously. It is dusk and the action of the play is continuous, without a break in time. Against this cold and stormy background the first action of the play will be a fierce *conflict* where the twin sisters verbally combat each other. Though in modern dress, the scene recollects *The Vikings at Helgeland,* which opens, against a stormy background, with the two warriors, Sigurd and Ørnulf, engaged in combat. But before the combat between the sisters begins, we are confronted with a scene of *waiting* as Gunhild sits tensely by the window while the sound of pacing overhead by another waiting figure is heard. At the metallic sound of sleighbells Gunhild rises, exclaiming "Erhart! At last!" But it is Ella who interrupts Gunhild's vigil, as she will Borkman's in Act II.

The contrast between the two sisters represents a perennial female dualism going back to Ibsen's first play, *Catiline:* the contrast between the "Aurelia" (Ella) and the "Furia" (Gunhild) identities who emerge frequently in Ibsen's plays. This dualism includes such notable figures as Dagny and Hjordis, Betty Bernick and Lona Hessel, Beate and Rebekka West, Thea Elvsted and Hedda Gabler, and Irene and Maia of *When We Dead Awaken.* This dualism is as much rooted in the Western imagination as it is a personal obsession of Ibsen's and continually appears in our literature (and opera). In drama, we find it as early as Sophocles' *Antigone* and *Electra,* in the contrasting sisters, and it was present in the saga literature. In Ibsen, the contrasting women stand for alternative temptations to the masculine will, the "Aurelia" figure being gentle and supportive but luring the hero away from heroic action, while the "Furia" figure, though vengeful and dangerous, nevertheless inciting the protagonist to heroic action. *Hedda Gabler* perhaps sets out this dualism most clearly.

Ella's gentle features and abundant, though white, hair and her expression of suffering rather than of hardness contrast with Gunhild's colder, harder aspect. Usually the Aurelian heroine is unfitted for combat. Ella is the striking exception. She and Gunhild resume their long-abandoned battle within minutes of their meeting, fighting for possession of the young male, Erhart, as they once fought for possession of his father. Ella fights for the value of Love and her nature retains a selfless concern for others, whereas Gunhild ("I am always cold") is icily self-centered and single-minded. Though a whole host of others shared in Borkman's fall, Gunhild is overwhelmed only by the dishonor done to the name into which she married. To set right this injured honor, to create a new living work, Erhart, that by its brilliance will forever dispel the darkness of dishonor, is the single purpose for which she lives.

In the past Borkman had been like a "king" deferred to "throughout the land." But this glory and magnificence (*herlighet*) was shattered (*ramlet*) by the disaster of his fall. This fall seems a permanent one, but Gunhild passionately and hysterically anticipates a restoration (*oppreisning*). The persistent height-depth, falling-rising, darkness-light, storm-and-wreckage imagery that surrounds the history of this kingly figure strongly suggests a legendary rather than a prosaically actual event. The very movement of the four acts is built upon the metaphor of ascent-descent-ascent, each change of elevation being a "turning point" or peripety (see diagram).

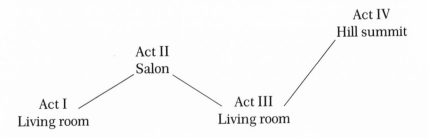

Act IV
Hill summit

Act II
Salon

Act I
Living room

Act III
Living room

The hero who Gunhild envisages will effect the brilliant resurrection is Erhart, the glorious boy (*herlige gutt*), who will restore "all that can be raised up" (*oppreises*). In this role he also will be the avenger (*hevner*) who will make pure all that Borkman has soiled. Such language, straining toward the mythopoeic, continuously weaves an archetypal pattern within the realistic one. The play's greatest stylistic incongruities derive from this collision of the archetypal with the everyday, and it is only when the realistic level is subordinated to the archetypal that the incongruities drop away. But the incongruities are an intentional effect and account for much of the fascination of the play.

Erhart had been rescued by Ella "when the storm broke over the house," but he later was reclaimed by his mother in order that he should live not for "happiness" but first and foremost that he should shine (*lyse*) so high (*høyt*) that none in the land should glimpse the shadow cast by his father. In spite of her confidence in Erhart's mission, Gunhild confesses that the memory of the old catastrophe breaks over her "like a storm" continuously. This repetition, within her mind, of the storm breaking over the house parallels Borkman's continual hearing of the hammers at work in the mines: two inward worlds that cannot communicate with each other.

As the sisters fiercely recount this old history, we suddenly are alerted to the sound of the "sick wolf" pacing above, and it would require something of a cultural lobotomy *not* to see the archetypal overtones in an action where, against a driving snowstorm, we hear the sick wolf pacing above the heads of the two women whose lives he has devastated.[8]

The vertical scenography is significant. Like Wotan, Borkman inhabits a realm of intellect, loftily "above" that of the passions, as he claims in his duologue with Ella later in Act II. In Wagner's cycle, Wotan has to *descend* to the passionate levels of Alberich, Sigmund and Sieglinde or Mime and Fafnir. Valhalla, created from Wotan's *thought*, stands high above the world of the *Ring* cycle, the world whose conflicting passions will bring about catastrophe. Alberich's realm of metallic power, like Borkman's visionary metallic kingdom, is *underground;* but Borkman's "kingdom" will be mountainous, so that Borkman is associated both with heights and depths: He is a *miner*'s son who climbed *high,* has even *soared*—as when he describes his most audacious exploit as a balloon voyage. He contemplated his most fateful action *below,* in a bank vault; yet with Ella, he spoke of his vision of a transfigured world while standing with her on a *height,* the hill with the tree. He was dragged *down* into disgrace and incarcerated but returns to live in the *upper* salon, reestablishing in his imagination his old proud vision. Ella will bring him *down* into the living room to confront Gunhild and the world of passions, but he rejects this realm and, with Ella, *climbs* the hill to speak once again his vision of a transfigured "kingdom." This vertical action and imagery is too emphatic to be ignored by interpretation, and, in fact, the last four plays in the cycle all involve heights and depths and all end with actions of ascent and the gradual recovery of the earthly landscape.

Though for eight years Borkman has not ventured out of his salon, his great cape and felt hat wait in the hall. The cloak and felt hat were Wotan's accoutrements, too: He appears in these in Wagner's *Siegfried,* and Borkman will wear them when he finally emerges in the moonlight. Much of Borkman's perversely visionary nature, so discomfiting to many critics, derives, I think, from this Odin/Wotan aspect of his nature; that is, his thought does reexplore the dimensions of the human imagination that could once give rise to the Odin myths.

Jacob Grimm, seeking to restore the northern myths after their long banishment from European high culture (they continued a subterranean existence in folk culture), saw Wotan as the figure who stands out most distinctly. As "Wish," he stands in closest contact with women who do the god's bidding, with the "wand" that unlocks the gold-hoards, with the mantle that carries him through the air (cf. Borkman's "balloon voyage"). The old legends of the gods remain and "to this day supply healthy nourishment to youth and the common people."[9]

In marked contrast to Borkman and the two sisters, Mrs. Wilton, in her way, is on as great a "scale." I noted that when she first appears onstage, a lamp is placed in the garden room, bringing to life for the first time the green hues of the natural world. No motive is given for thus placing the lamp in the garden room, which will not be entered: Gunhild merely directs the maid to do so when Mrs. Wilton is announced. Dressed in an evening gown beneath her fur coat, Mrs. Wilton establishes the presence of a completely different world to that of the Borkmans: one of sensuousness, munificence, and sexual fulfillment. She resembles the Bertha/Holda figure of northern myth as described in Grimm's *Teutonic Mythology* who, accompanied by her herald Eckhart (the name at least resembles "Erhart"), undertook riotously pleasurable journeys. Grimm also noted the affinity of this northern deity with the southern goddesses Aphrodite/Venus, Artemis/Diana, and Hecate, who cast spells and would "lead the ring of dancers."[10] Some such association is suggested in the curious little scene in which, trying to lure Erhart to the ring of dancers, Mrs. Wilton playfully warns that she will cast a spell on him:

> When I'm going along, I'll talk to myself—right out of my innermost will, and I'll say: "Erhart Borkman,—take your hat this instant! . . . he'll pick up his hat like a shot.
>
> (Fjelde, 962)

Erhart, not long after, desiring to leave the house and its Dance of Death, looks about the room and asks, "Where did I leave my hat?" The phrase that Mrs. Wilton uses is that she will cast *runes* over Erhart, and his laughing response, "Oh, really! Will you try *that* again," tells us that this is not the first "spell" episode between them. Clearly subordinate to her, Erhart is "under her spell" in the conventional sense, too, and because of his youthfulness, he is somewhat ill at ease in his role as her lover.[11]

It is uncertain if Erhart is Mrs. Wilton's only consort. In Act I Gunhild tells Ella that Mrs. Wilton's husband is dead, while in Act III she taunts her with the fact that this husband is still alive, which must be a slip on Ibsen's part, for there is no reason why Gunhild should lie. Mrs. Wilton admits that people say she is "wicked" (*uskikkelig*), which implies that Erhart is not her first lover. Erhart's youthful masculinity recollects such youthful consorts of older female goddesses as Tammuz, Attis, and Adonis, who especially were worshipped by women. Mrs. Wilton tells the company she has been "delegated by the ladies" to send for

Erhart and bring him to "room after room of shimmering festivities," rooms which are "teeming with young ladies" (Fjelde, 961), somewhat like a Venusberg. The struggle by *all* these ladies for the young man—Mrs. Wilton and her "ladies" on one side and Ella and Gunhild on the other—gives Erhart a gentle and somewhat passive aspect in strong contrast to his patriarchal father. Even on his journey south he will be shared by two females, Mrs. Wilton and Frida Foldal. Any reader of *Emperor and Galilean* will know that Ibsen was well versed in the mythology of the south, including the cults of Cybele-Tammuz and Aphrodite and Adonis. In *John Gabriel Borkman* there may be a contrast between a "matriarchal" south and a "patriarchal" north in the "binary" structure of the two contrasting trios, with, in each case, a male figure flanked by two females.

As Erhart exits in attendance on Mrs. Wilton, Gunhild and Ella, who had striven urgently to repossess him, now turn their attention from him completely, to resume their mutual hostility:

> GUNHILD (*after a short silence*) You've retaken him soon enough at any rate, Ella.
> ELLA. I wish I dared believe that.
> GUNHILD. But you're not going to hold him for long, you'll see.
> ELLA. Thanks to you?
> GUNHILD. To me, or—to her, that other one.
> ELLA. Better her than you.
> GUNHILD (*nodding slowly*) I understand that and say the same. Better her than you.
> ELLA. Whatever the end result for him—
> GUNHILD. That scarcely matters now, I think.
>
> (Fjelde, 966)

It is as if two spirits which urgently had tried to repossess a living young man now subside into indifference about his future. However, they will not be forced to relinquish him until Act III.

The conflict of passions in Act I had been played out in the lower realm of the house. For Act II we ascend to Borkman's more "intellectual" realm, where that remarkable figure paces up and down over the lives he has ruined, waiting, like a brooding, deposed monarch, for the repentant world to receive him again. At this height of consciousness Borkman will three times undertake his self-vindication: to Frida, to Vilhelm Foldal, and, finally, to Ella, the account gaining in depth and complexity with each retelling. To Frida, his account is the most simple and impressive; that of the miner's son, the visionary who, with his hammer that sounded like the midnight bell, intended to free the metallic spirits of the earth from their enchantment. He urges upon her his own pride in isolation: to remember that, though she does not join in "the dance of life," she has "ten times more music" in her "than all the dancers put together."

His impressiveness is amplified by the scenic background: the walls of the salon "covered with old tapestries, depicting hunting scenes, shepherds and shepherdesses, in faded, mottled colors" (Fjelde, 967). The faded tapestries with the pastoral and hunting scenes might suggest the natural world which Borkman, through his indifference to the world of passions, has blighted. This, we saw, *was* how Rousseau depicted the man who turned from the natural to the mineral, industrial world, renouncing the "green fields and flowers, the azure sky, amorous shepherds and robust laborers." Such a faded natural scene also visually "extends" Ella's description of the barren, love-deprived world caused by Borkman's betrayal. We notice that it is the female characters—Frida, Ella, and Gunhild—who exit or enter through the tapestried door (as if through this landscape), and it is the value of the feminine realm that Borkman most has offended.

Borkman's physical appearance could sustain the archetypal associations I have suggested for him. He is "distinguished, with a finely chiselled profile, piercing eyes, and curling, greyish white hair and beard" (Fjelde, 967). The impression is of distinction and power and this impression will remain, however perverse and even ludicrous he will appear at later moments. He is, he proudly declares, a miner's son (*en bergmann's sønn*). "Bergmann" derives from "berg" (mountain), an identity that contains both height (mountain) and depth (mines). In Ibsen's youthful poem, *The Miner* (*Bergmannen*), written in 1850, the miner feels

the compulsion to dig with his hammer down into the mountain
until he hears the ore sing:

> Nedad må jeg veien bryde
> til jeg hører malmen lyder

> Downwards I must carve my way
> Until I hear the ore sing

To Frida, Borkman repeats the words of Ibsen's poem: Der nede
synger malmen . . . Når den blir løsnet. Hammerslagene, som
løsner den,—det er midnattsklokken, som slår, og gjor dem fri."
("Down there, the metal sings . . . when the ore is loosened. The
hammerblows that loosen it—they're like the midnight bell that
sets them free.")

In the poem, the miner digs deeper and deeper into the depths
of the mine, which also is the heart's chamber hidden from the
world (*det dulgtes hjerteskammer*) and away from the confusing
light of the heights, searching for life's mysteries in its depths. In
Act V of *Emperor and Galilean*, Part 1, Julian turns from the
false light of the church and searches for the truth in the depths
and darkness of the catacombs. The metallic ore, gleaming in the
darkness which draws the miner from the world and its "glory"
(*dagens prakt*), quite clearly is a symbol for the buried spiritual
forces within the mind and within the depths of the world-spirit.
As Paul de Man reminded us, for Hegel the emblem "for inte-
riorized memory is that of the buried treasure, or mine."[12] For
Hegel, too, each individual mind was a world-mind, its buried
treasure being the universal possession of humanity.

Julian's descent to the depths and darkness of the catacombs
at Vienne was a search, like the miner's, for a source of truth not
to be found in the deceptive day-world above, where, in a blaze of
light, the wily priests of the corrupt church were busy creating
the lie of Helena's sanctity. In *John Gabriel Borkman*, where
Ibsen returns to this Hegelian metaphor of the buried treasure
within the mine, it is an actual world of metallic riches that
Borkman sought to control and release. That is, instead of the

metals taking on or symbolizing the spirit, the spirit has taken on metallic form, longing to be roused to life as actual metallic riches. (A memorable moment in the British National Theatre's production of the play was when Sir Ralph Richardson addressed the dark auditorium as his dark kingdom, so that we in the audience were the buried treasure Borkman lamented he had been unable to set free.)

The music that Borkman continually hears is that of the metallic spirits lamenting the postponement of their release, for, he declares, the ore "wants to come up into the daylight and serve mankind" (Fjelde, 968). Grimm, in *Teutonic Mythology*, notes the Germanic tradition of the buried ore imploring release, and connects this tradition to legends surrounding the god Odin/ Wotan. Of Wotan, Grimm observes, "The mythical aspect of *mountain prisoned* treasures, as of *mountain prisoned* heroes and gods, has led us to Wuotan the supreme maker and giver of all things to whom are known all hidden treasures."[13]

The name of Borkman's rival and enemy, Hinkel, at whose house Frida announces she will play and where Erhart was supposed to dance (for all this later will be revealed to be a subterfuge) derives from the verb *å hinke* (to limp) suggesting another of Ibsen's satanic references and, in this northern play, perhaps also a reference to the mischievous, limping god Loki, linked by tradition with the devil. William Archer noted that the Hinkel subplot seems designed to carry far more dramatic action than Ibsen actually supplies, for it seems elaborately built into the expositions of Acts I and II only to be abandoned by the succeeding acts. To have more thoroughly developed the Hinkel subplot would have required the elaborate dramatic plotting of the cycle's earlier style, and, in *John Gabriel Borkman,* this would have attenuated the effectively stark archetypal rhythm of the play. Yet the Hinkel story is important to the *archetypal* story of the love-power conflict, the bartering of Ella for gold and the false friend who toppled Borkman from the heights to the abyss.

After Frida exits, the powerful and dignified impression of Borkman is put in jeopardy, as if the hero must first undergo mockery as well as trial, before he can claim the right to heroic

status. Pacing the floor a number of times, Borkman hears someone approaching:

> *[He] quickly picks up a hand-mirror, studies himself in it,
> and adjusts his necktie. There is a knock on the sliding
> door. Borkman hears it, glances hastily toward the door,
> but remains silent. A moment later, the knock sounds
> again, louder this time.*

(Fjelde, 970)

Assuming the famous Napoleonic stance, his right hand thrust
into the breast of his coat, Borkman prepares to greet his visitor
impressively, only to have his whole stance deflated when that
visitor turns out to be "only" Foldal. Foldal's aspect, "a bent, worn
man, with mild eyes and long, thin grey hair" (Fjelde, 971), creates the strongest contrast with Borkman's forceful appearance;
but it is Foldal who will most endanger, through unconscious
parody, Borkman's tragic stature.

The relationship between the two is farcical and pathetic, revealing Borkman at his most vulnerably human. His grandiose
self-justifications continually are punctured by Foldal's inno-
cently devastating comments, so that their relationship is like
that of a disgraced king and his fool. It is not only the name, *Foldal*, that suggests a fool identity to serve Borkman's kingly identity;[14] his whole demeanor before Borkman sustains this identity.
His comic pathetic faith in his poetic vocation reminds us that
behind the medieval fool-identity lay the viking monarch's *skald*
or poet. The fool's relationship with his king was an uneasy one:
He could speak unwelcome truth, but, if he overstepped the
limit, he could be whipped or banished from the court, and this
latter happens to poor Foldal, who, after blurting out unwelcome
truth (his inability to believe in Borkman's restoration), is imperiously banished: "I've no more use for you" (Fjelde, 979).

One purpose of Ibsen's early dramatic career had been the
resurrection of the viking past, with its mythic and pagan consciousness, so that it would help to transform the spirit of the

modern Norwegian nation. This was the theme of his Prologue written in 1851 for a fund-raising celebration held to launch Ole Bull's Bergen theater. Ibsen proclaimed that, with the aid of drama, the northern king and his skald, frozen in winter and waiting to be released into modern life, *would* be resurrected, together with all the glories of the northern past. In this ardent enterprise Ibsen, as poet, continued to take part until his last re-creation of the northern world, *The Vikings at Helgeland*. The modern nation, Norway, however, went its own way.

To remain loyal to a past cheerfully ignored by the modern nation and "irretrievably different from present needs and concerns" would be both farcical and noble, and there is something of this situation, I believe, in the contrast between the older generation in the play passionately holding onto their past history of aspiration, suffering, and conflict and the amoral pragmatism of the younger generation, wholly indifferent to the past of their elders. Thus, from one point of view, Borkman and his companions are ludicrous and grotesque, and the play presents this judgment. But the play also presents the other point of view by which the characters attain the dignity of tragic expression. The dramatic method whereby Borkman is both mocked and finally honored is a subtle one and can lure interpreters (especially moralistic ones) into simplistic judgment; for it is only too easy to select the evidence that builds up a case against Borkman and to ignore the counteracting evidence that establishes, also, his authentic impressiveness.

Subtly ironic is the manner in which Borkman "appropriates" Foldal and expresses his indignation at the contempt his protégé suffers from his family. Foldal's situation is a bathetic version of Borkman's. He shared the "fall" that destroyed the financier and now shares his exile from the world, suffering, like Borkman, the hostility of his wife. He will lose a daughter to Mrs. Wilton as Borkman loses his son, and at the end of the play he will experience, in milder form, an "epiphany" paralleling Borkman's. To Foldal's daughter Borkman had conveyed his vision of the metal in earth waiting for liberation: to Foldal he expands this to describe his vision of the *world* he would have transfigured:

All the mines I could have controlled! Drilling new shafts, endlessly! Waterfalls! Stone quarries! Trade routes and shipping lines, girdling the globe. And all of these, I alone should have managed.

(Fjelde, 974)

In his account of his ruin through Hinkel's treachery over their love rivalry, Borkman treats as relatively unimportant what Ella will inflate into enormous significance. "Enough of these old, idiotic stories," he says, and, moments later, he as loftily belittles Foldal's central article of poetic faith: that somewhere in the world "the true woman is waiting to be found" (Fjelde, 978). The quarrel that ensues between the two repeats, now bathetically, the earlier history of two friends quarreling over the theme of "woman" and of Love-value.

With Foldal's dismissal, Borkman presumably has accepted the condition of total solitude until death. Putting out a lamp, he stands in semidarkness, a figure of tragic loneliness; but there follows a knock on the door and Ella emerges from the tapestried landscape, her lighted candle making her a center of moving light. This emergence from the tapestried landscape gives Ella the aspect of an apparition, of someone emerging from Borkman's own faded past, as if resurrected by his recent remembrance of her story. And this will be the brief resurrection, too, of Borkman.

And it is with Ella that Borkman will be forced into the most searching reexamination of this past as he proudly exonerates himself before her vehement accusations. Merely to note Ella's accusations and not to feel the force of Borkman's self-vindication (and its effect upon Ella) is to substitute Ibsen's subtle and complex play with a simplistic one. Borkman commences by again imperiously brushing aside the realm of *passions:* "Let's not get into feelings and such . . ." and immediately presents his defense of his longing for *power (evnen).* Power, to Borkman, was as much an absolute value as Ella's Love or Gunhild's Honor. Each of these characters expresses a loyalty to the single universal they personify, with an almost fanatic exclusion of other values. Thus Ella describes her loss of Borkman's love as an enormity in the world, as the unnamed crime against the Holy Ghost; but her assessment of the offense against her can no more be endorsed uncritically by the audience than can the self-valuations of Borkman and Gunhild.

Borkman describes his great aborted gamble as a godlike aerial voyaging, a balloon journey over a shadowy, perilous ocean. This *highest* of his aspirations immediately is denounced by Ella, both the aspiration and the denunciation rivaling each other in *scale* of expression. To her impassioned outcry that Borkman is guilty of a double murder, of her soul and his own, Borkman replies *"with cold self-control"*:

> How well I recognize that overbearing passion in you, Ella. I suppose it's very natural for you to see this the way you do. You're a woman. And so it seems to your mind, that nothing else in the world exists or matters.
>
> ELLA. Yes, nothing else . . .
>
> BORKMAN. But you have to remember that I'm a man. As a woman, to me you were the dearest in the world. But in the last analysis, any woman can be replaced by another.
>
> ELLA (*regarding him with a smile*) Was that your experience when you took Gunhild to marry?
>
> BORKMAN. No. But my life's work helped me to bear *that,* too. All the sources of power in this country I wanted at my command. The earth, the mountains, the forests, the sea—I wanted to subjugate all the riches they held, and carve out a kingdom for myself, and use it to further the well being of so many thousands of others.
>
> ELLA (*lost in memory*) I know. All those many evenings that we talked about your plans—
>
> BORKMAN. Yes, I could talk with you, Ella.
>
> ELLA. I used to joke about your projects and ask if you wanted to wake all the slumbering spirits of the gold.
>
> BORKMAN (*nods*) I remember the phrase. (*Slowly*) All the slumbering spirits of the gold.
>
> ELLA. But you didn't take it for a joke. You said: Yes, yes, Ella, that's exactly what I want.
>
> (Fjelde, 986)

In spite of her accusation against Borkman, Ella, we see, is won over again to his vision as they re-create, between them, their past communion. Her spirit is stirred and expanded by the scale of Borkman's vision, just as his vision is deepened by the Love-value of Ella. Love now floods his perception of the metallic power he longed for so that his last speech to that power will be a declaration of love. It is Ella who has revived this in Borkman, who "brings out" of him aspects of his vision that he could not communicate to Frida or to Foldal. He had dreamed of bringing a whole new world to life, begetting upon the metals a new world order. Year by year, with Hinkel's help, he had climbed "toward the enticing heights [I] longed for" until his rival "toppled [me] into the abyss." With this fall, Borkman's new world vanished also. Ella pronounces that their whole relationship has had a curse (*forbannelse*) laid upon it.

This imagery of long gradual ascent to enticing heights, of a fall into an abyss and the curse upon a relationship, is part of that process of weaving the mythopoeic pattern behind the realistically presented one, establishing its terms so that they can be taken up fully later. This process is continued in Ella's succeeding comments:

> You're the guilty one. You put to death all the natural joy in me . . . All the joy a woman should know, at least. From the time your image began to fade in me, I've lived as if under an eclipse. Through all these years it's grown harder and harder—and finally impossible—for me to love any living creature. Not people, nor animals, nor plants. Only that one . . . Erhart . . . I've never known any compassion— since you left me. I'm wholly incapable of that. If a poor starving child came into my kitchen, freezing and weeping, and begged a little food, then I left it up to my cook. I never felt any urge to take the child in myself, warm it at my hearth, and enjoy sitting by, watching it eat its fill. And I was never like that in my youth; I remember so clearly. It's you who've made this sterile, empty desert within me—and around me, too.
>
> (Fjelde, 987–88)

The generalizing, even universalizing, effect of this syntax, in which we see a world under a solar eclipse (*solformørkelse*), where people and animals do not receive the blessing of love from Ella, a winter world in which "*if* a child came into" her kitchen (thus implying a recurrent, not a single, episode) it was not fed by her, and in which a sterile desert has been created within and around her, suggests that Ella was a potential force for natural warmth and love that has been extinguished from the world. And the external scene of the play is a winter world of snow. In both the Eddic and Nibelung sources there is the tradition of the "curse" upon those who possess or attempt to possess the buried treasure, and of the punishment of gods and men for the sacrifice of love for gold. Of course, if "real life people" spoke as Ella, Gunhild, and Borkman speak, we would not search for archetypal but for psychopathological explanation: But on the stage space of Ibsen's theater, such speeches, at which not just Borkman but the whole audience is paying attention, and which are "paced" and timed to maintain a rhythm and build up a dramatic design, will not be *heard* in the way we hear real-life speech.

On the strictly psychopathological level of interpretation, which some have attempted, one would have to decide that the elder trio suffers from multiple megalomania; but it is far more rewarding to experience the play as a *psychomachia:* a conflict of spiritual forces, going back to the furthest past of our race, which far transcends psychological, sociological, or moral explanation. To attempt to judge Borkman, for instance, in conventional moral/psychological terms is to prevent the power of the figure on the stage from fully working on us. We should respond to the gods and demons of Ibsen's theater with the same thrilled but fearful attention, feeling the same ambivalence toward these alarming apparitions, as the spectators of oriental theater feel toward *their* god-and-demon-filled stage. I have suggested that Ibsen's theater has something in common with shamanistic ritual and this is why it is so successful as *theater*. The visionary longing for dominion over the earth, the equally as powerful longing for a world transformed by the power of love and the desire for honor and glory, which are the animating principles of Borkman, Ella, and Gunhild—and which are opposed by the equally as imperative demands for erotic fulfillment and happiness represented by the younger trio—are the subjects not only of the modern individual's most inward dreams and fantasies but also of the earliest mythic expressions of the race.

And with an imaginative production, the archetypal dimensions of the drama can be experienced by audiences who will be moved and excited by an action that, on the strictly realistic level, contains inconsistencies and incongruities that any competent critic can point to. All drama that achieves archetypal significance—all major drama, that is—will find itself having to sacrifice strict realistic credibility to establish its more universal intentions. The competent drama critic or academic interpreter, coming to Ibsen with preconceived notions as to Ibsen's place in the evolution of dramatic realism, and convinced as to what is or is not permitted by realism, probably is able to see less of the play than the uninstructed playgoer with a good capacity to respond to theater. I have been part of an audience to *John Gabriel Borkman* and have seen how the play gradually trains its audience to accept, excitedly, the visionary last speeches and gestures of the play: of Borkman's ascent to the height, his address to his ghostly kingdom, of the emergence of the invisible metal hand that clutches his heart, and of the final reconciliation of the twin sisters over the corpse of the man they have fought over. In the counterpoint of realistic and mythopoeic speech and action, it is the latter that establishes itself as the dominant "melody."

It is this larger-than-life aspect of the characters that makes somewhat incongruous, on the *realistic* level, the desperate battle of the sisters for Erhart's allegiance. As Ella gains Borkman's consent to Erhart adopting the Rentheim name, the tapestry door is flung open and Gunhild appears, passionately to oppose the project. The sudden apparition in the invisible doorway has much of the effect of a supernatural manifestation, uncannily on cue. (In naturalistic performance this apparition is uncomfortably melodramatic and needs careful handling. Wagner can get away with similar sudden appearances and disappearances because he has created a stage on which everyday reality is never allowed to intrude. But Ibsen is undertaking a more hazardous enterprise. He wishes to lead his audience from one level, the realistic, to another, the mythopoeic and archetypal, and it must be conceded that, until we reach the highest flying level some of the stages of the ascent are alarmingly bumpy.) Thus, Erhart's situation is worked up into one of extreme urgency, as Ella cries out, "John Gabriel—Erhart's bound to go down in this storm," an appeal which convinces Borkman that, for the first time since his incarceration, he must descend and confront Gunhild. Yet, in the ensuing action, Erhart, far from being in danger of going down in the storm, is all too evidently sunnily immune, and easily abandons the world of the sisters altogether.

Act III is divided into two actions: In the first Borkman appears in the living room and, with fine demonic force, vindicates himself before Gunhild, pronouncing his own acquittal. His merely *legal* crime was justified, he asserts, because he alone had the vision and power to release the "buried millions" (*bundne millioner*) that "lay everywhere, deep in the mountains, all over the country, crying out to me, crying out to be freed" (Fjelde, 997). Only his long self-incarceration in the salon is a matter for reproach, a waste of eight valuable years in which he should have gone out and encountered hard reality again and, once more, to have "begun at the bottom and raised myself up to the heights again—higher than ever before—in spite of what intervened" (Fjelde, 997). To Gunhild's cold response that he merely would have repeated the disgrace of the past, he asserts:

> Nothing new ever happens. But whatever has happened never repeats itself either. It is the eye that transforms the action. The newborn eye transforms the old action.
>
> (Fjelde, 997–98)

The spiritual change within the perceiver changes the nature of the thing perceived. But Gunhild denies that Borkman is reborn or has any role to play in the world: He is dead and his past shame is to be obliterated by means of a *monument*, the same action of the monument serving to erase the past as Helene Alving attempted in *Ghosts*. This monument is to be Erhart, who, however, now "bursts open the hall door" (*river ilsomt entredøren opp*) to oppose his youthful joy-of-life against his mother's manic and life-denying idealism. The somewhat ghostly aspect of the play, where Ella, Gunhild, and Borkman in turn futilely beckon toward Erhart like exiled spirits seeking to inhabit living flesh and blood, was noted by Bernard Shaw, who commented: "This melancholy household of the dead crumbles to dust at the knock of the younger generation at the door. . . . The fresh air and the light break into the tomb; and its inhabitants crumble into dust."[15]

Erhart's reactions to the overtures of the elders, until Mrs. Wilton's appearance, have a strangely formal and even mechanical quality. His stubborn bid for independence against their implorations to join them dutifully in love (Ella), honor (Gunhild), and power (Borkman) has much of the quality of an allegorical conflict. The scene indeed seems an ironic inversion of the conventional temptation scene in allegory where the young knight is tempted to be unfaithful to such virtues by being unchaste. Here, on the contrary, the young knight of Venus (an unrepentant Tannhäuser) must withstand the ghostly temptations to fidelity, love, and honor before he can claim his sensual prize, which he does, at last, by calling Mrs. Wilton into the room. In the bitter quarrel that follows between Gunhild and Mrs. Wilton, the latter easily is victorious and the life-forces of Erhart, Frida, and Mrs. Wilton now journey to the warmth of the south, choosing a life of casual alliances, lived for the moment only, in contrast to the rigid and fixed allegiances of the elders. What is discarded by the hedonist trio is the life transcending, the visionary; and it is with this latter that the play now remains, allowing it a supreme utterance. In a fine study of the play, Charles Leland has insisted on taking the play's tragic rhythm in good faith and thereby according the protagonists, including Borkman, the high status that such a rhythm confers. This status is not arrived at easily: As we saw, the play daringly permits other, less flattering perspectives on Borkman before presenting him, at last, as a tragic hero.

The play that began in late evening now ends, outdoors, in the dark of night; the moon shining through the scudding clouds, making a continuous play of light and shadow on the scene and characters. Though, as Jan Kott has observed, the play does not need mechanical stage devices to project the scenery, for "Landscape here is evoked by two contradictory voices: Borkman's and Ella's,"[16] imaginative staging of the winter scene would carry much of its meaning: the starkness of the snow-covered background and the dead tree being played off against the human drama.

There is one final brief flurry of agitation as Gunhild cries out after the fleeing sleigh carrying Erhart south, after which the play proceeds on a superbly *reflective* level, anticipating the mood throughout of the Rubek-Irene scenes of *When We Dead Awaken*. Borkman, "*as if awakening,*" refuses ever to return to the house, or to any interior, again. (The next play, incidentally, will be entirely out-of-doors.) To the literalist, this only can mean that Borkman has gone mad; but it is evident that Ibsen does not think Borkman is mad. He is being driven now by the awakened spirit, and with this awakening he fully recovers his visionary power and his human greatness. He will not be a "mature and responsible" bourgeois, to be sure, sensibly concerned about his own health and Ella's; he will be more like a *tragic* hero who will articulate the idea of a *tremendous* loss, moved, like the old Oedipus, to a hard but enthralling intransigence which sees beyond the horizons of the everyday vision.

This emerges in his exchanges with Foldal, following the latter's Chaplinesque appearance, limping, with a broken umbrella, without his spectacles, to narrate naively the circumstances of Frida's flight south and of his own accident. Borkman, hugely amused, sees everything falling into place. In Act II Borkman had described the collapse of his empire through the treachery of Hinkel in the following words:

> FOLDAL. But he [Hinkel] rose to the heights.
> BORKMAN. And I went to the depths.
> FOLDAL. Oh, it's a terrible tragedy—
> BORKMAN (*nodding to him*) I guess, almost as terrible as yours, when I stop to think about it.
> FOLDAL (*innocently*) Yes, at least as terrible.
> BORKMAN (*with a quiet laugh*) But from another perspective, it's really a kind of comedy, too.
>
> (Fjelde, 976)

In *that* exchange, Borkman's awareness of the tragicomedy of his situation had been sardonic and resulted in a somewhat cruel, though secret, joke against Foldal, who had written a terrible tragedy. Now, in Act IV, Borkman's laughter is not at Foldal's expense: On the contrary, with big-hearted tenderness, he carefully keeps his friend unaware of the implications of Frida's traveling with Mrs. Wilton and Erhart, and his vision of the tragicomedy of things is Promethean in scale. Unlike Borkman, poor Foldal would be wholly incapable of taking in the larger scheme of things, which includes acceptance of the scandalous *ménage à trois*. Kept in ignorance, Foldal is permitted his limited epiphany, his joyful perception of a wonderful pattern behind the misfortunes of his life. This is not a full *anagnorisis* such as Borkman will undergo, for Foldal never was large-spirited enough to see life in its totality, as Borkman now can. It is his fine responsiveness to the comic pathos of Foldal's situation and of the larger ironies of the human condition that assures us that Ibsen intends Borkman's "awakening" as authentic.

After Foldal hobbles happily out of sight, overjoyed that the sleigh that ran over him carried his daughter, Borkman sends after him a tender benediction and farewell: "Goodbye, Vilhelm! It's not the first time in life you've been run over, old friend" (Fjelde, 1018). Borkman's action now, of leaving the house and ascending the snow-covered hill, is suicidal; but he and Ibsen are responding to a poetic logic where, as in *Brand*, the attainment of *physical* height symbolizes a *spiritual* ascent: a topographic notation typical of the European idealist tradition. The house disappears from the stage before our eyes—the only such stage effect in the whole cycle—and this, I believe, signals the cycle's abandoning of the last confining habitation of the human spirit. To get to the height, he and Ella, Borkman announces, must "go up the winding path" (*krokete stien*).[17] At the top, he will look again on his buried treasures and bring to life again, in his own spirit, the world he once sought to create but which now lies lifeless under the snow. The scene around him changes to accord with his changing perception, giving way to a wilder and wilder landscape, until he reaches the height where, in the now-clear moonlight, there is revealed "*an expansive landscape, with fjords and high, distant mountain ranges towering one after another"* (Fjelde, 1020). Borkman, like a magician, now brings his whole ghostly kingdom to life, seeing smoke from the steamers that would have sailed out of the transfigured fjord, to "make the whole round earth into one community." He *hears* the uncreated factories whirring as the night shift continues the unceasing activity of his "empire," which itself becomes infinite:

> Do you see those mountain ranges over *there*—far off. One after another. They leap skyward. They tower in space. That's my deep, my endless, inexhaustible kingdom!
>
> (Fjelde, 1021)

Borkman's *religion* had been to transfigure the world through other than human means: through the metallic and mineral forces of the earth, just as Wotan had sought the same means to establish *his* empire over the world. This displacement of love from human to metallic forces, from love to power, is an aberration; Hegel declared that such work received spirit into it "as an alien, departed spirit, one that has forsaken its living suffusion and permeation with reality and, being dead, enters into these lifeless crystals."[18] This also was the verdict of Rousseau upon this form of spiritual activity, but, with Borkman, the aberration is an impressively visionary one. Though Ella indicts this aberration— with an intensity as megalomaniacal as Borkman's—the indictment would have no force had Borkman's love not been a magnificent thing. It is just this displacement of instinctual powers from the immediate gratification that Erhart and Mrs. Wilton seek, onto alternative forms (sublimation), that has created the most impressive achievements of human history. As Derrida comments on Rousseau's indictment, "And let us not forget that the violence that takes us toward the entrails of the earth, the moment of mine-blindness, that is, of metallurgy, is the origin of society. For according to Rousseau, as we shall often confirm, agriculture, marking the organization of civil society, assumes the beginning of metallurgy."[19] Every great and distinct human culture, for instance, is an aberration, founded upon the creative distortion of our "given" instinctual and natural identity. In *When We Dead*

Awaken, Ibsen will confront instinctual and *natural* man and woman (Ulfheim and Maia) with intricately convoluted *cultural* man and woman (Rubek and Irene), surveying, in the contrast between the two pairs, as it were, the history of the species. The great industrial-capitalist world of the present, which the Borkman spirit might have transformed into a civilization, is only the latest of our long succession and distortion of instincts.

It is only the visionary and dynamic imaginations in the human herd, the *demonic* ones, who are capable of such magnificent aberrations. Every great culture that has made its mark upon the world is an imaginative transformation of our humanity, what Reinhold Niebuhr, in *Beyond Tragedy,* termed "a tower of Babel." To remake our human identity as Hegel insisted men in the French Revolution had set out to do is to wield the powers of the gods, and Ibsen, working to bring about "a third empire of spirit" that would transform our species, was not unwilling to take on such godlike power.

In *Civilization and Its Discontents,* Freud pessimistically saw this process by our species of displacing and distorting instinctual energies into necessarily repressive cultural forms as both essential and fatal to civilization; creating psychical and social pressures that inevitably will erupt and destroy us. The long self-examination that Ibsen has been conducting in the cycle, which, like the *Phenomenology,* also is an examination of our species, represents, I believe, his effort to name the forces operating upon the modern spirit, forces that go back into our pre-history and of which the earliest mythic expressions were the first embodiments and the foundation of all that followed.

Borkman's betrayal of the "warm living human heart" of Ella, for "the kingdom—and the power—and the glory" of his empire, can stand for humanity's repeated betrayal of instinctual life for transcendent achievement. Erhart, by refusing to make this betrayal, will never have to face the indictment that Ella makes to Borkman; but neither will he raise his companions to the heights that Borkman and his companions painfully attain.

"The kingdom—and the power—and the glory" are, in traditional Christianity, the province of God only. The act of appropriating this divine province on behalf of humanity is a Faustian blasphemy, a leaguing with dubious powers (as with Solness's "helpers and servers") to which a number of Ibsen's heroes are driven, beginning with Brand. Julian, in *Emperor and Galilean,* boldly appropriates the same words from the paternoster to use in his campaign *against* Christianity. In the same way, we saw, Ibsen's "third empire of spirit" is a "blasphemous" endeavor, like Hegel's, to relocate the divine onto the earth. Borkman's choice of words therefore suggests that his "crime" against Ella is inseparable from his greatness. In the most thrilling speech in the entire cycle, Borkman, in what is at the same time a hymn and a declaration of love, carries us to the heart of his vision. Lamenting that his great, aborted empire "now lies there—defenceless—exposed to the rape and plunder of thieves"—that is, to men and women lacking his vision, he feels that empire stir to life in response to his grief, in the form of a *breath* from the earth-spirits:

> Det pust virker som livsluft på meg. Det pust kommer til meg som en hilsen fra underdanige ånder. Jeg fornemmer dem, de bundne millioner; jeg føler malmårene, som strekker sine buktede, grenede, lokkende arme ut efter meg. Jeg så dem for meg som levendegjorte skygger—den natt da jeg sto i bankkjelleren med lykten i hånden. I vill frigjøres den gang. Og jeg prøvde på det. Men jeg maktet det ikke. Skatten sank i dypet igjen. (*med fremrakte hender*) Men jeg vil hviske det til jer her i natte-stillheten. Jeg elsker eder, der I ligger skinndøde i dypet og i mørket! Jeg elsker eder, I livkrevende verdier—med alt eders lysende følge av makt og aere. Jeg elsker, elsker, elsker eder!
>
> (S.V. III)

> That breath works like the air of life on me. That breath comes to me like a greeting from captive spirits. I can see them, the millions in bondage: I can feel the metallic veins stretching their curving, branching, tempting arms out to me. I saw them before me like living shadows—that night I stood in the bank vault with a lantern in my hand.

You wanted to be set free then. And I tried to. (*His hands outstretched*) But I'll whisper this to you here in the stillness of the night. I love you, lying there, smothered in the depths and darkness. I love you, you riches craving life, with all your shining retinue of power and glory! I love, love, love you!

(My translation)

From the underground comes a *breath* that acts upon Borkman like the "air of life" (*livsluft*): the vampire theme of the breath of the dead awakening into the world of the living. This breath is the greeting from the enslaved (*underdanige*) spirits, the bound (*bundne*) millions of ghost slaves craving liberation. The veins of ore stretch out their curving, branching, luring/tempting arms, with the suggestion not just of imploring release into the living world of men and women but also of luring the beholder into a ghostly trap, as in the numerous fables of the spirits of the hoards who seek to trap those from the living world. Grimm records many of these northern myths and fables, often associated with Odin/Wotan, of treasures asking release and (as Borkman laments) sinking back again:

> It is supposed that the treasure *moves* of itself, i.e. slowly but steadily strives to come to the surface. . . . At an appointed time the treasure is up and waiting to be released; if then the condition fails, it is snatched away into the depths once more. . . . It ripens in most cases every seven years, in some only every hundred, and that especially under a full moon.[20]

Grimm notes that to get into the mountain where the treasure is concealed, "one usually needs a plant or root to clear the way,[21] which might provide the significance of the dead tree by which Borkman and Ella now stand, as they used to stand when the tree was alive and when Borkman might have gained the treasures and achieved power. Now, under a full moon, they survey the kingdom again. For Borkman, it does come to life again and begins to move. To Ella, it must remain forever dead.

Ella will charge that Borkman betrayed the world of the living for that of the dead. In the image of the ghost slaves lifting imploring and tempting arms to Borkman, who responds to them from the depths of his heart, we see the appalling and magnificent perversity of one who could be so deeply moved by the imprisonment of metals. When he stood in the bank vault contemplating his crime, these ghostly images appeared to him like animated shadows, the flickering light of the lamp making the shadows move as if alive. They begged to be set free from their slavery, but he lacked the power and so they sank back into the depths and darkness. Now Borkman addresses this shadow world again in the stillness of the moonlit night with his great declaration of love—a demon addressing demons. He wished to bring all these spirits and powers and "all their shining retinue of power and glory" up into the world, using the *limited* resources of the bank to get access to the *unlimited* resources of the infinite hoards of life-craving riches (*livskrevende verdier*) which still lay "smothered" (*skinndøde*), needing the air of the upper world in order to breathe and live. By betraying the living, human world to serve this shadow world, Borkman has turned the living, Ella and Gunhild, into mere shadows, a form of the living dead. (It is perhaps this attempt to raise a dead world to life that accounts for his second name, Gabriel.)

As Ella accuses Borkman of killing the power of love "in the living human heart" that beat for him, and as she prophesies that "you will never ride in triumph into your cold, dark kingdom!" (Fjelde, 1022), a cold, invisible, metallic hand eerily reaches upward from that kingdom and clutches Borkman's heart in a demonic love response. That action suggests more than the conventional punishment for the sinner of dragging him down to the infernal regions, for the powers that Borkman sought to release were not necessarily infernal, but potentially liberating. If Borkman is deficient, as many critics hasten to insist, it is the deficiency of a hero still far above *our* level; and he is deficient because the spirit of modern humanity, which Borkman exemplifies, is crucially deficient.

The closing image, of the two sisters, hands outstretched in mutual forgiveness as they stand on either side of the fallen hero, has, I claimed, a sculptural quality which further enhances the essentially non-naturalistic nature of the play and may represent an anticipation of the "sculpture" metaphor of the next play. *John Gabriel Borkman* reminds us that the major characters of the cycle exist apart from the categories of respectable mediocrity with which our psychological and moral judgments are at home. Like all major dramatic characters, they hazard commitments of the spirit that can run the risk of guilt and unhappiness and even of self-destruction, like Sophocles' Ajax or Euripides' Herakles: But the dramas they thereby instigate light up and exemplify essential (archetypal) aspects of our spiritual life.

Such moments as Ella's fierce, rhetorical denunciation of Borkman, his majestic self-exoneration and declaration of love, his death and the tragic reconciliation of the twin sisters over his corpse resemble the epiphanies of Greek drama, a revealing of the powers that our everyday life obscures or evades. Throughout the cycle we come upon such manifestations of spirit. The forces that were so tragically divided during Borkman's life and which I designated Power, Love, and Honor are brought together in Borkman's great address to the metallic powers, where he invokes the retinue of *power (makt)* and *glory/honor (aere)* in a declaration of *love*. These are values for which men and women from the beginning of human history have been willing to sacrifice happiness: the happiness of oneself or of others. These forces animate and agitate human activity endlessly, however diverse the forms they take in one human culture after another. When each of these forces elevates its value exclusively and to the utmost, as each does in the personifications of Gunhild, Ella, and Borkman, tragic conflict is inevitable.

The realistic action of *John Gabriel Borkman* is a modern (i.e., nineteenth century) one, but the archetypal patterns raised by this realistic action return the modern moment to its archetypal heritage. To the vision of Borkman, "The earth is like glass beneath his feet, and the miner's son can see clairvoyantly the cold arms, the winding veins of precious metals reaching longingly out to him, entreating release into the daylight and the service of mankind" (Fjelde, 940) beneath the surface, and hidden from the ordinary gaze. Likewise the poet, Ibsen, looking at his contemporary world, is able to see the forces, both alluring and dangerous, going back to the distant past, that also crave release to serve once again a liberated humanity.

The emphatic use, in all four last plays, of a "vertical" action and landscape seems linked to a movement of *spiritual* ascent by characters for whom consequential *horizontal* extension is ruled out: that is, the major protagonists—Solness, Allmers and Rita, Borkman, Ella and Gunhild, and Rubek and Irene—seem to have reached a "sticking place" from which the only possible movement is ascent, in contrast to the horizontal movement permitted to Hilde Wangel, Borgheim and Asta, Erhart and Mrs. Wilton, and Ulfheim and Maia. In the cycle, the invitation to the most tremendous horizontal voyage was made by the Stranger in *The Lady from the Sea,* a play that I have seen as the "turning point" in the cycle. Horizontal exploration entails leaving one's home base, as Hilde Wangel does, irrevocably, in *The Master Builder*. Vertical movement means exploring the levels of the given, to which one is fixed. The conjunction of these two movements in Ibsen's last plays and which, in *John Gabriel Borkman,* is actually represented by two contrasting trios, of different generations, would seem to set up a contrast of two modes of exploration: one (the horizontal) into the future with little of the burdened memory of the past; the other filled with the past and making its peace with it, at the "highest" level of reflection. The perilous enterprise the poet asks us to share with him is to take part in a vertical journey in which we have to leave behind, as dead weight, our usual moral and psychological presuppositions as we ascend to a more adequate and authentic self-exploration.

I have described Ibsen's intentions in terms unfashionable in Ibsen studies and in current critical theory. In my view Ibsen neither wished to moralize about his world nor to present us with secretively confessional "codes" about his private life and his personal, inner problems and doubts. I believe, instead, that Ibsen wished above all to give the greatest possible significance of achievement to the identity of dramatic poet that he took upon himself, just as Brand sought to give the identity of priest the deepest and highest significance. This represented a form of aesthetic heroism, of striving always to live up to, and not to debase, his adopted identity, so that it could become a supremely valuable presence within, or essential aspect of, our humanity. It was in this way alone, as he wrote to Brandes (using a Borkmanesque metaphor), by "coining the metal" within oneself that one would best serve the human community. This project of artistic self-realization, beside which the world could be considered as "simply non-existent," might seem to some a monstrous egotism in which the achievement of the supreme artwork is gained at the expense of the development of the self within the human community. But Ibsen did not simply remake his self by becoming a supreme dramatic poet: He changed the nature of the human community. And if the depth, width, and truth of his exploration of his universal humanity meant resurrecting also such disturbing forces as those explored in *John Gabriel Borkman,* that only increases the value of his psychoanalysis of the *Weltgeist.*

Notes

PREFACE

1. Charles Segal, *Interpreting Greek Tragedy: Myth, Poetry, Text* (Ithaca, New York: Cornell University Press, 1986), 49.
2. Ibid., 49–50.
3. Ibid., 50.
4. Eric Bentley, *The Playwright as Thinker* (New York: Harcourt Brace & Co., 1946; reissued by Harcourt Brace Jovanovich, 1987, with original Preface and new Afterword), 78.

CHAPTER 1   Introduction

1. John Deeley, *Introducing Semiotics: Its History and Doctrine* (Bloomington: Indiana University Press, 1982), 111.
2. Roland Barthes, *The Responsibility of Forms,* trans. Richard Howard (New York: Hill & Wang, 1985), 38.
3. Keir Elam, *The Semiotics of Theater and Drama* (London: Methuen, 1980), 10.
4. Roland Barthes, S/Z, trans. Richard Miller (New York: Hill & Wang, 1974), 16–17.
5. Wlad Godzich, Introduction, *Blindness and Insight,* by Paul de Man (Minneapolis: University of Minnesota Press, 1983), xii.

6. T. S. Eliot, "The Function of Criticism," in *The Selected Prose of T. S. Eliot*, ed. Frank Kermode (London: Faber & Faber, 1975), 74–75.

7. Michel Foucault, *The Order of Things: An Archaeology of the Human Sciences* (New York: Random House, 1973), 43–44.

8. Ibid., 44.

9. Paul de Man, *Blindness and Insight*, 17.

10. Ibid., 26.

11. Paul Ricoeur, *Hermeneutics and the Human Sciences*, ed. John Thompson (Cambridge: University Press, 1981), 175–76.

12. Jacques Derrida, *Writing and Difference*, trans. Alan Bass (Chicago: University of Chicago Press, 1980), 28.

13. Ibid., 29. For an account of how this passage in Nietzsche and its doctrine of the passing of old forms and of the transfiguration of the past relates to Ibsen's *The Master Builder*, cf. Brian Johnston, *The Ibsen Cycle*, 297.

14. G. W. F. Hegel, *The Phenomenology of Mind*, trans. J. B. Baillie (London and New York: Macmillan & Co., 1931), 75.

15. Donald Philip Verene, *Hegel's Recollection: A Study of Images in "The Phenomenology of Spirit"* (New York: SUNY Press, 1985), 9.

16. Ibid., 25–26.

17. Ibid., 36–37.

CHAPTER 2   Ibsen's Realist Aesthetic

1. Charles Rosen and Henri Zerner, *Romanticism and Realism: The Mythology of Nineteenth-Century Art* (New York: Viking Press, 1984), 149–50.

2. *The Oxford Ibsen*, ed. J. W. McFarlane (London: Oxford University Press, 1960), 1:603.

3. Rosen and Zerner, 147.

4. Ibid., 148.

5. Ibid.

6. Ibid., 150.

7. Henrik Ibsen, *Letters and Speeches*, ed. Evert Sprinchorn (New York: Hill and Wang, 1964), 144–45.

8. Paul de Man, *Blindness and Insight*, 72.

9. Ibid., 70–71.

10. Wayne C. Booth, *The Rhetoric of Fiction* (Chicago: University of Chicago Press, 1983), 95.

11. Ibid.

12. Rosen and Zerner, 145.

13. For example, Austin E. Quigley, *The Modern Stage and Other Worlds* (London: Methuen, 1985), 91–114.

14. Jan Kott, *The Theater of Essence* (Evanston: Northwestern University Press, 1984), 59.

15. Rosen and Zerner, 164.

16. Richard Hornby, *Patterns in Ibsen's Middle Plays* (Lewisburg, PA: Bucknell University Press, 1981), 40–41.

17. Harley Granville-Barker, "The Coming of Ibsen," in *Ibsen: A Critical Anthology*, ed. J. W. McFarlane (Harmondsworth: Penguin, 1970), 103.

18. *Letters and Speeches*, 103.

19. Sigurd Ibsen, *Human Quintessence* (New York: B. W. Huebsch, 1972), 3–4.

20. Ibid., 20.

21. Ibid., 14.

22. Ibid., 27.

23. Ibid., 44.

24. Ibid., 40.

25. Ibid., 55–56.

26. Ibid., 90–91.

27. Ibid., 92.

28. Ibid., 93.

29. Ibid., 96.

30. Rolf Fjelde, trans. *The Complete Major Prose Plays of Ibsen* (hereafter Fjelde) (New York: New American Library, 1978), 1058.

31. Sigurd Ibsen, 96.

32. Ibid., 95.

CHAPTER 3   Text and Subtext

1. Sigmund Freud, "Some Character Types Met With In Psychoanalytic Work," *Henrik Ibsen*, Penguin Critical Anthologies, 397.

2. Ibid., 396.

3. Derek Russell Davis, "Ghosts, Osvald and Schizophrenia," *Henrik Ibsen*, Penguin Critical Anthologies.

4. Fjelde, *CMPPI*, 579–80.

5. *The Oxford Ibsen*, IV.438.

6. *Contemporary Approaches to Ibsen: Reports from the Fourth International Ibsen Seminar*, IV.96, Oslo, 1979.

7. Charles Altieri, *Act and Quality: A Theory of Literary Meaning and Humanistic Understanding* (Amherst: University of Massachusetts Press, 1981), p. 156.

8. E. D. Hirsch, *Validity in Interpretation* (New Haven: Yale University Press, 1967), 121–24.

9. *Contemporary Approaches to Ibsen*, IV.85–100.

10. Trans. David Grene and Richmond Lattimore.

11. Errol Durbach, *"Ibsen the Romantic": Analogues of Paradise in the Later Plays* (University of Georgia Press, 1982), 60.

CHAPTER 4   Text and Supertext

1. Verene, 116.

2. *Letters and Speeches,* 24 September 1871.

3. Jennette Lee, *The Ibsen Secret* (New York: Putnams, 1907), 3–4.

4. Theodor W. Adorno and Max Horkheimer, *Dialectic of Enlightenment* (New York: Herder, 1972), 19.

5. Roland Barthes, *The Responsibility of Forms,* 77.

6. Verene, 13.

7. Ibid., 24.

8. Ibid., 25.

9. George Santayana, *Selected Critical Writings,* ed. Norman Henfrey (Cambridge University Press, 1968), 1.112.

10. *Letters and Speeches,* 181.

11. Hegel, *The Phenomenology of Spirit* (Oxford: Clarendon Press, 1977) (Baillie, 89); T. S. Eliot, *The Sacred Wood,* 49; Claude Lévi-Strauss, *Tristes Tropiques,* 396; Sigmund Freud, *Civilization and Its Discontents,* 89.

12. Søren Kierkegaard, *Concluding UnScientific Postscript* (New York: Doubleday, 1968), 308–9.

13. Søren Kierkegaard, *The Present Age* (New York: Harper Torchbooks, 1963), 103.

14. G. W. F. Hegel, *The Philosophy of Fine Art,* trans. B. Bosanquet (London: Kegan Paul & Co., 1886), IV.268.

15. Ibid.

16. Verene, 37.

17. *Philosophy of Fine Art,* IV.136.

18. *Blindness and Insight,* 149.

19. Ibid., 149–50.

20. Peter Gay, *The Enlightenment* (New York: Alfred A. Knopf, 1966), 425.

21. Thucydides, *The Peloponnesian War,* Edited in translation by Sir Richard Livingstone (New York: Oxford University Press, 1960), 115, 109–17.

22. Bruno Snell, *The Discovery of the Mind in Early Greek Philosophy and Literature* (New York: Dover Publications, 1982), 40.

23. Matthew 4:24.

24. Roland Barthes, *On Racine* (New York: Performing Arts, 1983), 148.

25. Robert Scholes, *Textual Power* (New Haven: Yale University Press, 1985), 58.

26. T. S. Eliot, "Francis Herbert Bradley," *Selected Prose of T. S. Eliot,* ed. Frank Kermode (London: Faber and Faber, 1975), 199.

CHAPTER 5   Providence in *Pillars of Society*

1. G. W. F. Hegel, *The Phenomenology of Spirit,* trans. J. M. Miller (Oxford: Clarendon Press, 1979), 244.
2. T. S. Eliot, "Gerontion," in *The Complete Poems and Plays of T. S. Eliot* (London: Faber and Faber, 1969), 36.
3. Henry James, *The Scenic Art* (New York: Hill & Wang, 1947), 252–53.
4. Verene, 97.
5. Lewis Mumford, *The City in History* (New York: Harcourt Brace and World, 1973), 234–35.
6. *Theater of Essence,* 58, 59.
7. Cited by Jonathan Culler, 139.
8. Michael Meyer, *Life of Ibsen* (New York: Penguin Series, 1985), 36.
9. John Howard Lawson, *The Theory and Technique of Playwriting and Screenwriting* (New York: Garland Publications, 1984), 67.
10. Aeschylus, *The Eumenides* (trans. Paul Roche).

CHAPTER 6   *A Doll House,* or "The Fortunate Fall"

1. *Theater of Essence,* 32.
2. The character Torvald Helmer has much of the aesthetic squeamishness of the "beautiful soul" Hilmar Tønneson, of *Pillars of Society.* His fondness for pretty word-pictures, however, with which to adorn and to evade reality, anticipates the disposition of Hjalmar Ekdal of *The Wild Duck.* All three figures are types of the "aesthetic" temperament, and the assonance of "Hilmar," "Helmer," and "Hjalmar" seems to link them.
3. This central round table will remain onstage for the entire action of *Ghosts* as in no other play in the cycle. Directing the play (with a Palestinian/Jordanian cast at Yarmouk University), I found this central disc dictated the nature of the players' movements. There are many Greek details in *Ghosts,* which itself resurrects the ghosts of Greek tragedy: the Orestes story, *Oedipus,* and *The Bacchae.* As Rolf Fjelde reminds us, the shape of the Greek theater effected "a synchronization of dramatic setting and actual physical phenomena," for "the *oikoumene* itself was traditionally envisaged with a flat disc with, also, an altar at its center, in the shrine to Apollo and Dionysos at the world's navel in Delphi."

Now, I can understand an exasperated reader protesting that Ibsen cannot even move a table in his theater without the interpreter embarking on fantastic speculation: and that, furthermore, no such significance as I suggest could be conveyed to a theater audience. Often, however, an artist (James Joyce, Ibsen's disciple, comes to mind) will include a detail to satisfy his or her own desire to *extend the art form to its utmost*. I am suggesting not only a rich cultural context (the supertext) in which the cycle exists but also a great and wholly rational intention behind it (the psychoanalysis of the *Weltgeist*, of our collective psyche). The cultural *sequence* I claim the cycle invokes (the sequence invoked by Hegel in the *Phenomenology*) covers the decisive stages of our cultural/spiritual evolution. Thus, there is a reason why the first four plays should be progressively more and more "Hellenic" in theme, form, and supertextual content, moving from pre-tragic to post-tragic (comedic-Socratic) consciousness; why the second group, beginning with *The Wild Duck*, should develop themes and metaphors predominantly from Christian and post-Christian Europe, and why the third group, beginning with *The Master Builder*, should represent something of a "synthesis" of these two earlier sequences. Ibsen is, after all, the poet of "the third empire of spirit" and of *Emperor and Galilean*.

My suggestion of a "Hellenic" reference behind that central round table is connected to the demonstration of very many other Hellenic references in *Ghosts*. By visually "tying together" all these references, the central disc onstage would superbly concentrate them into the fateful Hellenic world.

4. Nora, knowing that Rank soon will die, asks, on his last appearance, what he will wear "at the next masquerade." He replies that he will be invisible. The primary meaning, of course, is that he will be dead, but it is worth reflecting that the spirit of a dead man will powerfully haunt the "next masquerade" in the cycle, *Ghosts*.

CHAPTER 7   The Physician and the Gadfly: *An Enemy of the People*

1. I am not denying, of course, that Thomas Stockmann also lacks many Socratic traits, above all the famous Socratic irony (not a very histrionic characteristic). This is in the very nature of archetypal repetition, as in Joyce's *Ulysses* or the modern plays of T. S. Eliot. Furthermore, as I argue, Ibsen's characters often evolve from one archetypal identity to another, as Thomas does in this play.

2. "If we are bad at the rituals of eating and drinking of the bodily digestion of the world, we will be bad at the spiritual digestion of its contents. The secrets at the Dionysiac frenzy were not logical propositions. . . . Even most of Hegel's commentators would have stayed home from such rituals and sought a more sober relationship to the gods. Although Hegelian commentators, unlike logicians of the abstract concept, have an interest in

the whole, they usually insulate the *Begriff* in their discussions from the primordial and passionate speech of the world" (Verene, 34).

3. The metaphor of the "ship of state," with the king or leader as its captain, was a commonplace of Greek tragedy (e.g., in *The Seven Against Thebes; Antigone*). Plato, in one of his most famous, and fateful, analogies, compared society to a ship for which democracy would be the worst form of government. This analogy was to have a long history in Europe (readers of Shakespeare—and Shaw—are familiar with it). Socrates observes:

> Conceive this sort of thing happening either on so many ships or on one. Picture a shipmaster in height and strength surpassing all others on the ship and whose knowledge of navigation is on a par with his sight and hearing. Conceive the sailors to be wrangling with one another for control of the helm, each claiming that it is his right to steer though he has never learned the art and cannot point out his teacher or any time when he studied it. (*Rep.* VI.488)

4. Thomas Van Laan, in a discussion of *An Enemy of the People* in *Ibsen News and Comment*, no. 4 (1983). Van Laan has recently returned to this theme in an account of the play in *Comparative Drama* (Summer 1986), 95–114. His argument, though more detailed, is no more persuasive than before. He makes a false antithesis between seeing the play either as "straightforwardly polemical" or deeply "ambiguous"—as if these were the only possible alternatives—and once again seems to think that ambiguity is a value in its own right. In many cases, an objectively functioning ambiguity, as we find in *The Lady from the Sea*, does work to superb artistic effect: In other cases, such as in political comedy—as with Aristophanes—it would be counterproductive and evasive. Ambiguity is not the sole alternative to polemic. Nor can I see a "tragic" overlay to Act IV of *An Enemy of the People*. At the most, the method in that act is *satiric* and not directed only at Thomas. Ibsen's references to Stockmann usually were approving: His one later statement that Stockmann was "*to some extent* a grotesque fellow and a 'Strudelkopf'" does not, as Van Laan claims, amount to "a hostile dismissal" of his whole character (and would not affect our reading of the play even if it did!). It is remarkable that Van Laan, in his eagerness to establish an element of villainy in Stockmann, does not once mention the reason for Thomas's intemperance which prevents him from Aslaksen's "moderation": that his town for purely materialist reasons is willing treacherously to lure invalids to dangerously infected waters. If intransigence and hot temper were sufficient to damn a dramatic character, very few in the history of tragedy and comedy would escape whipping. It is in the nature of comedy to establish its conflicts by histrionic gestures that would seem extreme in actual life.

5. Thus, in their physical confrontation, the image of the Eteocles-

Polyneices conflict is visually presented. Ibsen, himself a painter, frequently employs visual as well as verbal quotation, an aspect of his plays that deserves a separate study.

6. This issue, of Might versus Right, initiates the major discussion of *The Republic* (and thus of political philosophy itself in the Western world).

7. As early as *The Warrior's Barrow* (1850), Ibsen had called for a *sublimation,* not an abandonment, of the combative warrior spirit "on silver seas of thought."

8. Walter Kaufmann, in his Introduction to Søren Kierkegaard's *The Present Age,* 29.

9. The first Christian martyr celebrated by the Church, Stephen, died by stoning. This probably is only a coincidence, but Ibsen's fondness for *galskap* means we should not totally rule out such Joycean playfulness in his art.

10. The stones in the room when Kiil presents his "satanic" temptation to wealth and power may recollect Satan's temptation to Christ to convert the stones of the desert to bread.

11. Einar Haugen, "Ibsen as Fellow Traveller," *Scandinavian Studies* 51 (1979), 351.

CHAPTER 8   The Turning Point in *The Lady from the Sea*

1. *The Ibsen Cycle,* 207.

2. Rolf Fjelde, *"The Lady from the Sea"*: Ibsen's Positive World View in a Topographic Figure," paper read at the Ibsen Sesquicentennial Symposium in New York, Pratt Institute, 9–13 May 1976. Cf. also Sandra Saari, "The Mermaid's End," paper read at the same symposium.

3. Ibsen's own landscape paintings are notably "Romantic" in scenography. Cf. Otto Lous Mohr, *Henrik Ibsen som maler* (Oslo: Gyldendal, 1953).

4. *Phenomenology,* trans. Miller, 358.

5. *The Oxford Ibsen,* VII.9.

6. Fjelde.

7. "Hedvig's Suicide: A Re-examination of *The Wild Duck,*" *Theater Three* (Fall 1986), 57–72.

8. Jean Paris, *Painting and Linguistics* (Pittsburgh: Carnegie Mellon University, 1975), 17–18.

9. Ibid., 18.

10. Ibid., 19.

11. Ibid.

12. *The Oxford Ibsen,* VII.49.

13. *Philosophy of History,* 442.

14. *The Oxford Ibsen,* VII.49.

15. *Henrik Ibsen,* ed. McFarlane, 138–39.

16. It also gives Hilde an association with death, with linking onto the doomed and dying. Does she prepare Solness for death in *The Master Builder?* In Scandinavian myth, the Valkyrie (of whom the most famous was Hildr—Wagner's Brünnhilde) appeared just before a hero was to die, to prepare him for Valhalla. This is most movingly presented in the confrontation of Brünnhilde and Siegmund in Wagner's *Die Walküre.*

17. Fjelde, *"The Lady from the Sea."*

18. This "psychic bigamy" recalls the threat of the woman in green in *Peer Gynt* to share in the lovemaking of Peer and Solveig; but the outlaw hut of Peer and Solveig has more in common with the "freedom" value of the Stranger (an outlaw) than with Wangel's bourgeois world. For a discussion of the contrast between the "valley-bourgeois" and the "mountain-outlaw" realms in Ibsen's scenography, see *To the Third Empire.*

19. The argument might go as follows: The limited, fixed, more rigid nature of land life encouraged the evolution of the human community into equally rigid and limited forms of living—of territorial boundaries and possession, of tribal and national identities, stable domesticity, law, order, all of which sea evolution might have avoided. "The depths of the sea" serves as a refuge from limitation and confinement, intolerably closing around Hedvig in *The Wild Duck,* and that play's strong thematic links with *The Lady from the Sea* need to be explored. The Stranger, it might be, invited humanity, through Ellida, to reverse this evolutionary error, a situation more jocularly treated in Edward Albee's *Seascape.*

20. *The Lady from the Sea* offers two ideas of union: the Stranger's, freely willed and unconstrained, like that of Falk and Svanhild, Peer and Solveig; and Wangel's legally valid but constrained *contract.* The word "contract" (*handelen*), repeated by Ellida and Wangel, had a special significance for the spiritual phase ("Kantian," "Rousseauist") that, I claim, the play is exploring. There was a firm contrast between the universal Will, which freely assents to the social contract (developed, in Kant, into the Categorical Imperative), and arbitrary, constrained, authority-based contracts, which the Will cannot consider binding. For Kant, the exact designation of the free Will remained problematic, but he was convinced that it manifested itself in our moral life. Its commands were imperative but derived from the unknowable, noumenal realm. The division within the individual between "the categorical demands of the noumenal ego, or moral will, which assumes absolute freedom, and the inescapable limitations of the phenomenal ego, or man as a part of nature and therefore subject to his instinctual and sensual drives" (M. H. Abrams) creates the profound dualism of Kantian man—a dualism that, I claim, is the shaping principle of this play. This dualism was total: epistemological, moral, psychological, ontological.

21. Hegel echoed Friedrich Schiller's disapproval of Kant's seeming sever-

ance of the moral from the instinctual and natural. For Hegel, as for the Greek tragedians he is so fond of citing—and for Freud, later—our "laws" are not the calm and logical creations of categorical reason but evolve, often violently (as in the *Oresteia*), through the crises brought about by the clash of human passions and the suffering that results. "Because of our sufferings, we acknowledge we have erred," Hegel quotes from the *Antigone* when tracing the evolution of the Ethical consciousness in the *Phenomenology*.

22. This idea of presiding over the *closure* of an age appears in a number of Ibsen's and Hegel's pronouncements (Hegel's most famous being in the preface to *The Philosophy of Right*). With many of his contemporaries (e.g., Wagner and Nietzsche), Ibsen saw the spiritual traditions and values by which humanity so far had been guided or convulsed as now having lost their beneficial power over us and needing to be evolved into a "third empire of spirit." It is the theme of my Ibsen studies that this is Ibsen's dramatic subject.

23. Which may explain why Ibsen, so oddly, specifies a "Scotch tam" as part of his costume.

24. *Allegories of Reading,* 106.

25. Did "the flying Dutchman" claim Hedvig in *The Wild Duck?*

26. *Letters and Speeches,* 106.

27. Ibid.

28. Ibid.

29. Ibid.

CHAPTER 9   The Demons of *John Gabriel Borkman*

1. Verene makes the very interesting claim that, in the *Phenomenology*, the *Image* or *Bild* precedes the Concept in Hegel's text and even is the condition of the Concept's emergence. His account so closely resembles what I believe to be the interplay between Concept and Metaphor in Ibsen that I shall quote him at length:

> In apparency the seen shines forth. The form of apparency is the image, the *Bild,* not the concept, the *Begriff.* But the *Begriff* shines forth from the *Bild.* I can keep my head about me within the world of the seen by a grasp of the unseen. To have this grasp of the unseen I see it as phenomenon. My sense of the unseen always takes me immediately *beyond* the given seen such that it appears to me as phenomenon. *Erinnerung* (recollection) forms apparency as *Erscheinung* (phenomenon) through the *Bild,* through the night of its gallery of images. The movement, the dialectic of the unseen against the seen is my pathway, my travel (*fahren*) through the

Erscheinung. In other words it is *Erfahrung* (experience). *Erinner-ung* is the producer of the *Bild* which points to the *Begriff,* the unseen element that is the basis of speculative knowing. Recollec-tion is the constant companion of speculation as the image is the key to the concrete concept. These come about through the sense of the opposition of the seen and the unseen that takes consciousness on its voyage of discovery, its *Erfahrung.* (*Hegel's Recollection,* 10)

2. *Theater of Essence,* 37.
3. *Phenomenology,* 808.
4. Ibid., 707.
5. Ibid.
6. Kott, 57.
7. Quoted by Jacques Derrida, *Of Grammatology* (Johns Hopkins, 1977), 148.
8. The wolf was the most common, and the most famous, of Odin's metamorphoses. Odin's empire was destined to fall, but Eddic prophecies foretold that a new, bright, and warm world would succeed it.
9. Jacob Grimm, *Teutonic Mythology,* trans. James Steven Stallybrass (London: George Bell and Sons, 1883); first published in German (Berlin, 1844), III.xvi.
10. Ibid., III.934–35.
11. In Act III Mrs. Wilton will admit to being just *seven* years Erhart's senior: an obvious fib, for Ibsen has specified that she is in her thirties, whereas Erhart, whose moustache is just beginning, cannot be more than twenty.
12. Paul de Man, Introduction to Hans Robert Jauss, *Toward an Aes-thetic of Reception,* trans. Timothy Bahti (Minneapolis: University of Min-nesota Press, 1982), xxv.
13. Grimm, III.977.
14. *Fol*-dal does not "work" in Norwegian, of course, but the French connection is familiar enough to encourage a polyglot portmanteau pun. And I only suggest this because of other strong evidence of a "fool" identity to Foldal.
15. Bernard Shaw, *Quintessence of Ibsenism* (New York: Hill and Wang, 1957), 135, 136.
16. *Theater of Essence,* 56.
17. The dialectical journey of the spirit in the *Phenomenology* has been called "a winding stairway of despair."
18. *Phenomenology,* 704.
19. *Of Grammatology,* 149.
20. Grimm, III.970.
21. Ibid., 975.

Selected Bibliography of Books Cited

The compilation of an adequate modern Ibsen bibliography would itself be a separate undertaking, and indeed is being undertaken in "Ibsen Bibliography: Norwegian Literature; Theatre and Drama," *Scandinavian Studies,* annual supplements. The following bibliography is of those sources, critical and interpretive works important to the argument of this volume only.

Abrams, M. H. *Natural Supernaturalism: Tradition and Revolution in Romantic Literature.* New York: W. W. Norton, 1973.

Altieri, Charles. *Act and Quality: A Theory of Literary Meaning and Humanistic Understanding.* Amherst: University of Massachusetts Press, 1981.

Barthes, Roland. *On Racine.* New York: Performing Arts, 1983.

Bentley, Eric. *The Playwright as Thinker.* New York: Harcourt Brace & Co., 1946; reissued by Harcourt Brace Jovanovich, 1987, with original Preface and new Afterword.

Booth, Wayne C. *The Rhetoric of Fiction.* Chicago: University of Chicago Press, 1983.

Burke, Kenneth. *A Grammar of Motives.* New York: Prentice-Hall, 1945.

Deeley, John. *Introducing Semiotics: Its History and Doctrine.* Bloomington: Indiana University Press, 1982.

de Man, Paul. *Blindness and Insight.* Minneapolis: University of Minnesota Press, 1983.

Derrida, Jacques. *Dissemination,* translated with an Introduction and Additional Notes by Barbara Johnson. Chicago: University of Chicago Press, 1981.

———. *Of Grammatology,* translated by Gayatri Chakravorty Spivak. Baltimore: Johns Hopkins University Press, 1976.

————. *Writing and Difference,* translated with an Introduction and Additional Notes by Alan Bass. Chicago: University of Chicago Press, 1980.

Durbach, Errol. *"Ibsen the Romantic": Analogues of Paradise in the Later Plays.* Athens: University of Georgia Press, 1982.

Elam, Keir. *The Semiotics of Theater and Drama.* London: Methuen, 1980.

Eliot, T. S. *Selected Prose of T. S. Eliot,* ed. Frank Kermode. London: Faber and Faber, 1975.

Foucault, Michel. *The Order of Things: An Archaeology of the Human Sciences.* New York: Random House, 1973.

Freud, Sigmund. *Civilization and Its Discontents,* trans. James Strachey. New York: W. W. Norton, 1962.

Gay, Peter. *The Enlightenment.* New York: Alfred A. Knopf, 1966.

Grimm, Jacob. *Teutonic Mythology,* trans. James Steven Stallybrass. London: George Bell and Sons, 1883; reprinted by Dover Publications, New York, 1966.

Hegel, G. W. F. *The Phenomenology of Mind,* trans. J. B. Baillie. London and New York: Macmillan, 1931. Also published as *Hegel's Phenomenology of Spirit,* trans. A. V. Miller. Oxford: Clarendon Press, 1977.

————. *Philosophy of Fine Art,* 4 vols., trans. F. P. B. Osmaston. London: G. Bell & Sons, 1920.

————. *Philosophy of Mind,* translated with a Foreword by J. N. Findlay, F.B.A. Oxford: Clarendon Press, 1971.

————. *Philosophy of Right,* translated with notes by T. M. Knox. Oxford: University Press, 1952.

Hirsch, E. D. *Validity in Interpretation.* New Haven: Yale University Press, 1981.

Ibsen, Henrick. *Breve fra Henrik Ibsen,* 2 vols., af Halvdan Koht og Julius Elias. København og Kristiania, Gyldendalske Boghandel, Nordisk Forlag, 1904.

————. *Letters and Speeches,* ed. Evert Sprinchorn. New York: Hill & Wang, 1964.

————. *Samlede Verker,* 3 vols. Oslo: Gyldendal Norsk Forlag, 1960.

————. *The Complete Major Prose Plays,* translated and introduced by Rolf Fjelde. New York: Farrar, Straus, & Giroux, 1978.

————. *The Oxford Ibsen, Vols. I–VIII,* ed. J. W. McFarlane. Oxford: University Press.

Ibsen, Sigurd. *Human Quintessence.* New York: B. W. Huebsch, 1912.

James, Henry. *The Scenic Art.* New York: Hill & Wang, 1948.

Johnston, Brian. *The Ibsen Cycle.* Boston: Twayne Publications, 1975.

————. *The Third Empire.* Minneapolis: University of Minnesota Press, 1980.

Kierkegaard, Søren. *Concluding UnScientific Postscript.* New York: Doubleday, 1968.

Kott, Jan. *The Theater of Essence.* Evanston: Northwestern University Press, 1984.

Lawson, John Howard. *The Theory and Technique of Playwriting and Screen-writing.* New York: Garland Publications, 1984.

McFarlane, J. W., ed. *Ibsen: A Critical Anthology.* Harmondsworth: Penguin Books, 1970.

Mumford, Lewis. *The City in History.* New York: Harcourt Brace and World, 1973.

Ricoeur, Paul. *Hermeneutics and the Human Sciences,* ed. John Thompson. Cambridge: University Press, 1981.

Rosen, Charles, and Henry Zerner. *Romanticism and Realism: The Mythology of Nineteenth-Century Art.* New York: Viking Press, 1984.

Salomé, Lou. *Ibsen's Heroines,* edited, translated, and with an Introduction by Siegfried Mandel. Redding Ridge: Black Swan Books, 1985.

Santayana, George. *Selected Critical Writings,* ed. Norman Henfrey. Cambridge: University Press, 1968.

Schiller, Friedrich. *On the Aesthetic Education of Man: In a Series of Letters,* trans. Reginald Snell. New York: Frederick Ungar, 1965.

———. *Naive and Sentimental Poetry: On the Sublime: Two Essays,* trans. Julius A. Elias. New York: Frederick Ungar, 1966.

Segal, Charles. *Interpreting Greek Tragedy: Myth, Poetry, Text.* Ithaca, N.Y.: Cornell University Press, 1986.

Shaw, George Bernard. *Quintessence of Ibsenism.* New York: Hill & Wang, 1957.

Verene, Donald Philip. *Hegel's Recollection: A Study of Images in "The Phenomenology of Spirit."* New York: SUNY Press, 1985.

Weigand, Hermann J. *The Modern Ibsen: A Reconsideration.* New York, 1928.

Index

in, 23–24, 45; dialectial nature of his
drama, 45; on history, 80, 232–33;
metaphors and symbolism of, 171–
72, 177–78, 181, 194–96, 200, 202–
3, 214, 232, 237–38, 251–52; on personal and communal guilt, 122; on realism, 31, 34; and recollection, 76–
78, 98; and well-made play, 39; as
first world dramatist, 26–27
WORKS: last four plays, 3; the Realist
Cycle, 7, 10, 21, 91–92, 102
Brand, 69, 84, 111, 115, 125, 130,
139, 141, 190, 213, 248
Catiline, 208, 250
Doll House, A, 3, 24, 38, 39–40,
43–44, 136, 137–164, 167, 174
Emperor and Galilean, 33, 34, 38,
42, 46, 78, 80, 84, 89, 96, 110,
111, 172, 173, 190, 194, 213,
220, 228, 255, 257
Enemy of the People, An, 40, 111,
165–91 passim
Feast at Solhoug, The, 105
Ghosts, 3, 22, 35, 36, 39, 41, 47,
51–52, 57–58, 73, 87–90, 91,
120, 132, 136, 138, 142, 156,
164, 166, 167, 182, 184, 187
Hedda Gabler, 3, 33, 38–39, 40, 73,
139, 152, 200, 226, 233, 238, 240
John Gabriel Borkman, 7, 18, 45,
63, 73, 127, 235–77 passim
Lady from the Sea, The, 3, 12, 24, 40,
44–45, 48, 68, 91, 93, 95, 152,
193–233 passim, 240, 246, 276
League of Youth, The, 47, 111
Little Eyolf, 5, 18, 42, 44–45, 47,
73, 241, 246
Love's Comedy, 107, 111, 140, 221,
231, 238
Master Builder, The, 63, 89–90,
121, 205, 211, 220, 226, 233,
241, 276
Miner, The, 256–57
Peer Gynt, 107, 125, 190, 213, 228
Pillars of Society, 39, 45, 101–36
passim, 138, 142, 152, 160, 174,
215
Rosmersholm, 3, 5, 33, 40, 54–62,
85, 152–53, 194, 200, 209

Vikings at Helgeland, 243, 245–46,
250, 260
When We Dead Awaken, 44–45, 49,
63, 74–75, 102, 218, 225, 241, 244,
250, 270–71
Wild Duck, The, 3, 18, 35, 38, 40, 41,
93, 157, 167, 173–74, 178, 196,
202
Ibsen, Sigurd, Human Quintessence, 9,
12, 47–50, 54, 103, 193, 195, 205,
233
Impressionism, 32
interpretation, 14; dangers of, 24; and
meaning, 14–19, 21, 92, 118
Islam, 7, 242

Jaeger, Henrik, 70
James, Henry, 2, 26, 30, 41, 44; on Pil-
lars of Society, 107–8, 125; on John
Gabriel Borkman, 243; The Ambassa-
dors, 33; The Awkward Age, 41;
What Maisie Knew, 41
Jesus, 95–98, 188–90, 201; as messiah,
226–27
Johnston, Brian, The Ibsen Cycle, 10,
90, 193 n.1, 240
Johnston/Freeman, 216, 224
Jonson, Ben, 85
Joyce, James, 2, 68, 78, 90; on Ibsen,
93, 99, 119, 135; Ulysses, 14, 31, 168,
190; Finnegans Wake, 68
Jung, Carl, 76

Kafka, Franz, 3
Kant, Immanuel, 20, 26, 48, 197–202,
205, 222, 229
Kaufmann, Walter, 63, 185
Kennedy, Andrew A., 86
Kierkegaard, Søren, 82–84, 86
Kleist, Heinrich von, 30
Kott, Jan, 29, 40, 119, 141, 238, 245,
267–68
Kristeva, Julia, 119

Lawson, John Howard, 125
Lee, Jennette, 70
Lévi-Strauss, Claude, 82
Lichtheim, George, 67

unconscious intention, 61–62

Verene, Donald Philip, 24–26, 75–76
Victorian art, 42
Virgil, 138
Voss, Heinrich, 25

Wagner, Richard, 6, 30, 78, 119, 238; *Tristan und Isolde,* 155; *The Flying Dutchman,* 196, 238; *Ring Cycle,* 247, 249, 252–53

Weber, Max, 248
Weigand, Hermann J., on Ibsen's "modernism," 1
Weltgeist or "world soul," 26
Wilde, Oscar, 2
Wordsworth, William, 7, 31, 42

Yeats, William Butler, 84

Zola, Emile, 112